TAKING STOCK

TAKING
STOCK

A True Tale of Seattle's Investment Community

JEFFREY PORTEOUS

NORTHWEST CENTER FOR RESEARCH JOURNALISM
SEATTLE

First published in 1989 by Northwest
Center for Research Journalism,
Seattle, Washington

LIBRARY OF CONGRESS CATALOGING IN PUBLICATION DATA
Porteous, Jeffrey
    Taking stock.
    Includes index.
    1. Brokerage Industry of Seattle - History and Business.
ISBN 0-9624935-0-3

Printed in the United States of America
Designed by Linda J. Porteous and Holli Brown
Endpapers by Steve Atkinson

And so, for L...
and for Z as well.

Ich und Du.

ACKNOWLEDGEMENTS

In general, those who helped most with this book are the Seattle brokers who appear in the following pages, I thank them all for their patience, their kindness, and their excellent humor. I also wish to thank Mike Kunath - who first conceived of this project - without his faith in the venture, and confidence in its outcome, this book could never have been accomplished. Warm thanks go to Joan Gregory and Rosella L. Stern, but for their editorial touch, the book couldn't have been finished. They are not responsible for any errors that may remain. A heartfelt thank you to Holli Brown, Dr. Robert Keller, Robbins Harper, Marilyn Adams, Jim Adams, Bill and Alice McNeil, Tobey Dickson and Jim Porteous, Francine, Bjorn B., Rand Jack, Camille Colaizzo, Kathy Henwood, Katy Goodwin, Wayne Luckman, Patsy and Jim and old Charley.

And finally, to my mother, who taught me what I know of getting the show on the road.

CONTENTS

INTRODUCTION

After six months in the area's libraries, searching for documents telling the history of Seattle's investment community, I had filled three drawers of a four-drawer filing cabinet with material. Much of this material was fascinating, excellent in its coverage of Wall Street, almost equally good on a century of Seattle business. Hardly any of it, however, told the story I had undertaken to tell - that of Seattle's investment community.

In the fifth month of this research, on Monday, October 19, 1987, the stock-market fell 508 points. Taking a 5:00 a.m. cab into town the following day, I paid a visit to the Shearson offices in The First Interstate Building, walking around with a tape recorder and a notebook. From Shearson I proceeded to Schwab & Co. From Schwab to Kunath Karren Rinne & Atkin. From KKRA to PaineWebber.

Realizing I'd been handed my first chapter, I knew as well that I would tell this part of the story as reportage, using the present tense. I also knew I would end the book in the same manner. This material would eventually form Books One and Three in the volume. But the book's second chapter was to begin its "historical" section, Book Two, the major portion of the work. And I knew only too well the contents of that four-drawer filing cabinet.

So where was the material for Book Two to be found, data that might tell of the earliest days in the community? And if this material didn't exist, how was the story to be told? The first clue that there might be an answer to these questions came from the bottom of a bureau drawer in the city's Madison Park district. It was a scrapbook, an old company album with the word "publicity" scratched on its spine. This was the scrapbook of the William P. Harper & Son Company. Having already scoured the area's archives (Pacific Northwest Collection, Seattle Downtown, University of Puget Sound, Seattle University, The Museum of History and Industry), I knew that in all likelihood this was as much material as I would find for this first chapter in the investment community's history.

The scrapbook contained assorted newspaper clippings, some going back to the last century, a single prospectus, and a few letters, both business and personal. This was the collection of first, William P. Harper, and then his son, Paul Coates Harper. Luckily, this chronicle was supplemented by Paul Coates' personal scrapbook, an album containing mementos from Harper's turn-of-the-century college days at the University of Washington and Stanford, magazine clippings, more newspaper columns, posters, hand bills, etc.

Two scrapbooks - and nothing at all in the libraries. So, how was this story to be told? How to fill the critical gaps? After examining the facts I had, I began asking questions. Who were these men? What had they done? How had they done it? What were the times within which they acted? And perhaps as importantly (and in order that this story be told - I could see no way around this), what might they have been thinking? The more I pressed the little material I possessed, the more it seemed to disclose, and the more these particular personages seemed bent on telling their own stories. Eventually, after more rewrites than I care to remember, they began demanding it. I finally had to get out of their way, and my own, and let them do just that.

And, of course, from that point on, it began to read like fiction. With the completion of the Harper chapter, the form was determined. After that, I had little choice in the matter, only, so it seemed, the opportunity. I would anchor each chapter in fact, starting with the found documents: a chance discovery of board minutes, a cache of someone's personal sales reports, old desk diaries, a company's forgotten income statements. As well as hours and hours and hours of tape recorded interviews.

Out of these facts I wrote this book. If it reads like a "true tale," I've done the work as it offered itself up to be done. If, however, it has the feel of "history," there's a reason for that as well. It largely is.

The individuals portrayed in this book are real. The author has spent considerable time interviewing all available persons and has attempted to portray the brokerage business as it existed and now exists in Seattle. The conversations in this book have been recreated after extensive investigations into the various individuals and events about which the author seeks to write. The author has used his best efforts to recreate the conversations as they have been recounted for him, and sends his apologies for any minor discrepancies.

BOOK ONE

"Money? Why it's a way of life..."

ROSS SUTHERLAND
*
Seattle yachtsman,
sportsman, working
stockbroker, Age 91.
1988

Chapter One

FAT TUESDAY
ON THE PHONE

1

SEATTLE, 5:35 A. M., TUESDAY, OCTOBER 20, 1987. THE NEW brokerage floor of Shearson/Lehman Brothers' downtown office is just coming alive. Gary Farber, a 34-year-old Shearson stockbroker, is already stripped to his white-on-white shirt. Telephone to his ear, he speaks with his New York office for several long seconds before finally hanging up. "How you makin' it?" asks a colleague, sticking his head into the broker's office. Farber quickly straightens himself in his chair, his wired smile riding the nervous energy flooding the brokerage floor this morning. "You gotta keep your sense of humor," he says, his legs crossed, his black tasseled foot tapping out Morse code as he speaks.

"Hell Gary.." exclaims a voice from the office next door. "We're off the map!" The voice is that of Jim Adams, Farber's partner in the giant Shearson system. Adams is a bond salesman, and like his partner here on the First Interstate Building's 39th floor, the bond broker has also kept his sense of humor this morning, managing a smile as indicators begin pointing in unfamiliar directions. "This is seein' history like never before," Adams announces, glancing at the columns now frozen on the screen of his Quotron, "we're off the charts. No one's ever been here before!"

Adam's quote machine isn't working properly, its innards still giving yesterday's record read-outs. "Scary," laughs Farber, standing in his partner's office, venting the apprehension all are feeling on this morning of October 20, 1987. Black-Monday-Plus-One. Adams quickly punches several buttons on the machine's keyboard. No luck. It is now twenty minutes away from the opening bell.

From a speaker in the office ceiling, the corporate "shout-down" can be heard, a kind of national chorus to the action in the rooms below. This is more than a coast-to-coast link-up: every branch office in the Shearson/American Express national organization forms part of the loop. However, much of the broadcast seems to come from New York. Odd words and phrases leap out: "Blown away...chaos...catastrophe...panic." Then, "I don't think this is a worldwide financial collapse," comes the message from Shearson's main office in New York City.

The 40-year-old Adams, wearing gold, aviator-style eyeglasses, quickly begins checking lists, phoning out-of-town clients, attempting to allay their anxieties, to settle the panic of this financial passage. "We're gonna be here tomorrow and next week and next month," he assures them. Then, 10 minutes after the opening bell, before anyone has time to take a second breath, the market races up 24 points.

In the adjoining office, Farber's busy right foot continues its cadence. He seems energetic, cheerful, and thoroughly wired. A call from Mike Kunath comes in, a local money manager. The man wants to buy Boeing. The price of the stock is low; the market is rising. Leaning over his desk, Farber immediately begins making calls.

There is a lithograph hanging on the wall behind Farber's head. Strategically placed, the work is a cartoon portrait of two ducks, each armed with a brush and a pail of bright red paint. The two have covered the entire floor of their living quarters with the red paint, all but for the doorless corner in which they now find themselves - trapped - their eyes wide, puzzled expressions spread across their cartoon bills. The piece is captioned, "The Failure of Marxism."

FAT TUESDAY ON THE PHONE

6:55 A.M. The market roars up 110 points in the first 25 minutes.

"Look at that," says Farber, staring at his Quotron. "The spreads are ridiculous!" In an efficient market, the spread between buying and selling prices is very tight, this morning it has begun to unravel. Farber, trying to place his order for Boeing, had found 48,000 shares ahead of him, a measure of the huge volume now flooding the system.

"Usually, when the market's real bad," Farber explains, "you want it to open down, get some strength into it, and rally. But what can happen, at some point today, is the sellers are gonna want to get out. In '29, on the day after the break, the market spiked up, then fell even further. That's what we're afraid of now."

Wall Street has an apt term for such rallies following badly broken markets. They are dubbed "The Dead Cat Bounce."

7:07 A.M. Its eyes rolled to the back of its head, the DOW is presently bounding 133 points off the pavement.

Word is passed among Shearson's brokers of a branch wide meeting called for 7:30 a.m.. The gathering is held beneath the bright grid of the building's overhead fluorescence, amid potted Ficus, pastel filing cabinets, and the secretarial desks that fill this corner of the giant brokerage floor. Shearson's Ross Rogers, the 39-year-old branch manager, begins with a warning: brokers should not assume that they own anything, or, in fact, that they have sold anything to clients. The problem is still yesterday's crushing overload of data, which has so crippled Shearson's data system, it is now barely able to limp along, dragging one foot, information D.O.A. by the time it's received. With client confirmations running hours behind, nobody wants to get caught out.

Standing with their backs to the office's glass-paneled walls, the Shearson brokers appear restless, edgy, expectant; the sound of loose change being jingled in pants pockets. To all outward appearances, however, none seems entirely glum, despite the apprehensions of financial disaster now permeating the brokerage floor.

5

TAKING STOCK

"Briefly, from the standpoint of the branch," Rogers informs his people, "margin calls are not a problem at this point."

Margin calls, though not threatening disaster to the broker, are a serious enough threat to the market. Simply put, "margining" allows clients to buy securities with money borrowed from their broker. As long as markets rise and stockprices go up, everything goes well. But in a sharp downturn, brokers are forced to send their clients "margin calls." These distress signals require either that money be deposited in the client's tumbling account, or that stock be bargained-off to cover debts. As stock is sold, prices go down; as prices go down, stock is sold. This cycle had been repeating itself all day the day before, feeding directly into the panic.

Finished with equities, Rogers turns the meeting over to Adams. Now comes news of the enormous market in bonds.

"Long treasuries are up to 92 1/2," Adams begins. The bond broker is in his shirt sleeves and tie, a clipboard and a white, stick-pen in hand. "We've had a dramatic move in the bond market. Flight to quality is the name of the game, but in real honesty, it's flight from fright. That's the reality," he confides. "I talked to an old-timer last night who said just watch the spreads between the bid and the ask. That's the measure between how secure or insecure this market is. If you looked this morning as they opened the AT&Ts and the Phillip Morrises - AT&T was 26 at 31. That's a measure of how uncertain they are. The bond market itself is coming narrower and narrower. But, they're continuing to spread treasuries by 3/8s to 3/4s. And that's a very wide gap.

"Still," Adams concludes, hoping to offer some assurance, some ray of optimism to his listeners, "having said that, the feeling I get is that this is an enormous overreaction, finally, to a colossal bull market.

"I mean, and I've said this before," he adds, the reflection of the overhead lighting now mirrored in his eyeglasses, his hand tap-tap-tapping at the clipboard with his ball point pen, "But, we're off the map. These are uncharted waters. Nobody's ever sailed here before."

• • •

6

FAT TUESDAY ON THE PHONE

8:40 A.M. The market has turned back from its peak of an hour ago, back and straight down. For a moment the DOW was up 133 points from Monday's subterranean close. It is now up 9.

"You know one of the things they did this morning?" asks Farber, standing in Adams office. "I don't know if it's just today, or if they won't make it tomorrow, too. Nobody can buy uncovered puts. Which means institution's portfolio insurance is down the drain for today."

The "put option" that nobody may now buy is an instrument designed to rise in value in proportion to the fall of the market. The sale of puts is suspended as mass purchasing of these options pushes the market inexorably lower. Their loss, as Farber explains it, leaves institutional managers one final decision to make.

"They can't insure against the market moving further down today," the young broker tells his partner. "Which means it's kiss-and-tell-time. You gotta either stand up... or bail out." Adams nods, then swivels back in his chair and picks up his phone.

9:10 A.M. A man's stricken voice comes crackling out over the shout-down. "Have we checked with the exchange? Do we know when they're closing? Rumors are they're closing the exchange any minute! Can we confirm that?"

"Sir, as of right now, we have not heard that." This is a young operator's voice, her familiar Brooklynese coming from Shearson's headquarters in Manhattan. Though obviously under pressure herself, she now attempts to calm her frightened caller. "They are...they must be rumors only, sir. We are certainly not confirming that...If we get more information, we'll be right back on the box."

The first voice: "Are you checking with the exchange!"

"Yes sir, we are."

Then a third, an irate male voice is heard: "They're not gonna close the exchanges! Stop trying to start that rumor!" Then silence.

TAKING STOCK

Farber stands in Adam's office, eavesdropping as the older man works the phone. "...there is nothing except struggle, and the hope we'll be OK. And, you get to this point in time, and I keep saying we're in uncharted waters, and that's exactly where we are. It's kinda like being on the airplane? And the plane settles down pretty hard? I always look at the pilot to try and see if he looks nervous, right? Because, what the hell, I mean, why get nervous anyway? We'll come out of this OK..."

At length, Adams puts down the receiver. "Your account?" Farber asks. "It is now," Adams responds. "Her broker left. Shearson's had it two weeks. Her portfolio's now down $160,000...and she's laughing." Adams says this, and laughs himself, though it is evident he feels some portion of this woman's frustration, even mounting distress, as he turns once again to his Quotron. "I doubt she's laughing on the inside," he tells his partner, who returns to his own office. Leaving Adams, who watches the huge sell-off now flashing on the screen of his monitor, and once again picks up the phone.

9:20 A.M. London is down 240 points.

9:25 A.M. The DOW is now down 25 points, compounding Monday's 508 point loss.

On the wall, to the right of Farber's desk, hangs a second print. Less noticeable because of its placement, it too features a pair of cartoon ducks. Only these two birds are hip, turned out in dark glasses, cool designer shades. And though once again the characters sit side-by-side, now it is upon an enormous mountain of money, staring out over a cartoon sea - perched, silent, transfixed - watching the setting sun in the form of a green and radiant dollar sign. The print is entitled "The Failure of Capitalism."

"Jesus, Gary!" Adams hollers from his desk, staring at the screen of his Quotron. "D'you see Boeing? It's down 3 1/2 points."

"This is ugly," says Farber. Then he smiles, and straightens his tie. And picks up the phone.

2

NORTH OF SHEARSON'S BROKERAGE SUITES IN THE FIRST
Interstate Building, and 38 floors below, a crowd has gathered inside
the public room of Charles R. Schwab & Co.. Finding little room to sit,
people are forced to stand, packed side by side in this street-level room,
gazing up at the flickering lights of the electronic tape, or queuing up for the
shop's two Quotrons.

Charles R. Schwab & Co. advertises itself as America's largest discount
broker. Instead of the array of services offered by a Shearson, the San
Francisco-based company simply offers deeply discounted brokerage
commissions. That, and three tiny rows of seats, two well-used Quotrons,
and an electronic broad tape displayed high on the wall of its functional,
Third Avenue public room. Once upon a time, all brokerages operated in this
manner - at ground level, with a public ticker for those of the curious
stepping in from the streets. Targeting the modern version of this immense,
if less affluent end of the market, Schwab's accomplishment lies in rein-
venting this wheel - and taking in a billion nickels. Moreover, because of the
scaled down nature of Schwab's system, each investor's coin comes without
its attendant headache. Nothing, after all, is recommended - that being the
province of the "full-service" brokers. Schwab simply executes orders, and
offers a roof under which the curious may gather. This particular Tuesday,
judging from the crowd, people are *very* curious.

9:50 A.M. "Where's the market?"
"Up!"
"Up? How far up?"
"66."

TAKING STOCK

"I don't believe this."

The market has again turned, attempting to reclaim lost ground, though the crowd, their eyes on the overhead tape, seem to have little faith in the numbers.

"This is artificially supported."
"Wait 'til the program sales come in."
"No, I think it's holding pretty well."
"Wait awhile."

An old man seated in the room's front row is smiling. "When nobody wants it," he declares, staring up at the tape, "that's when I'll buy it." Standing in front of him, an attractive young woman has stationed herself at one the room's two Quotrons. Not more than 25, she busily works the quote machine with her left hand, while making tabulations in a small, dog-eared notebook with her right. A collection of bracelets jangles about her wrist as she types companies' NYSE codes into the Quotron, and though from time to time she glances up at the overhead tape, she never seems to miss a beat on the instrument, and never once looks down at the keys.

The crush continues. The windows of the room become edged white with steam; the crowd, clutching copies of the morning's Wall Street Journal, stare up at the flickering broad tape, fewer and fewer talking. Then there's a shout.

"Market's sliding off!"
"When nobody wants it!" comes the announcement, "that's when I'll buy it!"

Outside the brokerage, a Schwab customer walks to the curbside and stands, waiting for the traffic light to change. Above the noise of Third Avenue's traffic, a ferry is heard leaving its berth on the waterfront, the bass rumble of the boat's steam-whistle broadcasting this fact to the city. It is 10 minutes after 10 in the morning, October 20, 1987, Pacific Standard Time.

3

THE PARTNERS AT KUNATH, KARREN, RINNE & ATKIN ALL agree: Initiative must be taken. The strategy they devise is to focus on gains made in the bond market, a by-product of yesterday's frenzy in the DOW. Pairing off, the four principals in the investment counseling firm begin making calls. The firm's clients, their troubled voices amplified over speakerphones, nearly all begin with the same question: "What happened?"

"A major correction, of course," KKRA partner Michael Kunath says. Sitting forward in his chair, facing the grill of a speakerphone, Kunath tamps tobacco into the bowl of a corncob pipe as he speaks. "Even historic. But let's not lose sight of something here, let's not forget the fact that more went on than just equities yesterday. It was also a big, big day on the bond market." This observation is met with silence, a stony reticence assuming the guise of a large and immovable object at the other end of the line. "Naturally," says Kunath, " the news is all going to be focused on the stock market, on the DOW. It's what you'll hear, it's what you'll see on TV. But you don't own the DOW. ... At the same time, what you won't see on TV is that treasuries rallied, they were up a bit over three points. That's an enormous swing in the bond market. An historic rise. As I said, a big, big day."

"Yes? ...Well, I hadn't thought of that," the client admits.

"And," Kunath continues on, "about 30 percent of the portfolio is going to the short-term treasuries. Jointly, we'll be close to twenty-five percent in cash, yielding approximately six, no, six and a half percent." Kunath, joined by his associate Jeff Atkin, begins closing in, tossing off figures, citing facts. Yes, there was damage, and yes, unfortunately some were hurt, but please pay attention, the two men seem to warn. Do not be distracted by the obvious, for look over here! The response to this direction - is a tentative smile coming over the speakerphone. Tentative, but real nevertheless.

"Yes, I see, Mike, and..."

The two partners lay aside their client folders; Atkin checks off a name in a book.

"...and thanks for taking time out to call."

Calling, as one partner puts it, "seems the prudent thing to do." Perhaps, in a business predicated upon keeping clients happy, it is the only thing to do. For the unpleasant fact remains: unhappy clients join other firms' clienteles, something few young companies can afford. As Kunath and Atkin work their client lists, partners Ned Karren and Bruce Rinne are busy on the other side of the room. Surrounded by the sound of printers and the ringing of unanswered phones, the four men confer, flip through files, waiting for clients to pick up their calls.

"Hello?"

"Is this the former Mr. P?"

"Yes?" The voice, though relaxed, remains uncertain.

"The man who used to be a millionaire - Thursday last?"

"Well! How you making it, Michael?"

"Jesus Christ," laughs Kunath, pleased to have found the retired banker at home. "It must have been about a week ago I said, Don't you want to sell your Microsoft? Naaw, you said, I'm gonna live and breathe with that one."

"It's worse off than the rest of 'em."

"The carnage was something else."

"Incredible!" exclaims the retired banker. "You hear anybody talking about where a bottom might be?"

"Not really," says Kunath. "Over at Shearson yesterday, their guru, Elaine Garzarelli, was talking about 1900. But she was a bit early. We went right through that."

"So it's anybody's guess."

"Well, I hope we do better than that."

"But long-term."

"Long-term? C'mon," says the investment counselor. "We're in the middle of a dust storm. I mean, as of right now, the market's edging up, but nobody's got a handle. Though my gut feel, I mean if you really want long-term, my feel is that what was begun by Kidder and Salomon last week in cutting back, I think we'll see more of that. Probably a lot more of it. There'll be people on the street. And I think it's probable we'll see some brokerages go upside-down. Major brokerages."

"So Mike," asks the ex-banker, his voice oddly calm now, nearly serene. "What's your plan?"

"Well," Kunath says, shaking a wooden match from its box and striking it on the desktop, "we'll stay on the sidelines." Narrowing his eyes at its sudden flare, Kunath draws on his pipe, then adds the blackened match to several dozen charred companions at the bottom of a gilt-edged tray. "Whether it's for a week or a month. We'll just have to wait to see..."

"Yes, Mike? See what?"

"What the fallout finally is."

The immediate fallout, if slight, is apparent. At the other side of the room, KKRA's Ned Karren has stepped away from his desk to attend to an enormous wall chart. This chart, actually a great many charts worked together, is a mural-like work composed of three-color addenda, four-part extensions, and a half-dozen enamel, magnetized arrows pointing in a half-dozen different directions. Covering the last fifteen years of the market's activity, and, in some instances, its minute-by-minute currency, Karren's chart also covers the entire length of a twenty-foot section of wall. During the days of mid-August, the days of the 2700 DOW, the partner would mount to the top of a large packing case and stand on tiptoe to flag his daily notations. At the present moment, Karren is squatting on the same brown cardboard box, pen and protractor in hand, tracing the bottom of a clifflike trend-line three feet off the carpeted floor. A controlled and cheerful man, seldom given to the use of strong language, the 47-year-old Karren now looks drawn, and has begun using the word "bloody" to describe the action of the last 36 hours.

12:13 P.M. The battered DOW, having twice attempted huge gains, loses both to renewed selling. It is the parable of the elephants wishing to exit through the same small door, all at the same time. But stampede or not, even in a crush there is room to maneuver.

TAKING STOCK

The "put option" Gary Farber had seen being taken off the market earlier may be one of Wall Street's more abstract and imaginative inventions. In effect, a put guarantees its purchaser the right to sell a number of shares of stock at a predetermined price and date. The seller of the put (the other half of this contract) agrees to purchase these shares, at the same price and on the selfsame date. People buying puts are betting that the value of the shares will fall below the locked-in price, enabling them to pocket the difference when selling. It being a zero/sum game, the sellers of puts are betting that prices will jump, then netting them a profit when they buy at an attractively low number.

Purchased as insurance against down markets, the effect of using puts is simple and direct: no matter how low a portfolio may fall, its puts will have an equal and opposite rise. However, the options have the reverse effect whenever markets climb. Used correctly, their rewards can offset unexpected downturns in the market. Make the wrong call, however, and losses can be compelling.

Early in the morning on Black Monday, October 19, before the conflagration became general and a full day before these "insurance" options were prohibited by the exchange, one of KKRA's partners parlayed a singularly prescient hunch. He maneuvered to purchase 400 puts. He was betting, before anyone <u>knew</u> what was going to happen, that prices would fall, and fall sharply. It was a masterful intuition, considering the DOW was about to fall farther than on any day since the index was invented. Roughly one million dollars was the price the partner paid for the options. Waiting at the bottom of the market's nearly bottomless plunge was a $2.4 million dollar profit. All that had to happen for the partners of KKRA to insure their clients from any losses whatsoever was that the stockmarket had to fall, and fall hard. That, of course, was exactly what happened. But (and it's that kind of story) there was a final and unforeseen hitch - the market didn't fall straight down.

Over the rollercoaster course of Monday's selling panic, there were three periods during which the market actually reversed itself and rose. To have foreseen that these upturns wouldn't herald a sudden, even meteoric rise, was nearly impossible for professionals who had spent the last five years of their lives hanging onto the highest flying market ever known. What was such a professional to think? That on this day, a Monday like any other, the strongest, longest-running bull market in the history would suddenly bellow and be dead of cardiac arrest before it struck the ground? Not likely.

Over the course of an hour, the facts had been as close as the nearest Quotron: the market had clearly stopped its fall, suddenly marshaling its enormous strength - and was then (late in the morning) engaging in a potent and precipitous rise - in fact, it had been rising nonstop for nearly an hour. So, to avoid being burned in an apparently reigniting market, the partner reversed himself and sold off the firm's 400 puts. And then he watched through the rest of that afternoon, as his once certain $2.4 million vanished even more completely than the DOW.

"Quiet Please, Market Open," cautions a blue-and-white neon sign hung high on the west wall of the KKRA partners' room. Below this sign, a bank of windows overlooks Elliott Bay. In the clear, still summery air, the distant Olympic Mountains float above the bay, rising from the far peninsula now visible behind the treelines of Bainbridge Island.

However, this view from the 21st floor of the Fourth Avenue Financial Center is soon to be obstructed by construction of the fifty-seven story Washington Mutual Tower. Against this eventuality, the partners of the counseling firm have hung a blueprint on the wall, the diagram's spidery lines portraying the entire top floor of Seattle's Key Tower. A marble fireplace is sketched here, and a Japanese rock garden, three times as much room, a shower...

The move to this penthouse suite had been on the partners' minds for some time, and they have hung their new floorplan with a certain fanfare. Today, however, no one speaks of it, no one now looks at it tacked to the wall. Instead, the inevitable question is heard again and again, the same answer offered over and over. "What's happening? Tell me. What happened?"

"A major correction, of course." The room fills with the clamor of printers and phones ringing over conference lines, the smells of pipe tobacco, of shaving fragrance and sweat. "But let's not lose sight of something here," a voice is heard to say, the words coming rapidly, smoothly.

"It was also a big, big day on the bond market."

4

DRONING AWAY, THE ELECTRIC FAN SITTING AT THE FAR corner of PaineWebber's bond desk has been turned to its highest setting. Always on, the machine is always turned to its highest setting, as from time to time Robbins Harper indulges a habit for low-tar cigarettes. This afternoon, Harper, vice-president for institutional sales at PaineWebber, indulges, paces, and talks on the telephone all at the same time. Trailing his curling phone cord behind him like a tether, the 43-year-old broker talks with a local money manager. This is institutional business.

"You want a bid on 8 1/2 million GMAC 6.65, 11-4-88s, right? And you want an offer on 15 million current long treasuries. That everything? ... I'll be back." Harper, jotting a note as he speaks, puts down the receiver and punches the direct line to his corporate trader in New York. Receiving his bid on the corporates, he swiftly hits a second line, extracting a price from his government trader for the 30-year treasuries. He is back to the caller in two-and-a-half minutes. At this level of play though, no one grows old on the phone. In those same two and a half minutes, Harper's caller has obtained two other bids. On this occasion, with regards to these particular securities, Paine-Webber's numbers are more attractive - and the caller's business stays here. Working with his traders in New York, Harper is paid to be here whenever his callers ring, and Harper's phones have been ringing all day.

Though it is now Tuesday afternoon, the nation's bond departments are still running from Monday's quake in the stock market. Never a matter of simply moving money out of equities, wealth must have some place to go - some placid harbor, some refuge from hazard in the street. Bond departments provide that harbor, acting as tenderers of every kind of debt: corporate bonds, municipal bonds, money market instruments, and, at the top of everyone's agenda today, United States Treasuries - interest-bearing IOUs whose repayment is guaranteed by the "full faith and credit" of the United States Government. Money managers, fund managers, institutional investors - all have been calling throughout the day, eager for the safety of government bonds, anxious to fill their portfolios with the long treasuries, to ally themselves and the fortunes of their clients with the ultimate fortunes of the government itself. Of the industry's two emotions, the identical twins of fear and greed, fear had just won out and was now running up and down the streets, spooking the country's shareholders. It was to prove a bountiful day on the bond market.

"No, no, I'm fine," Jeff Wilson tells a client on the phone. "We're doing all right. No, really! It's OK." Wilson is Harper's associate on the institutional sales desk. Thirty years of age, Wilson has also had clients calling. The majority of these calls have been institutional. A number, however, have been from Wilson's retail customers, clients concerned with the young broker's well-being. Of these callers, a few have been elderly, and a great many more female and not elderly at all. Pleased that his welfare should warrant such concern, the young broker has been uniformly patient with each.

"Everything's OK. No no, I'm doing fine. In fact," he confides with a smile, "we're doing really well."

The two institutional bond brokers _are_ doing well. Having sold off their entire inventory before lunch, they have begun scouring the street, attempting to buy product for their clients at any price. Since the fall in stocks the day before, the bond market has become white-hot, with sellers commanding higher and higher prices for their remaining inventory. Supposedly "orderly" markets in bonds have taken on the appearance of raffles, prices often blurring before the buyer's eyes.

A few hours before, Harper had had a client in the market for two million Ginnie Maes. Having found a trader willing to sell the mortgages, Harper also found the woods filled with buyers then baying after the same "safe" issue. In the course of this clamor, prices had begun to move in the space of a single call. Each time the price was driven up, Harper was forced back to his buyer for approval in order to remain in this chase. Returning in a matter of seconds to the seller, Harper would find his former price driven even higher. This had gone on like a game of demented Ping-Pong, until the broker had finally advised his frustrated client to wait until morning.

A telephone rings on Harper's desk. "Robbins Harper..." A local money manager wants a bid on $12 million of short-term corporates. Again the reflexive pushing of buttons, the shouting over speakerphones. The result: a swift "No Sale." Harper's trader passes on all $12 million.

Hoping to get out of his corporates, Harper's caller desires 30-year, 0-coupon Treasuries. But, with ebbing interest rates, so does everyone. The bond broker listens, and politely wishes the man luck. It is a commodity the money manager may need. His short-term bonds have become increasingly unattractive, and he's much too late, for, with interest rates already falling, the party has long started without him.

Bond prices, unlike stock prices, all move together. No matter what type the bond, all are collectively riveted to interest rates. But bonds, though their prices move in unison, all have different dates upon which each matures. Lined up from tomorrow to 30 years hence, this time-line becomes the broker's "curve." To own long bonds when rates are coming down is to have assumed the correct position on this curve. This is called "lengthening," and on this bullish day in the bond market, it is the game-move the nation's players have attempted to make. In fact, unlike the unfortunate money manager who just called Harper, most had made it hours ago.

2:57 P.M. Equity brokers from PaineWebber's retail floor have been walking back to ask for treasuries throughout the day. Their clients have been insisting on them. Harper and Wilson, occupied with their own institutional business, have done what they could. Now, a lull settles in. Harper sits down. Wilson picks up the morning's sports pages.

There is no view from this corner of the 1111 Third Avenue Building, no windows opening out to the mountains, or to Elliott Bay, or to the city itself. With no light other than the ceiling's inset fluorescence, it is a room that conveys little sense of time, and no sense of its geographical moorings, an office that could exist anywhere in the net: Zurich, Tokyo, Johannesburg, Milan. Conceivably, a Tibetan bond trader could be placed here, if she or he exists, and bonds would get traded. For it is a compartment as refined to its essential function as a breaker panel. During market hours, with the switches thrown and power up, the room becomes a relay in the financial circuitry of the world, transmitting investments as silent streams of electromagnetic impulse, its human occupants strung like wires into the grid of the planet's wealth.

The sound of an incoming call. Once again Harper reaches for the phone. "Robbins Harper." The caller is an officer in SeaFirst Bank's Trust Department, someone Harper often talks to at market's close. "Well, *I'm* OK. How are you? ... Of course, the market was driving them all out. We rallied here all day long. ... Hell, I think they were worried about the end of the world, don't you? ... Uh huh, uh huh, yeah, I think that's part of it. I think also, with enough confusion out there, enough worry, there's a flight to what's perceived to be safety. ... I know, I think what's happening is less a break in the market than a bit of a breakdown in the system. And personally, I don't much want to see that happen. Then we might have real problems on our hands..."

"No no, not at all. I'm fine," Jeff Wilson may be heard reassuring a client after Harper hangs up the phone. "Really! It's OK. We've done pretty well today. No, I'm not, really. Of course I mean it!" Wilson insists, smiling. "Trust me," he says. "My word is my bond."

• • •

"Robbins!"

"Yes, Mr. Wilson...?"

"We're gonna be in a book..."

"Well, it certainly looks that way."

"That's great! Think they'll spell my name right?"

Harper laughs as he begins bringing up the Tokyo bond market on his Telerate. He is holding the shaft of a ballpoint on which he has affixed nine different colored pen caps, one on top of the other, making the instrument several inches longer than it would be otherwise. Harper uses it to reach out with his left hand and peck at the Telerate's keyboard. In so doing, the institutional bond salesman displays a length of snowy, monogrammed french cuff. The cuff is clasped with a silver, initialized stud. On his hand, the broker wears an old-fashioned, gold signet ring, his scripted initials engraved on its face.

"So, tell me, what does the P. stand for?"

"The P.?"

"In William P. Harper. Your great-grandfather, right? I don't think I ever knew."

(Laughs) "You doing the interviewing now?"

"What can I say? You're a celebrity, Robbins."

"The P. huh? Pennsylvania...?"

"Real good, Robbins."

"Penn. The P. stands for Penn."

"William Penn Harper?

"From Pennsylvania."

BOOK TWO

Chapter Two

.

THE QUAKER AND THE CLUBMAN

WINTER 1887

COMING IN ABOARD THE STEAMER GEO. E. STARR, WILLIAM Penn Harper had watched the evening's rain slowly turn to snow on the windows of the ship's passengers' cabin. For the month of December, out here in Seattle, you might plan on one or the other, thought Harper. So, at least he'd been told back in Ohio. Though, it seemed he now had something he could tell *them*, if he ever saw the Ohio town again. You'd do well to expect both at once, he thought, looking out at the shape of the approaching city, the bay and sky then gray in nearly every direction.

The weather had closed down at the ferry's departure from Victoria, the paddlewheeler heading south through a string of forested, seemingly uninhabited islands. By dusk, the boat had reached the northern headland of Elliott Bay, the sidewheeler beating its way into the harbor, the bass rumble of the Geo. Starr's steam-whistle announcing this fact to the city. Standing on deck as the boat proceeded to its berth at the tip of Main Street, Harper waited out in the cold with Evangeline and the children, finding himself turning up the collars of his daughters' coats, once more winding the boy's woolen scarf around his neck, providing the same answers he'd been parceling out for days. That they'd wait and see. That this strange city was to be their new home now.

TAKING STOCK

There was much that was not strange to this family of Ohioans, however: signs on the passenger dock signaling such wares as Harper had inventoried in his store in Ohio: "Ghiradelli's Chocolates," "Sloan's Liniment," even 5-cent "Owl Cigars." He'd certainly sold enough of those in Mansfield. And the ever-present "Dr. Prices," the company's name painted in white, block letters at the landed end of the pier. It was there, at the far end of the high, covered dock, that the city began its climb above the bay, rising on a series of hills that encompassed the harbor. Even through the falling snow, the family could read the lamp lit signs of the town's commerce, the children pointing out over the steamer's rail: "The Golden Rule Bazaar," "Seattle Safe Deposit Company," "Brown's Iron Bitters." ("Paul Harper, thee can have Mr. Brown's Bitters," Harper's youngest daughter had teased the boy.) And there - a sign on an immense, domed mosque declaring this enormity the city's "Opera House." Opera. Harper *hadn't* expected that. And across from this colossus stood a YMCA. But then, what had he imagined? What had any of them imagined: Evangeline, the two girls, even seven-year-old Paul? The place was as raw as he had expected - yet it was large enough, the mansard roofs of the city still visible on even it's highest cliffs, the tiers of the wooden town spilling down the surrounding hillsides.

As the ship's plank was lowered to the tip of the passenger dock, Harper found himself sighting along the ends of the city's wharves. He could see the lights of freight-liners, lumber haulers, paddlewheelers and packet-boats riding at their berths - the city's commercial and passenger docks busy, even on Sunday, and even in this snow. Which was just the thing... busy. Yes, precisely the thing, and the exact reason they had come.

· · ·

William Penn Harper had arranged to have a house waiting for the family, a large and comfortable rental home surrounded by a block of imported fruit trees. The house and orchard was located at the intersection of Ninth Avenue and Pike Street. Ungraded and unplanked east of Seventh Avenue, these roads would sink into mud with the coming of March, turning again to muck with every autumn. Yet, for months after the Harpers' arrival, such predictions seemed cause for hope. For all the family of Ohioans ever saw was snow.

This was Seattle's winter of 1887-88, the coldest in pioneer memory. Lake Union had frozen that December, a three-foot crop of ice being quarried from its hardened surface. The long, frozen nights had forced the city's shopkeepers to sow the town's sidewalks with salt, turning these icebound promenades to slush, their wooden surfaces then becoming something very like sponge. It was into this freak season that the transplanted Easterner set out to establish himself: arising each morning, brushing out his salt-and-pepper beard, attiring himself in fresh linen and his best, heaviest woolen suit, finally donning the black derby hat he'd purchased soon after landing. Thus appointed, Harper would head down Pike, balancing atop the glistening berms left behind the town's horse-pulled snowplows, walking into the city to look for work.

With the passage of winter, the drifts that had besieged the Harper home gave way to a gumbo-like slush. As Pike's mud became nearly bottomless beneath the murky, interminable drizzle of March, William. P. hired on as a collection agent for Jacob Furth's Gas and Electric Company. Soon, the former storekeeper and farmer found himself carrying an account book for the financier's power company, hiking down the city's boardwalks.

"Hello...Mr. Hillen? Mr. Peter Hillen, the scissor-grinder? William Harper, sir. William P. Harper. I have a bill here from the gas company that would seem to need your immediate attention. Yes, that's the amount. No, no one desires to shut you off. My friend, I just work for this company."

Thus, the Quaker and would-be entrepreneur, labored for Furth's gas and electric company for three-and-a-half years. To William Harper, however, working for Furth was less an occupation than a way in which to provide himself time. For unlike his colleagues at the electric company, the Quaker had an advantage: he had money. The first of this had come from selling his family's Pennsylvania farmland, then selling his own dry-goods store in Ohio. He had come West with enough capital to buy property on Queen Anne Hill, enough money so that his wife would never have to work, and enough to send his children on to college. But no more. Certainly not enough that he himself needn't work each day, guarding his principle in the bank.

For, of course, Harper wanted to start a business. It would have to be one with very few expenses, he knew, and it would have to return his investment very quickly. In short, he couldn't afford to fail. He hadn't enough money to allow himself the luxury. So...he hestitated, spending the three years he worked for Furth imagining buying every business he encountered. And for three years he found reason to reject each one: its price too high, its inventory certain to tie up too much of his capital. Understanding his requirements, remembering as well his experience in Ohio, he found himself besieged with reasons not to try. And so, looking down from his home on Queen Anne, raising his family, William Penn Harper continued to work.

A similar tentativeness, however, couldn't be said of the city. Booming since the fire, the city was putting up new construction nearly as fast as the old had burned. This boom continued on through the summer of 1889, then into the fall and winter. When Harper realized he'd been in the city almost four years, working, and waiting for something to happen.

On New Year's eve, 1891, as the Harper family was sitting to dinner, their Christmas tree caught fire, William. P. immediately rushing the burning tree outside. In doing so, Harper suffered burns on both hands. Confined to bed for several weeks, unable to work, he spent his days gazing from his bedroom window, looking out at the city below.

What, he found himself wondering, looking off at the big, two-and three-story apartment houses being constructed at the base of Queen Anne Hill - what occasioned these ventures? For the ex-storekeeper, the answer was automatic: Money. The movement of money in the creation of profit. Harper felt this was so. Here was the fuel feeding the young city's expansion, a fact so pervasive it existed beneath notice, a commonplace. Yet who supplied this essential? Even simpler - the banks. And who provided it to them? Well... he did. And others like him. All who kept their earned savings on deposit, earning interest. Though undoubtedly the banks made a larger profit on his funds than they'd ever returned him in interest, loaning his capital to the contractors he now watched out his window.

What, he then asked himself, if he weren't to do as he had done in Ohio? What if he were not to buy a store? What if he weren't to buy anything at all? Rather, what if he did the opposite? What if he sold, or rather, rented the only thing he really possessed? Though he was not a banker, had never been trained as such, yet what might prevent him from doing with his own money that which the banks did every day, and capture the profits for himself? Why shouldn't *he* make loans, taking mortgages in return? These concerns existed in the town right now. And surely he had seen them in Ohio. He could make loans to the building trades, they seemed to be in constant need of them. Or, perhaps, any business in need of money.

How difficult could this be? Besides, what else had he? His job collecting bills? He would sooner return to Pennsylvania, go back to farming. No, he thought, returning to his idea with all the force of new discovery. For it seemed then, lingering in bed, that all that was required to accomplish this, was simply to go out and do it...was finally to go out and begin.

"Evangeline!" The Quaker called to his wife, reverting to the language of his religion. "Mother, I think thou had best come in here. I have something to discuss with thee. And thou surely art the one to hear it." He laughed (cool, clear laughter,) "I'm certain it's going to concern us all."

· · ·

Players, even amateurs pioneering on the financial frontier of 1892, found their scarce capital could commandeer a lordly 10 percent. Borrowers caring as little for this rate as they may have cared for the city's rain, could always go to New York. Money was reportedly cheaper there, and it was rumored not to rain as much. Harper, however, wasn't doing business with people much able to go to New York, William P. Harper's stratagems would involve things closer to home. The city's properties - the houses he had walked by year after year - would form his security, his guarantee of repayment. He would carry within his frontier loans, like a pistol beneath a cutaway-coat, a fail-safe lien on each recipient's house. If borrowers defaulted on loans, the courts would call in the obligations and force the debts. Simple enough, and it seemed to work. Harper's Loan Company loaned out money, Harper's Collection Company collected debts. It was Newtonian. What went out, soon came back - with interest.

But the traffic didn't stop there, and in certain significant ways it had just begun. Harper quickly learned there were more things to do with encumbrances than simply make them. He could sell them. Like the alchemist's feat of turning lead into gold, he quickly discounted the mortgages he had made and sold them as investments. His profit was a percentage of his initial interest. But the arrangement's real advantage for Harper lay in the immediate return of his principle, for this was money with which he could make further loans. Which was precisely what he did, and did, and then did again.

The 12,000 souls present on Harper's arrival in 1887 had become an population of 60,000 citizens by 1892. The new city's first clearing house, established in 1889, recorded deposits of $1.8 million in 1890. By 1892 the number had increased to $4 million. Volume land sales in Seattle surged from $3 million in 1887 to $23 million before 1892. These same half-dozen years saw the assessed value of the city's property climb nearly 700 percent, from $7 million to an unheard-of $46 million.

Then, in February of 1893, James J. Hill sent the young city a valentine: his Great Northern Railroad steaming into town. With this first real competition to the Northern Pacific, visions of slashed transportation rates, of immigrant multitudes intent on buying up pieces of the city, began dancing through property holders' heads. To the 250 real estate agents in the town, to the city's bankers and newly launched mortgage-men making their 10 percent, the future seemed well assured.

It seemed everyone shared in this confidence. Recalling the first exuberant years of the new decade, Governor Ferry's young daughter Eliza wrote, "Social life was in a gay whirl. A real estate boom had caused many optimistic businessmen to erect large and expensive homes, erecting them with scant capital..." But the future had been something less than assured, as Eliza Ferry recorded as well, "[then] this '93 panic....When the mortgages fell due during the bad times, the plight of these people was often tragic."

A shock along Wall Street had caused a panicky run on the nation's gold supplies. The resultant tremors had savaged Seattle's economy before the year was two months old. Dubbed "The Depression of the '90s," or "The Panic of '93," its bottom, in July of that year, saw the railroad empires of the Northern Pacific and the Great Northern collapse into receivership. So did six of Seattle's street car companies. Before the summer was over, 600 of the city's newly unemployed began a march across the nation. An "army" of the hungry and homeless, their aim was to shame the federal government into help. This army was met by Federal Troops in Spokane, however, its march halted before it could leave the state.

In Seattle, meanwhile, those businessmen who had leveraged properties in the boom watched the value of their holdings fall anywhere from 40 to 80 percent. Unable to sell at prices they'd paid a short time before, with tenents able to pay rent in suddenly short supply, many received an additional shock: mortgage bankers demanding payment. To meet this debt, new money had to be raised in the panic, properties forced into the market, sold quickly and on the cheap. For those unable to raise the capital, the outcome was invariably the same: bankruptcy. And the deflation didn't go away, it stayed on like an evil smell, hanging around the city for years.

However, barring death or the actual apocalypse, if a newly established loan agent were not in debt, remained unleveraged in a lien-free home, managed somehow to remain on his feet...what then? At worst, having repossessed defaulted homes, such an agent ended up in the rental business. And in 1897, William P. Harper found he owned a great many such homes. This was his situation as the news from the Klondike broke, bringing half the footloose population of the nation streaming through Seattle, hurrying to Alaska or heading back from it, but either way demanding someplace to rent, someplace to buy: Anywhere - Overnight - Now! Harper didn't have to step outside his door, the rush came pouring through it.

Though the wave would eventually pass, the Alaskan mines remained, the city continuing to profit from these northern gold-fields for a many years. In 1902, having expanded his firm's activities, a now prosperous William Harper considered bringing his young son, Paul Coates Harper, into business. Unlike William P., who had had little formal education and whose interests shuttled between family, business, and church, young Paul Coates had acquired a wider range of tastes. As a college student, the boy had been a popular fraternity member at the University of Washington, a cigar-smoking guard on the varsity football squad, and a First Lieutenant in the University Cadets - just missing an appointment to West Point. Young Harper was a talented boxer as well, and quite unlike his Quaker father, had a reputation as a something of a brawler. In his junior year at the university, he had been expelled for having a row with a senior classman. The fight had taken place at 9:30 in the morning, on the grounds of an old flour mill near the city's Ravenna Park. It ended after four rounds with Harper's larger, heavier opponent refusing further punishment. As a prize, Harper had received a speedy transfer to Stanford. In 1903, Paul Coates was in his senior year at the California college, majoring in geology, when his father, business forcing his hand, summoned him back to Seattle. The boy returned before earning his degree, determined to pursue a career in business.

Soon after the younger Harper's return, father and son acquired a large downtown property on the parcel sliding into debt. With the land and building's defaulted bonds selling for cents on the dollar, Paul Coates engineered the purchase of the Third and Pike Heussey Building for $155,000. Next came a profitable line of insurance, father and son becoming agents for the Hartford Company. As the city's financial district developed, stretching north up First Avenue, the Harpers left their ground floor offices on Main Street and moved up into the castlelike Haller Building on the corner of Columbia and First.

In 1906, "Harper's Real Estate, Loans & Rentals" incorporated as "William P. Harper & Son." The company was organized to loan money, to buy and sell real estate, to sell insurance, to operate safe deposit vaults, to borrow money, to issue notes, and to buy and sell commercial paper. Almost as an afterthought, the two men empowered themselves to deal in stocks and mortgage bonds, the year 1906 seeing their profits in this mortgage-bond business climb steeply, then climb again. In the summer of that year, Paul Coates acquired a 20-acre property on 800 feet of Mercer Island lakefront. Christening the elegant vacation-estate and its parklike setting "Ensenada," young Harper and his bride of two years, Alice Dickinson, began spending months at a time there, commuting to the city by boat. It was then, when the Harpers' business was nearly running itself, gliding on swells of national and local prosperity, that, as in deja-vu, the country's economy ran aground once again.

If less grim than in 1893, the effects of "The Knickerbocker Trust Panic" were grim enough. In 1907, however, it wasn't the area's builders that were first affected, but its bankers.

"Prior to October 28th," wrote A. L. Mills, the president of Portland's First National Bank, "the Pacific Northwest had watched with interest, but with no concern, the rich man's panic on Wall Street. But on October 28, all was changed. Telegrams poured in from bank correspondents all over the country. 'Cannot ship you coin or currency against your balance... Advise you organize for your own protection.' And in a flash, business was paralyzed."

Perhaps. William P., however, having watched this deflation with interest, had also taken precautions. Besides, without any real debt, by 1907 the company had simply made too much money to be seriously stopped. In fact, if the city's growth were again to be checked, Harper & Son would attempt a remedy.

Nine months after the 1907 collapse, an article by F. W. West, dean of the city realtors, appeared in the financial pages of the Post-Intelligencer.

"Building materials are cheaper beyond a doubt than they were a year ago, but no man can go ahead and build without money. National banks are not permitted to lend money on real estate, and the state bank is surrounded with restrictions. What is needed, is some sort of agency to bring the man and the dollar together. A bank that will bring together the people who have money to lend, or to deposit in small sums, and the people who wish to negotiate loans on real estate for building purposes. With such an institution as that, the city would go ahead with greater speed...."

To William P., who had contemplated a mortgage bank as his next and natural step, it seemed West was speaking to him alone. He cut the article out, pasted it onto the facing page of a company scrapbook, and scratched June 30, 1908 at its top. On the book's spine, Harper wrote the word "Publicity." He could well have written the word "Prophesy"; it would have cut closer to the mark.

On the fifth of March, 1910, 21 months after the appearance of West's article, William Penn Harper and his son Paul signed incorporation papers for a bank. Christened "First Mortgage & Savings," it took West's idea into action, specializing in receiving the town's smaller depositors, loaning money to the building trades, and turning out first-mortgage bonds. As a matter of form, the state had granted First Mortgage & Savings banking powers running for the next 50 years. To Harper's son, who had plans of his own, this seemed just time enough. To the Quaker, who had at last allowed himself to dream of the bank, imagining it as the well-laid end to all his carefully fitted plans, it seemed just the beginning.

. . .

SPRING 1916

THE POINT WAS, HE HAD TO GET TO SELVIN OVER AT THE P-I, speak to the man before deadline over there. It was important. And now, as Paul Coates Harper realized, listening to the series of clicks at the other end of the line, the fool operator had mis-routed his call. He'd just have to wait, it was too far to run over there (not that he was going to run anywhere anyhow). But this having to see to everything was getting to be too much. Though, who else was going to? thought P. C. Harper, looking over at his father, the old man half-asleep at his desk - or was he just sitting there, staring off into space? Jesus, thought P. C., tapping his signet ring against the base of the black, candlestick-like phone at the center of his desk. Well, they'd better find him a line soon - the paper wouldn't wait, not for him or anyone else. Standing, taking up the telephone in his hands, Harper began to pace the few feet the phone's cord would allow, holding the black, cuplike receiver to his ear as he walked back and forth, trailing the telephone's wiring behind him.

As it happened, William P., his hair now completely white, was not asleep. Neither was he half asleep. Nor, despite what P. C. may have thought, was the old man looking off into space. He was looking at his son, watching these proceedings from his desk across the office. William P. understood that when things became rushed, or went suddenly wrong, his son had a habit of blaming everyone but himself. This aspect of Paul's character seemed unfailing. William P. also knew that the best thing to do, the only thing actually, was to say nothing. In such a state, the boy wasn't about to listen to anyone. Nor was William P. about to try. The Quaker couldn't help but watch, however. So, he found himself studying the boy - a man in his thirties now - tall and slim with the Harper family's premature grey to his hair. He had his mother's eyes, however. That was obvious, thought the old man, though the elegant, beribboned, gentleman's pince-nez, that was all his own - pure P. C.

William P. smiled. And smiled again as he recalled a shivering boy on the bow of the old Geo. E. Starr, standing bundled in the black wool scarf he'd wrapped him in. The boy had followed his father on deck, following him outside that miserable evening they'd first arrived. When he had been what? What could Paul have been? Seven or eight? Twenty-nine years ago...He remembered all of it. The hours of waiting...all of them - Evangeline, the children - every one of them so young. Yes. The boy beside him leaning from the bow railing. The sidewheeler's white railside. Yes, he remembered. Chafing to arrive. Impatient, good Lord, impatient even then...

"That...would be...entirely wonderful," said young Harper, standing with his plank-straight back to the old man, leaving little doubt as to how entirely un-wonderful he thought the operator to be. "That is correct. Edwin Selvin. Financial Section. Yes, tell him P. C. Harper," the young banker said. "Tell him P. C. Harper's on the line."

• • •

By Monday morning, the P-I's financial editor, Edwin Selvin, had run his friend's story beneath his own byline, carrying Harper's information to the town. "Bank Moves From Haller To New Home On Pike Street," announced the the April 17th edition of the paper. "Paul Harper, vice president of Mortgage Trust & Savings, recently oversaw...the bank's handsome new quarters...lavishly finished in white marble, quartered oak and bronze...located on the ground floor of the Third & Pike office building owned by Wm. P. Harper & Son."

Over that same, rain-filled weekend, Mortgage Trust & Saving's 36-year-old vice president had also managed to move the Washington Abstract Company over into the bank's former offices in the Haller. P. C. had arranged to purchase this title insurance company several months before. If buildings were to be built, bonds sold, then of necessity property titles were to be searched. As owners of the mortgage bank - and the title company - the Harpers would provide a convenience for local builders, and two paydays for themselves with each transaction. With the young banker's enterprising eye for detail, little of this missed Selvin's desk at the P-I.

"Five-story Building Planned for Fourth Avenue," announced the paper's financial pages. "Mortgage Trust & Savings To Put Out Another Realty Bond Issue," "Paul C. Harper Explains Essentials," "Mortgage Trust Finances New Building," "P. C. Harper Tells Of Merits...."

The merits Paul Harper had so described, were aspects of a system he'd imported from the East. This was a formula he felt would fit the still cash-poor Pacific Northwest. In a guest column written under his own byline, headed "Small Investor's Needs Cared For," and published on Selvin's pages in the P-I almost a year to the day before moving the bank, Paul Coates gave the city a primer in this new scheme. "During the past few years," Harper began, "the bank has found it more and more difficult to obtain mortgages of medium size to supply for safe investment. At the same time we have been offered many very desirable loans of larger amount. The obvious thing to do, was to combine the two demands in the form of ["bonds and mortgage,"] long used in handling loans in the Eastern cities of this country."

["Bonds and mortgage."] The idea was exotic enough that the banker set the phrase in quotes, bordering it in brackets. However, Harper's new plan offered no great intrigue, his was simply a proposal to slice a large, locally unmarketable mortgage into so many affordable bits. Under Harper's plan, each of these "bits" would become a first mortgage bond, offered by Mortgage Trust in $250, $500 and $1,000 denominations. Here was a method by which the city might develop itself - removed from a dependence on eastern money, which was the plight of every western settlement, undercapitalized and trying to grow. Here were bonds all could afford, each low-priced note backed by a single sizable lien.

"There is no priority of one note, or "bond" as it is still called in the East, over any other," Harper went on, as if translating from a foreign language. "No one has a first claim and the others second. All are equally secured by the mortgage. Now add to each of these notes its own coupons, representing interest due, and you have the essentials of the mortgage coupon bond."

And why should the town's aspiring middleclass invest in "Eastern" bonds? Harper, having gauged his newly moneyed, newly conservative clientele, had a ready answer: They were safe...

"Loans are only made upon close-in, well-selected property, and never exceed 50 percent of appraised valuation," Harper wrote. "Each mortgage runs to the Bank as trustee for the bond holders, and each calls for the insuring of the property and for title insurance to the full amount of the mortgage."

Having disclosed the innerworkings of his securities, there remained for the banker-cum-columnist one final explanation; if his plan were to work, it was important he put it right. "Many people have an idea that a single mortgage is more desirable than these bonds," Harper wrote, going after his scheme's real adversaries: the town's single mortgages, and the young investment community's freewheeling economics.

To raise cash for construction in turn-of-the-century Seattle, a prospective builder first delivered himself up to one or another of the city's several banks. If his proposal was sound - the possibility of its returns intriguing enough - an awaiting loan officer would quickly attach a lien to the builder's property. At the instance of signatures being applied to various bottom lines, this lien then took on a life of its own, becoming, much as diamonds or gold, a thing of value. Merchandised as a "single mortgage," considered solid and reliable, the obligation was then sold to the bank's wealthiest clientele as investment.

From the investor's point of view, this was straightforward enough. Here was an unembroidered venture these investors could stroll by each day - free to lay a boot to its cornerstones, peer in its windows, check its occupancy rates - safe in the knowledge that should bad lead to worse, they'd come out acquiring city rental property at cents on the dollar. All of which, however, evaded the fundamental question: Having acquired rental space on the bottom vanishing from the rental market...what then?

For investors unwilling to take this risk, Harper was proposing something new, a radical kind of conservatism. Under the young banker's plan, if a piece of property fell into receivership, individual bond holders remained secure, easily cashed-out in any eventual sale. The plan's safeguards seemed self-evident, its disbursement of interest secure. But did it make sense? Was it advisable?

"Absolutely nothing...can be better safeguarded in every detail," the columnist insisted. "And the choice of close-in property with...steady market value of land and rentals make these bonds quite as safe as the single mortgage, and much more satisfactory."

Twelve months later, by 1916, the ambitious mortgage banker had lined the city's editors up like fish on a string. "Mortgage Trust Finds Plan Long Popular In East Meeting With Success In Seattle," announced the P-I. "Regrade To Have Apartment House, Bonds Offered By Mortgage Trust," hailed The Times. "Eastern Method Used By Mortgage Trust & Savings."

Soon the tags of "unfamiliar," and "Eastern," were no longer to be applied; Mortgage Trust & Savings being the picture of tradition itself. This symmetry could be seen in the huge volume of the bank's new first-mortgage bonds, in the mortgage department's development of larger and larger loans, and in the savings department, the driver in every other bank, keeping everything reasonably bank-like. Wheels within wheels. Once rolling, the organization had developed a momentum of its own.

It was this momentum that had carried the Harpers out of the old Haller Building and into their new quarters at Third and Pike. And it was there, ensconced in their "beautifully decorated banking room," surrounded by white marble, quartered oak and bronze, that William Penn Harper realized that momentum can also be created by things simply pulling apart - in a hurry. For less than two months after having completed the move, his son had pulled the whole bronze-clad bottom out of his father's oak and marble bank.

• • •

SUMMER IN THE MODERN AGE

BY JUNE OF 1916, THE FINANCIAL PANIC OF 1907, WITH ITS long and ugly slump, was finally over. A vast European conflict some had begun to call a "World War" had begun to demand the cheap, raw materials the Pacific Northwest could provide. The opening of the Panama Canal had increased the area's trade dramatically. In February, the first vessel passed through the city's new locks - an engineering wonder that connected Lake Washington and the Sound. Local boatyards had begun employing their shiftworkers around the clock, even as the city watched 8,000 men lockstep down Second Avenue in a "Preparedness Parade." Soon Seattle began to expand, to rise. Slowly at first, then with increasing haste, an acceleration good for almost everyone, everyone being an astonishing 348,000 citizens by that summer of 1916.

To an entrepreneurial mortgage banker in a satin-ribboned pince-nez, the times may have seemed ideal. The city was rising on tides of labor and money and just enough luck. Professionally, as business editor Selvin indicated in the pages of the P-I, these were commodities the shrewd young banker could combine on demand. Indeed, the demand for investment services seemed to be growing as precipitously as the town. It was this fact that may have led, not 60 days after the move to the corner of Third and Pike, to the bank finally coming apart.

> "Negotiations conducted during the past week between Ebenezer Shorrock at the Northwest Trust & Safe Deposit Co. and the Mortgage Trust & Savings Bank, resulted today in the taking over of the banking...of Mortgage Trust...by Northwest Trust & Safe Deposit."

TAKING STOCK

So ran the lead from an article on the business pages of <u>The Times</u>, June 30, 1916. The pretext given for the sudden sale was William P.'s unexpected ill health, which almost made sense. At least, it appeared to make sense, but for one hale and hearty fact: the 71-year-old president of Mortgage Trust wasn't ill. His son, however, had come to believe the commercial banking end of their business was something less than robust. By early summer of 1916, P. C. had finally understood this problem had been with them from the day they'd first opened their doors.

It had been in 1908, when realtor F. W. West had called for a new kind of bank, some new "sort of agency" that would bring people with small amounts of money to lend together with persons who wished "loans on real estate for building purposes." With an institution such as that," the builder had predicted, "the city would go ahead with greater speed."

This had been the Harpers' blueprint, the pattern upon which Mortgage Trust had been drawn. The dean of realtors had called for a new sort of bank; the Harpers had volunteered to become bankers. But if William. P. had ushered something new onto the scene, and if by his so doing, West's agency were then accomplished, then the question could be asked: What manner of new bank was this?

From his first day in business in the Seattle of 1892, William Penn Harper's trade had been that of making loans on real estate, marketing the resultant mortgages as investment. If long-held desires pushed him in the direction of banking, his business was something different: he had been a commission agent and middleman. Founding Mortgage Trust & Savings Bank had institutionalized that activity, it hadn't changed it.

It had, however, altered the Harpers' perceptions of their business, channeling the two men's energies into certain, well-worn paths. Finding themselves running a savings bank, the two bankers had expected their building loans to be driven by deposits, a rising tide of new, small depositors. Wasn't this the way a savings bank was to be run? Weren't deposits the force that drove a bank? In fact, as P. C. Harper began to see, this had never happened, not in the six years of the bank's operations, no matter how the city had grown.

So the younger Harper had begun by rethinking his business, starting at the beginning, going through the bank's account books year by year. He saw that by 1912, Mortgage Trust & Savings had listed $153,000 in its mortgage accounts, carrying $16,000 in savings. Three years later, by 1915, their savings had grown by $30,000. Yet the bank's real estate mortgage division had more than doubled that, increasing by $74,000. Over the next 12 months, the bank's mortgage business again climbed by another $70,000.

Then in the spring of 1916, while savings fell off, a $200,000 transaction on a Pine Street property put the mens' business on an entirely new footing. It was this transaction that forced young Harper to rethink the basic premise for their bank.

In March of 1916 P. C. had gone to see Daniel Kelleher, the prominent Chairman of the Board of Seattle National Bank. Harper had known Kelleher slightly, though the crusty Irishman was several decades his senior. The two were both clubmen, members of the Men's University Club, the Rainier, and Seattle Yacht Clubs. Though the patronizing banker had never discussed his business with Harper, nevertheless, over the course of these social evenings, Harper had managed to learn a fair bit about the chairman. First of all, he had discovered that Kelleher owned the Federal Hotel and its double lot on the southwest corner of Third Avenue and Pine Street. By making his own discreet inquiries, P. C. also found the chairman had made this profitable, if illiquid investment four years before. More importantly, P.C. knew that Kelleher had tied up much of his cash in this deal. This was money, Harper surmised, observing the pre-war boom then going on around him, that Kelleher would enjoy laying his hands on.

Ushered into the chairman's spacious office, Harper was confronted with the balding, heavyset Kelleher, presiding as aloof as Buddha behind his large and impressively empty desk. Asked what business he might have at the bank, Harper simply made himself comfortable in one of the banker's wing backed chairs, crossed his legs and lit a cigarette. He knew exactly what he could offer Kelleher, even better, he knew it was precisely what the old man wanted. Harper's opening gambit - a money-back-guarantee.

Why not, he asked the banker, have the public pay off Kelleher's Federal Hotel mortgage, putting the chairman's original purchase price back in his pocket? And what was more: have the public pay Kelleher a profit to boot. Mortgage Trust, he led Kelleher to understand, was prepared to do exactly this. It would be accomplished, Harper explained, by "securitizing" Kelleher's cumbersome mortgage; that is, breaking it up and selling it to local buyers as small-denomination bonds. Harper further proposed that these securities be callable. If Kelleher wanted his equity back, he could quietly take it back, piece by piece. In return for designing and seeing the $200,000 deal through, the young mortgage banker would, he explained, require a personal note from Kelleher for $20,000 - payable when the issue was sold. This was a requirement, to which the condescending chairman, then suddenly less so, promptly, even hastily agreed.

Priced between $100-$1,000, the bonds came out in April at six-and-a-half percent, the entire issue maturing six years later. Attractive, local, short-term investments - Harper sold them off in less than 90 days, putting nearly a quarter of a million dollars into Kelleher's account, taking his $20,000 in commission. With the war approaching, there appeared any amount of similar business to be done. As P. C. continued slogging through Mortgage Trust's account books, certain facts began to fall together, until at last they were all of a piece.

Whatever he and his father's original plans, one element of their business remained unmistakable: Their savings bank was doing nothing. At the same time, their bond department was carrying almost a half million dollars worth of the city's mortgage trade. The father and son's share of this was well over $30,000 a year. P. C. knew that his friend, Ebenezer Shorrock, President and chief executive officer of Northwest Trust, paid himself an annual salary of $5,200. This was generous compensation for the president of a Seattle bank. Yet it wasn't a third of what Harper made himself. Still, he and his father had bothered themselves with the running of a bank.

In fact, as the younger man then began to see, the Harper's business lay in selling bonds and making loans on city real estate. It always had been. Paul Harper didn't have to wait for his vaults to fill in order to to do business, he could create deals. Positioning himself between builders and investors, he would secure projects, make commitments, slice his loans into so many affordable bits, then sell them off as mortgage bonds. By putting together larger and larger packages of these new, small denomination bonds, Harper could provide larger and larger loans, paying bondholder's an attractive interest, and affording himself a satisfactory profit. Clearly, by taking their mortgage business out of the bank, he and his father would eliminate regulation, reduce overhead, and immediately expand their margins. This was his *real* engine. If new, it was also precisely the need he filled in the city.

It was at this point that P. C. traded the banking division of Harper & Son away to Shorrock at Northwest Trust. He then put the company's new oak and marble bank on the rental market, knowing Wm. P. Harper & Son would have no future need of it. For Paul Harper had seen what his pioneer father had failed to see - it wasn't so much a bank they'd been running... but a brokerage.

• • •

In January of the new year, Paul Coates moved the city's pioneer bond house of William P. Harper & Son into the new Hoge Building. Seventy-two year-old William Penn, feeling a sudden chill, turned up the collar of his topcoat, clamped his old black bowler squarely on his head, and quietly absented himself before the move to the modern skyscraper was complete. With the retirement of his father, Paul Harper discontinued the company's offering of first-mortgage bonds on city residences; that had been William P.'s end of the business. Instead, P. C. branched into a full inventory of bonds: corporates, governments, and a varying line of local municipals. He then began moving onto larger projects, financing the city's new St. Regis Hotel, the Lumber Exchange Building, the General Furniture and the Seaboard Buildings.

The World War finally came with the first spring days of the year, Wilson delivering his declaration of hostilities against Germany. Orders for war materiel soon brought money into the city. Seattle's fledgling investment community, capturing its commissions selling war bonds, financing the city's mobilization and the economy's renewed build-up, began expanding outward from First Avenue, moving up out of its walk-in, ground floor offices. The tower of the L.C. Smith Building soon marked the financial district's southern rim; the heavily ornamented, 18-story Hoge Building its impressive hub.

Second and Cherry. In 1917, the address of the Hoge was pure prestige. John E. Price and Co.; Lumberman's Trust Company-Bank; A. B. Leach & Co.; Odom & Howe; Smith & Strout; Bond, Goodwin & Tucker; G. E. Miller

& Co.; Baillargeon, Winslow & Co. - all were investment houses domiciled in the building, all members of the city's booming investment scene. And each day at noon, as dependably as the workings of the finest Swiss clock, the whole pack would surge out of the Hoge on its way to a place called Manca's.

The little restaurant was famous in Seattle. In fact, among the town's brokers - who believed they'd made it so - the cafe had come to be a downtown club - its spartan atmosphere, generous meals, and an inexpensive supply of drink bringing in the district's brokers, bankers, and businessmen. Though anyone was allowed to dine there, its mid-day patrons also knew this entirely missed the point. For not everyone was a participant, initiated into the cafe's fellowship, with its busy, teeming, table-hopping lunches. But even membership was no mystery, fraternal or otherwise. At Manca's, it was simply a matter of being recognized.

"Well hell, hello Eddy," said Ebeneezer Shorrock. "I didn't see you there. Sit down."

"Must be 80 degrees waiting out there on that damn sidewalk," said Edwin Selvin, accepting the banker's offer, the tables and booths in the crowded restaurant already filled with its noontime crowd.

"A cold bottle of beer might revive you," said Shorrock, who, though he hadn't been expecting the editor from the P-I, knew Selvin well enough. "The trick is to order them early, before Victor runs out of ice."

"Four or five might bring me back to life," said Selvin. "But I don't want to interrupt your lunch, Eb."

"Not at all," said Shorrock, a tall man with a thin face and a graying mustache. "I hardly ever eat in the middle of the day. Anyway, its always good to buy the business press a drink."

Selvin, much younger, and a good half-foot shorter than Shorrock, appeared nearly twice as wide, the P-I's editor being built like a miniture bull.

"You haven't seen Paul Harper in here earlier, have you?"

"No," said Shorrock. "He always sits over there in that big corner booth with Baillargeon and Ed Strout. Though I don't see either Baillargeon or Strout now. Why? Paul have you doing a story on Harper and Son?"

"You know, Harper," said Selvin, smiling. "It's the company's 25th anniversary next month. He's been calling, and happens to mention it.

Anyway, I know he always eats here."

"I imagine P.C. doesn't let you alone."

"You know him, alright. But, of course, you bought their bank."

"I've known Paul Harper for 20 years. Since we went to the university together. I was there the day he got expelled from the place."

Is that so? For what?"

"For breaking a boy's nose."

"That a fact?"

"And his jaw, as I remember. This city hasn't always been the flower of civility we enjoy today, Eddy."

"I'm from Chicago, Eb."

"Paris compared to this place. I suppose you couldn't put it on the business page, but I could tell you stories, Eddy..."

"I could listen, Eb," said Edwin Selvin, who, catching Victor Manca's eye, asked for the two coldest bottles of beer in the house, then took out the notepad he always carried in his coat.

• • •

From his new office on the 13th floor of the Hoge, Paul Harper could see Ed Strout, Ceibert Baillargeon and Andrew Price, all three standing directly below him, clumped together talking to Henry Carstens. From this height, his friends appeared as the tops of so many heads. It was odd. Then as they walked up Second Avenue, their feet came into view, first one, then another, left and right, directly in front of their chins. It made them look like, well, P. C. didn't know what they looked like... Still, it was an odd perspective. And Harper, thinking about it, thought it must be the same view a pilot had in flying a plane.

Looking in the direction the brokers had gone, Harper searched north, past the Empire Building and the Savoy Hotel. Finally, up the streetcar filled avenue, P. C. could just see the tip of the Harper Building. The day was clear, and he paused for a moment, studying the building, catching himself thinking of their old bank. Then thinking of the old man.

The two of them had often been like oil and water. Even as a boy. When he'd been filled with the enthusiasms of a boy, talking of being an explorer,

45

a politician, a military man. All those tales he'd read as a child. Things his father had ignored, too modest to even allow them as possibilities. And when he'd tried to enter West Point... What was that he had called him? . . . A romantic. Yes, well, he was no romantic either. Romance was believing yourself to be a banker when you made your living as a middleman. He had certainly made more money in commissions in the last two years than his father had ever seen at the bank. He was paid for his services. He saw to that. No, romance was what they gave you when they didn't give you money. William P. could have all of that he wanted.

Taking the elevator to the ground floor, waiting as the operator raised the lift's latticed gates, Harper realized he was suddenly hungry. As he stepped from the car's open doors, he found himself walking faster. He was late. And the restaurant would be full. Though hell, why hurry? It was a beautiful day, and he was bound to know everyone there.

In 1921, the English author W. L. George, observed that "America feels business is the finest, as well as the most valuable function of man; she perceives in the business man the qualities of hero...doing the best that can be done by man." By decade's end, this American Best would be christened "Coolidge's Prosperity," though to many Americans, to those not failing in the country's wheat fields or farm belt, the times would be even better than "best." They would be grand.

It was a romance that lit the town in the twenties, filling the office towers on Seattle's Second Avenue, informing the cut of women's fashions, lending its style to the explosion of business success, fashioning the ambience of smart new restaurants, and the adventure of prohibition's after-hour joints downtown. As much opportunity as excitement, at its heart lay pure anticipation. "Never had there been a better time to get rich," John Kenneth Galbraith has written about the period, "and people knew it."

Tuesday, September 13, 1927. On the day Charles Lindburgh landed in the city, the young flier found Seattle plugged into the incandescence of the Big Bull Market, the feverishness of the advancing DOW having turned frontier Seattle's Second Avenue into Dreamstreet on the Sound. One had only to rise in the morning, pick up the paper, and... B-O-O-M, watch as the DOW sailed right off the page, the one-way market flying even further than Lindburgh.

By 1927, stock brokerages had begun taking on the trappings of urban celebrity, Second Avenue brokers become advertisements for an age, for the true new style. The town's pioneers, city fathers of wealth and years, began taking their business to brokers as young as twenty-five, anticipating these young men's results - then getting them. For somewhere in the decade, youth and optimism had stepped through the looking glass, the bull market converting both to a roaring infallibility. Boy-millionaires began populating the local landscape, building posh addresses and bankable names. One such address was the corner of Seattle's Second Avenue and Cherry Street, in the heart of the city's investment district, the names were Drumheller, Ehrlichman & White.

Chapter Three

THE ANGLE OF ASCENT

Dreamstreet

"IT'S NOT A DEPARTURE, GEORGE," SAID ROSCOE DRUM-
heller, waiting for George Harroun to fit himself into one of the boardroom's leather chairs. "Not from United Bond & Share. Besides, Ben feels,
and I agree, the words investment trust shouldn't be in the title. United
Founders has done well back East. People know it. I think United Pacific will
do just fine for us here in the Northwest."

"As always in these matters," replied the heavyset Harroun, "I defer to
your financial acumen, Roscoe."

"As always..." said Ben Ehrlichman, stepping into the carpeted boardroom
behind the two men. "And bill us for the flattery every quarter, right, George?"

"You wound me, Ben," said Harroun, turning to smile at the brokerage's
young president. "Cut me to the very quick."

"Thank God it's nothing very serious then," said the tall, opulently
tailored Ehrlichman, walking to the long conference table at the center of the
paneled room. "In any case, George, we'll be needing your talents this
morning. There's a few details with United Pacific still left to iron out, and I'd
like to finish up this afternoon. Earlier if possible. I'm still planning on seeing
Colonel Lindburgh at two."

"I thought we'd go out together," said Drumheller. "Perhaps drag George here along."

"If I may, I'll forgo the adventure, gentlemen," said Harroun, crossing one, sausage-like leg over the other, revealing beige silk socks gartered clear to the knee. "If the crowds are going north, I believe I'll remain in town for a quiet dinner. In my humble estimation, the best dining companion still remains a competent headwaiter. Which reminds me... friend Harper was telling me a story over lunch yesterday."

"P. C.?" asked Ehrlichman.

"The one. It concerns a certain scissor-grinder," said Harroun. "And may be of particular interest to you," he added. Glancing up at Ehrlichman, Harroun then began his story with a ponderous recrossing of legs, the man's hosiery looking more and more like bologna skins.

"It seems," he began, "that Harper had known this peddler when Paul was still a boy; in any case, knew him enough to say hello. The Harpers," Harroun added, looking knowingly at his two listeners, "have been here since Creation, you understand... Anyway, it seems that after all this time the man came to pay P. C. a visit. Walked into his office dressed in rags - evidently his usual rig - wanting to see Young Mister Harper. It turned out the scissor-grinder had just disposed of a $100,000 of equities. Radio, I believe it was. Asked that P. C. sell him governments. So...Harper sold them to him."

"All $100,000?" asked Drumheller.

"Indeed. $100,000 in Treasuries. Afterwards, P. C. contends he actually took this scarecrow to Rippey's. Being seated, which is wonderment enough, the old man looked at a dish of rolls placed on the table, and then proceeded to filch the whole lot, dump them in his pocket. All of them. Said he wouldn't have to buy bread that week."

"As if he couldn't afford it?"

"Peculiar isn't it. But it gets even odder. Paul Harper said the man's actual name is Hillen. Peter Hillen. Perhaps you recognize it? He told Harper he owned a sizable piece of United Bond & Share."

"One of ours," said Ehrlichman.

"A shareholder, yes."

"Isn't that something," said Ehrlichman.

"Something, yes," proclaimed Harroun. "But exactly what sort of something? I mean...Good Lord, Ben, an itinerant peddler. And a scissors-grinder at that..."

"But why not?" Ehrlichman laughed. "George! You ought to go downstairs and talk to our sales people more often. Ask them about their clients. It's not all rich, fat lawyers like yourself."

"That's not the question!" puffed the attorney, raising objections from the depths of his hidebound chair.

"No, you're right," said Ehrlichman, picking up the phone to his appointment secretary. "The real question is, why not everybody?"

• • •

"Why not everybody?" If the question still lingered, the markets had been supplying its answer for months, as volumes on the nation's exchanges grew larger and larger, carrying stock values to historic levels. Wall Street intellectuals and leading economists had begun to declaim a progressive and perpetual prosperity, a green and permanent plateau stretching as far as the eye could see. Why, the question had begun to be asked, why should the middle class work for the most modest of returns, when with a little help, the market could offer riches overnight? Why indeed? To Benjamin Bernerd Ehrlichman, the zealous young president of Drumheller, Ehrlichman & White, the key lay in pressing and pushing the city's investment community in directions it had not gone before. That young Ehrlichman's methods were new, certainly unheard of in Seattle, hardly seemed to matter...they had almost immediately worked.

"Seattle's Boy Millionaire," the local papers had begun to trumpet, "The Man Of A Thousand Ideas." By 1927 even Ehrlichman's enemies were calling him the best financial mind in Seattle. On this morning of September 13, 1927, the date of Lindburgh's flight to Seattle, the best financial mind in Seattle was being chauffeured into work from his Washington Park home. He had been looking forward to Lindburgh's flight for weeks, and now Ehrlichman was eager to get to the office, eager to begin. Dressed in a chalk-stripe blue suit and ten-button spats, kidskin gloves folded carefully in his lap, Seattle's 32-year-old investment tycoon had been reminded of his Christian

Science, the scripture he had memorized as a youth: "Man doesn't grovel in the dirt - he lifts himself." Exactly, thought Ehrlichman, his gaze falling on his Malacca walking stick lying on the limousine seat beside him. Picking it up, Ehrlichman felt its heft, tapping its silver tip on the Cadillac's jump-seat in front of him. Mindful of the Malacca cane, the kid gloves, the leather seat stretching out beside him, Ehrlichman suddenly smiled, mindful of something else, something the young millionaire would one day tell a local business reporter: "I could..." he had then confided, "I could easily have been a bum."

The old, old story - even if it wasn't true. But then Ehrlichman had believed it all his life. For Seattle's "Boy Millionaire," while still a boy, had known nothing of millions. His earliest years had been punctuated by Ehrlichman's father, Walter, deserting his family in Seattle. No letters would ever arrive, no money would be mailed to Ehrlichman's mother, Antoinette, nor would word ever be sent to his sisters - or brother - or himself. Ever. Instead, Ben, the dutiful, driven, and intensely ambitious oldest son, found work selling morning papers along Second Avenue. His brother, Rudy, would find work as a deck hand on the city's ferries.

In the spring of 1912, at the age of 17, his wage as newsboy no longer meeting necessities at home, Ben Ehrlichman once again found himself downtown looking for work, for real work this time. It had been raining off and on throughout the day, and the 17-year-old was wet and cold and finally despairing of again returning home empty-handed - when he spotted something. In fact, it was someone: an older, prosperously dressed gentleman leaving an office building at the southeast corner of First Avenue and Cherry Street. Catching up, Ehrlichman had asked the stranger if he knew of any jobs to be had. The man, Henry Carstens by name, asked the boy what skills he had to offer. Ehrlichman, as precisely desperate as only a wet, broke, ex-newsboy might be, blurted the truth: "I don't know how to do anything!" Apparently this was the answer Carstens had been waiting to hear. "You're just the fellow I'm looking for," he told the boy, asking Ehrlichman if he could come to work the next day. Of course he could, but where? The businessman gave Ehrlichman his card. On it was printed, "Carstens & Earles, Mortgage Bonds and Stocks, 1st & Cherry." "You can't miss it," Carstens said, and laughed,

Above: Ex-Shearson bond broker, Jim Adams, in his new offices at Oppenheimer. Right: Adams' partner, Gary Farber.

Top: KKRA's Ned Karren, conferring with partner, Bruce Rinne. Center: KKRA's Mike Kunath. KKRA's, Jeff Atkin, the clean-desk-man.

Left: Robbins Harper, divining the mysteries of the bond market. Below: Jeff Wilson, on the phone at PaineWebber's institutional sales desk.

FINANCIAL
FIRM GROWS WITH CITY

WILLIAM P. HARPER & SON
PIONEER INVESTMENT HOUSE.

After Third of a Century, Bond-
ing Company Now Is in
Wider Field.

WILLIAM P. HARPER, Upper.
PAUL C. HARPER.

Opposite page: The Geo. E. Starr, coming into Seattle, 1879. Photo by A. Curtis. Neg # 486. Top: detail from William P. Harper & Son ad. Column featuring William P. Harper and his son, Paul Coates Harper.

Founded 1892

Wm. P. Harper & Son

Municipal, Corporation, Mortgage
Bonds

Hoge Bldg.,   *Seattle, Wash.*

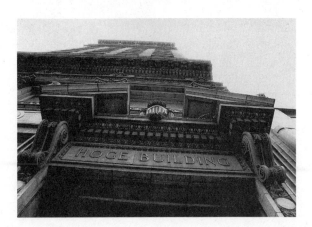

Top: The Quaker and the
Clubman. Bottom: The entrance
to the Hoge Building.

A young Ben Ehrlichman, making the first air delivery of the San Francisco Bulletin.

Career of Ben Ehrlichman Is Talk of Financial World

Former Broadway High School Student Climbs Ladder Rapidly to Head of Merger.

BEN B. EHRLICHMAN—who is he?

His name is on the tongue of almost everyone in Seattle's financial world today.

He's the 33-year~~~~~~ the United Group~~~~~ with $12,000,000 cap~~~~ volume of $47,000,00~~~~~

~~~~edited w~~~~
~~~~pioneer~~~~
~~~~d Dive~~~~
~~~~of S~~~~
~~~~p.
~~~~is he~~~~
~~~~poration~~~~
~~~~roup of~~~~
~~~~addit~~~~
~~~~ookane~~~~
~~~~ent of~~~~
~~~~White,~~~~
~~~~group.
~~~~ent of~~~~
~~~~rporatio~~~~
~~~~vice

United Pacific Ca~~~~ Company, vice ~~~~ United Medical and~~~~ Inc., all of them ~~~~ United Corporation~~~~ a Knight Templar and a thirty-second degree Mason.

Quits School Early.

In 1913 he was a sophomore at Broadway High Scho~~~~ quit his schooling at~~~~ to go out into the wo~~~~ living.

His rise in similar t~~~~
~~~~ry books.
~~~~tage of col~~~~
~~~~have an ind~~~~
~~~~n on his b~~~~
~~~~have as~~~~
~~~~as the ordi~~~~
~~~~ollege. He~~~~
~~~~$30 a mon~~~~
~~~~orked. He~~~~
~~~~the advice~~~~
~~~~ns & Earles~~~~
~~~~rs. It had~~~~
that his first job~~~~ school was in an inve~~~~

When he had lear~~~~ sell bonds, he joine~~~~ Guardian Savings Bank. Then came war. He enlisted and became an air pilot, serving as an instr~~~~ camps in this country. Returning, he took charge of the bond department of the National City Bank of Seattle. Later he transferred to Ta-

coma, where he became vice president in charge of bonds of the Puget Sound Bank there.

In 1921 he became interested with ~~~~~, then collector of ~~~~~ $25,600 of Drum~~~~ ~~~y formed the firm ~~~~ Ehrlichman & Co. ~~~~man, now a vice ~~~~xpanded firm was~~~~ ~~~~that la~~~~ ~~~~small r~~~~

~~~~ater m~~~~
~~~~23 W.~~~~
~~~~and th~~~~
~~~~le his~~~~
~~~~ued a~~~~
~~~~Ben Eh~~~~
~~~~uccess~~~~
~~~~to Sea~~~~

~~~~Princi~~~~
~~~~our co~~~~
~~~~it all w~~~~
~~~~severa~~~~
~~~~hrlichm~~~~
stant adherence to ~~~~ I believe, accounts ~~~~

~~~~ple was 'If a thing ~~~~ssible of achieve-ment.' With that principle one ~~~~ook at the apparent ob-~~~~ long as he satisfies him-self the course is right.

"We have never sold a man se~~~~ being sure he knows ~~~~ing. It is our prin-~~~~ggerate.

~~~~ys eliminated from ~~~~ men of the flippant ~~~~ outside of ~~~~redit on th~~~~ ~~~~e that the ~~~~r only whe~~~~ ~~~~and we h~~~~ ~~~~t they sha~~~~

~~~~ys devoted ~~~~ting our c~~~~ ~~~~e the offic~~~~ ~~~~tact with ~~~~ght to ma~~~~ ~~~~ur stocks, ~~~~ We haven't held any ~~~~r investors."

~~~~an has been married ~~~~ He has a daughter, Nancy, 7 years old, whose interests are his chief diversion.

~~~~entive for all this work and self-denial? First, his family. Second, "I enjoy achievement more than anything else in business, more than making money."

Roscoe Drumheller

Herb White

Ben B. Ehrlichman

Elwood Denny

Rudy Ehrlichman

Geo. Harrou

Ben Ehrlichman, as he appeared in Clarence Bagley's, History of Seattle.

Ben Ehrlichman's office in the Bailey Building.

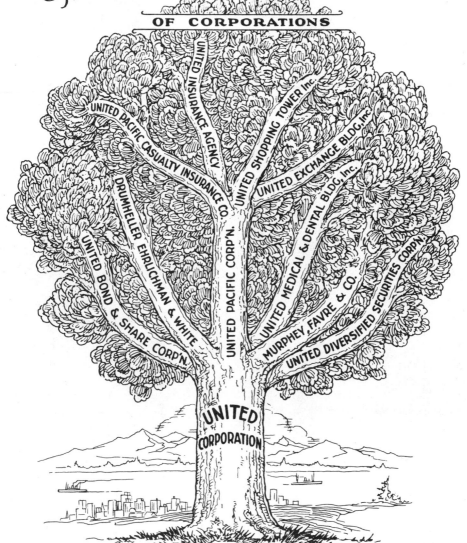

The UNITED GROUP
OF CORPORATIONS

(tree branches labeled:) UNITED INSURANCE AGENCY · UNITED PACIFIC CASUALTY INSURANCE CO. · UNITED SHOPPING TOWER Inc. · UNITED EXCHANGE BLDG. Inc. · DRUMHELLER EHRLICHMAN & WHITE · UNITED PACIFIC CORP'N. · UNITED MEDICAL & DENTAL BLDG. Inc. · UNITED BOND & SHARE CORP'N. · MURPHEY, FAVRE & CO. · UNITED DIVERSIFIED SECURITIES CORP'N. · UNITED CORPORATION

A GROUP of eleven Corporations, mutually benefited by their affiliation. Among the benefits accruing are: the associating of many hundreds of stockholders, who in various ways may patronize their own Corporations; the bringing together of preferred insurance risks, both individual and corporate; the advantage of having available for each enterprise a management skilled in finance and allied with strong banking interests — all this creating additional value in the properties and interests included in the United Group of Corporations.

Total combined Capital, Surplus, Reserves and Undivided Profits of the United Group, over $14,000,000

Top: Ben Ehrlichman, seated center, his nephew, John Ehrlichman at his knee, to the extreme right, Rudy Ehrlichman and George Harroun.

THE EXCHANGE BUILDING
FORMAL OPENING TOMORROW, MAY 5TH

Opposite page: Photo taken in 1929 showing the half-completed Exchange Building to the right, the Haller Building to the left, and Mancas' sign board appearing down the hill

Opposite page top: A
resident of Seattle's
Hooverville, 1931, photo
courtesy of Museum of
History and Industry.
Opposite page bottom: The
nine acres of Hooverville.
Opposite page bottom
right: News of Arthur
Bastheim's suicide.

This page right: A young
Jim Morford. This page
bottom: Charles "Chick"
Badgley.

Top: A smiling Mac Pringle after a good round of golf. Bottom: Bill Slater, during his years at Blyth.

pointing to the brass plaque on the stonework of the Lowman Building in front of them. "It's right here."

Ehrlichman was waiting outside the building the next morning by six.

• • •

"I heard two o'clock," said Elwood Denny, working the adding machine at the center of his cluttered desk. "That's what it said in the paper." As the 29-year-old accountant spoke, he worked the machine's keyboard with his left hand, pulling its black, lever-like arm with his right. "This morning's radio said people were already parking half-way out Sand Point Way."

"So we don't park," said an even younger Rudolf Ehrlichman, standing just inside his brother-in-law's hutchlike office. "We drive out this afternoon. Take the Cadillac past the gate. Or ask Ben. He must know someone or other at the air station. What time've you got?"

"I...9:45," said the nearsighted Denny, continuing his calculations as he looked at the clock on his office wall. Elwood then glanced at his brother-in-law, Rudy in the act of re-perfecting an already perfectly knotted cravat.

"Let's see," said Rudy Ehrlichman. "Three-and-a-half hours will get your stuff out by 1:15. Tell you what, you just stay here, I'll go over to the exchange with Morford today, I haven't even seen the new room yet. That should clear you from eleven to one, give you plenty of time. But Elwood, look, we better work fast. How many times does Seattle get the Lone Eagle, huh? Lucky..."

"Rudy..." Elwood Denny interrupted, this uncharacteristic action causing the accountant to stop his calculations, the agitation even causing him to ferret a sheaf of paper from his buried work area. He then began tamping the stack edgewise in the clearing left upon his desk. "Listen, I don't mean to upset any plans, but I have a lot to do here. I've still got the cash projections to finish for Medical/Dental Inc. and Ben's upstairs with Roscoe right now waiting for these United Pacific runs. I mean I don't want to give you the rush," Denny said, his eyeglasses magnifying his eyes, lending the bookeeper the appearance of an anxious owl. "But don't you have any calls to make?"

The younger Ehrlichman, tall and dark, with a military haircut that looked as if it had been administered by means of a bowl, then parted in the middle and slicked straight back, straightened himself in the doorway. Then he smiled. "You know Elwood, I'm just dumb enough to take a personal interest. But a smart guy like yourself, this is probably history in the making. Don't you want to be part of that? The whole city's going to turn out this afternoon. Why, you couldn't keep me away."

"Well of course, *sure* I'd like to go," said Denny, looking for someplace to deposit the documents he now held in his hands, to cover the fact he had taken them up in the first place. "But it depends on..."

"I mean, the thing about it, how many times you think Lindburgh's going to come to Seattle?"

"No one's arguing," submitted Denny. "But I've got..." he said, at last resigning the stack of paperwork to its original subterranean site on his desk. "I've got my hands full." The accountant then sat back in his chair, and taking off his eyeglasses, began to clean them with a handkerchief he'd taken from his suit. "I know Ben'll go. I mean, I suppose he'll go" he added. "Actually, I'm sort of surprised he hasn't sent the fellows out for haircuts and a shine."

"Sure," said Rudy. "And the thing is... You and me and Ben, maybe some of the other fellows, we all oughta ride out in the limousine."

"I... Yes, of course." said Denny, sitting up again, putting his glasses back on.

"So, Woody, what did you get stuck with?" asked Ehrlichman, seating himself beside the man's crowded desk. "What are we going to do here?"

Once again, the accountant began his calculations, once more working the wooden handle of the calculator at the center of his cluttered desk, the sound of the instrument's turning gears the sound of inevitable pay-off. Elwood Denny began to work faster.

· · ·

In 1912, Henry Carstens believed young Ben Ehrlichman to be the quickest study he had ever hired. Instructing the gangling youth a first time seemed invariably sufficient, the boy rarely needed to be told anything twice. Soon Carstens' new employee was asking to do more than clean the ink wells and perform the menial chores first assigned him, eager to discover just what, exactly, a brokerage was.

In fact, Carstens & Earles was a bond house. Located at First and Cherry in the center of the city's brokerage district, the firm's primary business lay in selling first-mortgage bonds. Here the boy was initiated into the world of debt finance, rehearsed in the correlations of par and premium and yield, drilled each day in the system of the city's bond market. To the mechanically adept office boy, the workings of this new environment suggested an elaborate, even elegant machine, a device to create profit where none had existed before. And far better it seemed to the young man from the penniless family, the apparatus was impartial, impersonal, indifferent, its rewards could go to anyone - even himself.

Ehrlichman apprenticed to Henry Carstens and his partner for four years, working on the first floor of the Lowman Building from 1912 to 1916, apprenticing until the boy who hadn't known "how to do anything" could quote labyrinthine bond tables from memory. Then, in the fall of 1916, Ehrlichman made a move, traveling a block north to Seattle's Guardian Trust & Savings Bank. Offered $7 more a month, and promises of rapid advancement, Ehrlichman began as the bank's assistant cashier. He stayed in this position for five months, before being awarded the managership of Guardian Trust's bond department. Because of his age, the bank was forced to obtain a special dispensation from the state legislature to allow for the boy's advancement. The promotion was picked up by the local papers, the several headlines emphasizing the manager's youth: "Seattle's Boy Banker," "Banker Barely Out Of Teens." Ben Ehrlichman was just twenty years old.

In the Seattle of 1917, Paul Harper notwithstanding, the principal buyers of bonds were the areas's banks, insurance companies, trustees and those few individuals able to commit some portion of their wealth to investment. A growing list, it was still one which omitted the majority of citizens in the town. That this was fact, drew no one's very fevered attention; it was simply the way things were. For the brokerage community, however, largely dependent upon the town's pockets of prosperity and wealth, the way things were was soon to change.

On April 2, 1917, President Woodrow Wilson declared a state of war to be in existence between the United States and Germany. By this time, the hostilities had already rolled over the European Continent for thirty-six bloody months, the conflict draining its increasingly bankrupt combatants of both men and materiel. Low interest loans were being made to the European Allies by Eastern banks, but, so the Allies insisted, the advances were too few, and far from generous enough. To remedy this, a month after entering the war, Congress authorized the issuance of "Liberty Loans," modestly priced bonds yielding the country's investors a three-and-a-half percent return. Dubbed "Liberty Bonds" by the public, the securities were initially put on sale for just over a month, from May 2 to June 15, Congress requiring a subscription of at least $2 billion be sold. A national promotion was begun, the first of its kind, with posters promoting these securities going up like flags all over the country. People who had never before purchased securities, people who'd never before ever *thought* of purchasing securities, bought the new bonds. By June 15, four million of the country's citizens had subscribed to over $3 billion of Liberty Bonds, surpassing Congressional requirements by over a billion dollars. Though unintended by Congress, this national flotation was seen immediately as a watershed by the securities industry, the sale heralding a new and far broader market: the huge center of the country's vast middle class.

It was this public, now primed and hungry for investment, that Ehrlichman served as head of the bank's bond department. He offered up everything he could stock on the department's shelves: corporates, municipals, and foreign governments from a half dozen different countries - Anglo-French 5s, United Kingdom 5 1/2s, Russian 6s. His customers, in the first flush of the wartime boom, began to purchase the securities as fast as the youthful Ehrlichman could offer them. As a result, the earnest young bond manager, ambitious and driven and tasting his first success, began to look past even his managership with the bank.

Whatever he might once have said (echoes of his introduction to Henry Carstens), Ben Ehrlichman had never been unaware of his own abilities - nor was he now unaware of his actual accomplishments. He knew as well that he'd been fortunate. Chancing upon Carstens had been a stroke of luck: his abilities had fit into the man's brokerage like a lightbulb in a lamp. But even after his move, and his promotion at Guardian Trust, Ehrlichman also knew his skills were often flattened to the simplest mechanics, that of functionary, facilitating the market's machinery in its work. If Ehrlichman was making more money than he ever had, the young man also felt pressed to do more than simply set the bank's wheels in motion.

By the time the country's troops had joined the war in Europe, few in Ehrlichman's bond department were in doubt as to what the ambitious young banker required: never doubting that he expected continued advancement, and an acceleration of his recent, rapid ascent. What Ehrlichman was given, however, was a JN4D Curtiss. What he received was a lesson in control.

· · ·

"Hold it, hold it, hold it. Now keep holding and give me right full rudder. All the way. *Full* rudder, corporal. That's it, keep it full. That's right, now ease up and level out. Ease back. Throttle back and level out. Okay, now check your wing tips. How do they look to you? Well well, imagine that. So, what do you think, Ehrlichman? Your first Immelmann."

What did he think? The 23-year-old was soon soloing the maneuver high over San Diego's Rockwell Field. If he had thought his first JN4D Curtiss was exacting, the old Jennies were nothing to turning a big DeHavilland on its tail, upside-down and out again. Word of Immelmann's Roll had come back with the wounded from Europe, this enemy maneuver soon being instructed by the numbers, the roll's fluid motion broken into its constituent parts. As Ehrlichman had expected, with practice these components had quickly fused, the numbers becoming automatic: full throttle to vertical ascent, straight up - then straight over, flying upside-down in the reverse direction from which the maneuver had begun - before rolling over into level flight. That the roll became reflexive, however, hadn't been the point. The point was pure control. Borne in at every turn, at every wingover and roll, this was the airship's visceral teaching: The Gospel of Total Control. Without it, Ehrlichman would remain a glorified groundsman, left on the tarmac. Having it, he would be awarded his lieutenancy, and his airman's wings to fly.

The single and central lesson of his training - and it had not been forgotten when the young lieutenant re-entered civilian life two years later. In 1920, with the war over and his days as a flying instructor and air mail pilot at an end,

TAKING STOCK

Ehrlichman went to work at Tacoma's Puget Sound National Bank. No less driven, nor less ambitious, Ehrlichman almost immediately began looking for something of his own. He watched as the nation's post war markets bottomed, observing as they then slowly began gathering strength. By the end of 1920, the country's corporate earnings were good and getting better, stock prices low, yields favorable. Ehrlichman, barely able to make ends meet on his manager's salary, was forced to look on as these opportunities delivered themselves up to those with money. Ehrlichman hadn't any money at all. However, he did have a reputation, once again winning notice for his ability in the market. It was on the strength of this reputation that Ehrlichman was invited to lunch one afternoon - though he'd never heard of the man who had invited him. Still, being curious, he found himself in January of 1921 sitting across a table from a middle-aged businessman. The man reminded Ehrlichman a bit of old Henry Carstens. And, oddly enough, the first thing the man had told Ehrlichman was that as far as finance was concerned, he hardly knew how to do anything...and that furthermore he was wealthy. And that his name was Roscoe Drumheller.

"No reason to beat around the bush," Drumheller began, sipping a cup of sugared coffee at the end of their meal. "We both know you have brains. On the other hand, Ben, I have money. The question being: why don't we combine the two? Why don't we do business together?"

No reason Ehrlichman could think of, knowing this to be exactly the break he'd been waiting for. That was not, however, what he told Drumheller.

"Mr. Drumheller, you say you want to enter the securities business," Ehrlichman replied. "That you suspect the market is going to attempt some unbelievable rise. And that, furthermore, you want to get in early. Then you tell me you really don't know the first thing about it...I'm not sure what to say to your proposal, Mr. Drumheller."

"Please...Call me Roscoe."

"All right, Roscoe. I'll make *you* a proposal. There's an investment banking school up in Seattle, The American Investment Banking College. It offers a six month course in finance. You go to school there, then bring me back your course grade. If it's good enough, perhaps we'll see about doing business together."

Six months later, the well-to-do heir of Eastern Washington wheat money hurried back to show young Ehrlichman his "A." Ninety days after that, on September 26, 1921, the bond house of Drumheller, Ehrlichman & Co. opened for business in Tacoma's Rust Building. Drumheller had put up $50,000; Ehrlichman put up his ability. In twelve months the two men had moved their head office to Seattle. Not a year after that, the country's financial markets began their seemingly endless rise.

• • •

In September of 1927, the Seattle offices of Drumheller, Ehrlichman & White filled the first two floors of the city's Bailey Building, a courtly stone pile on the southeast corner of Cherry Street and Second Avenue. The offices of the company's three principles took up much of the building's second floor. Downstairs was given over to the firm's customer's men, the term for brokers in the twenties. Across the floor from these were D.E.W.'s traders and the company's operations staff. As befitted the largest, locally owned brokerage in the city, the office was stylish. Gone were the blonde, rolltop desks of twenty years before, replaced now with luminous, heavy-legged furniture, velvet drapes, leaded-glass windows, and brass, shieldlike chandeliers. The effect achieved was one of elegance, gravity, permanence...and a wall of noise. For unlike the golden silences of a bank, the hush of one crisp note contentedly covering another, the stock brokerage was a hive, its workers busily, blatantly on the make.

The trading department at D.E.W. had been forced to place its new, electric broad-tape out in the hall of the neighboring Railway Exchange Building, prying a brick from the common wall the buildings shared and feeding the tape through the opening. The apparatus, linked by wire to New York, was so loud the traders hadn't been able to make themselves heard over the phone. Out at the center of the brokerage floor, D.E.W.'s customer's men spent the daylight hours welded to their *own* phones, cigars in hand, shouting across at the trading department as they pushed the firm's preferred stock through the town. Around the perimeter of the floor, at the center of every secretary's desk, stood the big black Underwoods, their carriage returns going off like ring-bells at a smoker. In addition to this, there came the chorus of speculators walking in off the streets - their voices rising through the open doors of the first floor's public room. What was coming? What was hot? When to get on? When to get off? This clamor would cease only for the opening of each day's session at the exchange, at which time the curious would crowd out the doors of the brokerage, leaving D.E.W. in something nearly resembling peace.

By September of 1927, the City of Seattle had had a stock exchange of its own for 21 months. The exchange had been formed in January of 1926, in a room in the city's Rainier Club. Ehrlichman had been responsible for the meeting, but more than being attributable to Ehrlichman, the desire for a local stock exchange was in many ways the child of the decade itself. By 1926, local exchanges had formed across much of the country, exchanges in Los Angeles and San Francisco doing business in larger and larger volumes as the twenties wore on. It was decided Seattle should be no less endowed. Hadn't the town supported a mining and grain exchange for a number of years? As fit the wave of mergers then sweeping the nation, a plan was envisioned welding these separate units into a single, overseeing body. By the end of its meeting, the Rainier Club group, naming itself the Seattle Bond & Stock Exchange, even designed a corporate seal, the mark being two concentric circles, having within their margins: "Seattle Bond & Stock Exchange." In the center was the phrase: "Corporate Seal - 1926." Thus sealed and delivered, the infant exchange was offered up to the city.

The feeling of the exchange's founders, including Dietrich Schmidt, Ben Ehrlichman, Stanley Minor, Harry Grande, L. M. Arnold, Fred Blanchett, Andrew Price, Kenelm Winslow, Paul C. Harper, Homer Boyd, Tom Gleed and Mansel Griffiths, was there might be a billion dollars of Northwest corporation capital spread between public utilities, industrials and local banks. All had bonds and shares, securities susceptible to trading on just such a local exchange. Finding still other enthusiasts, the 16 became 25, and ten months later the Seattle Bond & Stock Exchange opened in rooms taken from the Seattle Clearing House. With its business increasing, in March of 1927, the exchange had moved to permanent quarters on the Merchant's Exchange Floor in the Chamber of Commerce Building. And then, six months after that,

D.E.W.'s embryonic real estate division began combing the city's financial district, quietly visiting with owners of the district's oldest buildings, looking over city plats. Ehrlichman hadn't been entirely satisfied with the exchange renting a floor from the Chamber of Commerce. He had other, further ambitions for the budding exchange, executing the first rudimentary stirrings of a design. Though he told no one, this was to be a new office tower, built by Drumheller, Ehrlichman & White, built to display the exchange itself.

· · ·

In July of 1927, D.E.W. had purchased the city's recently completed Medical & Dental Building, a modern, 18-story office tower in Seattle's fashionable retail core. The deal had been the largest single real estate transaction in Seattle at the time, and Ehrlichman had immediately organized United Medical & Dental Building Inc. as a holding company for the property. Capitalizing itself with the sale of common stock, D.E.W. had raised $688,120, retaining 51 percent of the capital stock themselves, selling the remainder to the Seattle estate of C.D. Bowles. Having to insure the building, Ehrlichman began speaking of forming an insurance company of his own. If executed, the plan would demand a fresh infusion of money, perhaps a great deal of it.

Ehrlichman's purchase of the building had been part of a local investment strategy, D.E.W.'s formula of keeping a quarter of its "paid-in" capital at home in the Pacific Northwest. There was reason for this beyond that of simply attracting local clients. Ehrlichman wanted to ground the brokerage's financial activities in the commerce and trade of the Pacific Northwest. He envisioned a Northwest empire, the firm's financial dealings tying it to the equity markets of the world, but set firmly on the bedrock of the city's basic economies. Here would be D.E.W.'s insurance companies and real estate holdings, its interest in the city's local banks. To either buy into such businesses, or to start his own, Ehrlichman would need to raise a good deal of capital. But by then, he had the machine to do just that.

Since 1925, the United Bond & Share Corporation had been the single, largest producer of profit within Drumheller, Ehrlichman & White. In September of 1927, the company had a paid-in capital of $2.5 million.

TAKING STOCK

D.E.W.'s United Bond & Share was its first investment trust, and the very first in the Pacific Northwest. If there was a financial locomotive in the late 1920s, an example of speculative rolling stock by which the future investor might identify the period, it was the investment trust company. Largely unknown in this country before 1925, the trusts had first been created in Britain in the 1880s. The novelty of the investment trust was that it allowed investors of relatively modest means to pool their monies, the trusts placing the funds so secured. One of these early trusts may have held securities in five hundred to a thousand operating companies. Thus, each small investor could distribute his risk far further than if he entered the market alone. In addition, the managers of these investment trusts were understood to be financial experts, keeping their eyes on the daily ebb and flow of the market, capital markets the average member of the middle-class had little time to analyze or understand. This lighter risk and superior information so recommended itself, that by the turn of the century the trusts had become an accepted part of British investment.

That is how the investment trusts were promoted, and how, in short, they were first sold: the enticement of low risk and expert advice in harness for the small investor. To their promoters, however, all this was, in effect, beside the point. To these men, the trusts' real beauty lay in the correlation of shares sold to the public and the volume of the trusts' own corporate assets. For, in fact, there was none. The volume of stock issued could be any inflated multiple of corporate assets in existence. Thus freed to produce unlimited stock, the trusts proceeded to sell far more of their own securities than they bought in outside companies. This surplus capital often went into real estate, or onto the call market, or into the pockets of those less virtuous among these early promoters.

Imported over the Atlantic in the early twenties, by mid-decade these novelties stood ready to print-and-deliver. In the general public's rush to own stock, nearly any stock, here was an invention near miraculous in its ability to issue and distribute securities for investment. And perhaps just in the nick of time. For Wall Street was beginning to express an increasing apprehension: it seemed the country was running out of stocks to buy.

Certainly the velocity at which corporations were created in the 1920s - that their securities might be sold to the public - was in itself remarkable. Yet, despite this burst of entrepreneurial spirit, there were only so many start-ups that could conceivably issue new securities, and only so much capital existing companies could absorb. Nevertheless, the appetite for buying and trading rising stocks continued unabated; in fact, it grew geometrically. It was in this rush to board the skyrocketing DOW that some issues quickly assumed a "scarcity value." In the general speculative fever, these scarce stocks became so desirable it was hinted they'd be taken out of the market forever, to never appear again at any price. Nor were these fortunate few companies alone. By the late twenties, it had begun to look more and more as if there could be a shortage of common stocks across the board. That, it was explained, was why the nation's stock prices had flown so high. So, the public then asked, what was to be done? Their answer came in the form of nearly 160 investment trusts then preparing themselves around the country.

A decade later, when the newly formed Securities and Exchange Commission put out its seven-volume compendium "Investment Trusts and Investment Companies," the commission used the year 1927 as the starting line of the country's headlong dash into the trusts. D.E.W., however, hadn't waited until 1927. Ehrlichman had organized United Bond & Share in 1925. It had been his first investment trust, the first in the Seattle, and one of the earliest in the nation. It was late in the morning, on Tuesday, September 13, 1927, when Ehrlichman prepared to launch his second. Christening it the United Pacific Corporation, the young financier felt it useless to wait for some further sign from the market. Everything was ready, he'd see they put it into play the following morning. Once more he would direct each part. Once again - he'd control it all.

· · ·

At one hour past noon, on September 13, 1927, 30,000, Seattleites, half-mad for a glimpse of Charles A. Lindburgh, awaited their idol at Volunteer Park. Another 25,000 were keeping a frenzied vigil in the University of Washington's new athletic stadium, while 5,000 "officially appointed greeters" stood in the rain and wind of Sand Point Naval Air Station, waiting to see the Spirit of St. Louis fly into the airstrip.

Off to the side of Mayor Berthe Landes' and her contingent from city hall, downfield from the ranks of Sand Point's uniformed naval officers, Ben and Rudy Ehrlichman were standing, looking out over the crowd from the running board of a rain-beaded limousine. Like everyone present, the two men were looking to the south, the eldest sporting a homburg pulled low against the drizzle, looking back in the direction of the city for Colonel Lindburgh's arrival. The conscientious young pilot had wired ahead, saying this would be his route, and that he would arrive at exactly 2:00. It was already 1:53, and the crowd had been waiting in the rain for hours.

As the officials queued up on the shoulders of the muddy airstrip, the rain came down even harder. Standing, waiting, the crowd became restive, and wetter by the moment, and it was then they first heard the engine noise, but coming from the opposite direction, from the north instead. As the crowd turned, a single airplane appeared low over the hills above the airfield to the west. Before they could send up a shout, the craft was directly above them, a helmeted head peering out from the aircraft's side.

He was early, uncharacteristically off-schedule, and, as he flew over the field - and kept flying - apparently not about to land until the stroke of two. Instead, he circled out over the lake, pulling his famous monoplane into a climb, the crowd oohing and aahing as Lindburgh drilled his craft into the air, straight up into the rain.

Watching from the limousine's running board, Rudy gripped his older brother's topcoated arm, saying over and over, to himself, to Ben, "Isn't this fine! This is swell! Isn't this swell, Ben! This is absolutely tops!..." And Ben agreed that it was. And more. Standing out of the mud, up on the Cadillac's running board, the moment seemed somehow the apogee of much he had tried to do: his work, the crowd, the city - and now Lindburgh, stunting over the airfield. At the familiar sound of wheels touching down to the tarmac, Ehrlichman found himself and his brother nearly swept from their automobile. People were suddenly streaming around either side of it, running out to the end of the muddy airfield. Ehrlichman could see naval officers and businessmen, women with children - all rushing at once, converging in the direction of Lindburgh. Turning to Rudy, Ben saw his brother leap off the car's running board. "C'mon!" Rudy had shouted, looking back at his brother and laughing. And then Ben was running as well - as the little silver plane stopped, and turned, then taxied up the field to meet them.

Everything That Rises

T HE LAST REEL OF AN OLD HOLLYWOOD FILM: A CALEN-
dar hung on an office wall, a sudden wind riffling its pages - carrying
them off like so many leaves. The audience watches as September flies by,
then October, November - this cinematic wind blowing harder, mysteriously
picking up speed: 1927, 1928, 1929...

In the first few days of the new year, before handing over his office to
Herbert Hoover, President Calvin Coolidge put his particular stamp on things,
declaring the country's economy to be "absolutely sound," asserting that
stocks were "cheap at current prices." Certainly as late as September 3, 1929,
the country's economic indicators simply pointed in a single direction: Up.
The New York Stock Exchange witnessed 4,438,910 shares traded, the Dow
Jones Industrial Average closed at a dizzying 381.17, call money was 9
percent all day, and the rate at the banks on prime commercial paper reached
6 1/2 percent. All through spring and summer, the market had offered day after
day of this. Three thousand miles away, the fledgling Seattle Stock Exchange
was reporting its own unprecedented volumes. August had seen more than $2
million of stocks and bonds traded at the young exchange. Then in early
September, the numbers got even better. Fisher Flour Mills reported record
highs on the exchange, as did Sherman & Clay, the Pacific Coast Biscuit
Company, Richfield Oil Company and C.H. Lilly.

After nearly seven years of increasing prosperity, Seattle had grown
accustomed to its rising expectations. In the late twenties, this had meant a
tangle of construction in the city, downtown streets torn apart as new
buildings were erected. Standing back from the iron workers and masons, one
could see the new Northern Life Tower being built, the Dexter Horton Bank,
the Vance Building, the Leary Building, the huge new box of the Bon Marche,
the city's new Post Office and Federal Building. The largest of all, however,

65

was the block-wide wonder being constructed at the base of Marion Street, the building's entrances, to the east and west, fronting both First and Second Avenues. Designed in part to house the city's new stock exchange, this 23-story Goliath was Benjamin Bernerd Ehrlichman's dream of 1927 come true, and by September of 1929, the giant Exchange Building was already three-quarters built.

Here was to be Seattle's future as seen from the summit of the sky-high DOW, the building infused with the drama of the decade's bull market. On entering its Second Avenue vestibule, one beheld less a lobby than a black marble concourse, its south side bound by a curving wall of elevators. Architect's plans called for the operators of these "express-cars" to be stationed beside their vehicle's filigreed doors, each wearing the building's scarlet livery, and each topped with a crimson, pillbox hat. The John Graham Company had fashioned this showcase for Ehrlichman, creating a vision of luxury for the financier in the speculative age. The polished black marble in the lobby itself was even veined in green - rope-sized deposits of it - a color any investor might surely recognize. While the vault of the lobby's ceiling was turned in gold.

But then, like King Midas, everything D.E.W. touched had turned to gold, and in that fall of 1929, the boy-millionaire's face was all over the town's front pages. "Career of Ben Ehrlichman Is Talk of Financial World," headlined the Times. "His name," the paper reported, "is on the tongue of almost everyone in Seattle's financial world today. He's the 33-year-old president of the United Group of Corporations, with $12,000,000 in capital and an annual volume of $47,000,000 of business. He's the man credited with consolidating the pioneer Murphy, Favre & Co., and Diversified Securities Corporation of Spokane with the United Group. And not only is he president of the United Corporation, which controls the entire group of [eleven] corporations, but he is president of The United Bond & Share Corporation, United Pacific Corporation, vice-president of the United Medical & Dental Building, Inc. and president of Drumheller, Ehrlichman & White, the original company in the group."

Ehrlichman's creation was still founded on investment trust income, these shareholder's dividends insured by the rising market. Resting on this base, however, were the firm's three divisions. In 1929, the group's real estate department was no longer in its infancy, having grown to include the United Medical & Dental Building, the United Exchange Building, the United Shopping Tower - a new 12-story spire being constructed at Third Avenue and Pine Street, and the 16-story Rhodes Medical Arts Building in Tacoma. Each office building was boxed in its own holding company, these holding companies in turn held by either the United Pacific Corporation, Ehrlichman's second investment trust, or the parent holding company: The United Corporation.

The company's insurance division was its newest, and in its start-up, perhaps the costliest. This included the United Insurance Agency, a general insurance wholesaler; the United Pacific Fire Insurance Company; and the United Pacific Casualty Insurance Company, an underwriter of automobile insurance. All were controlled by the United Pacific Corporation.

The group's investment division, its real profit maker, was headed by the United Pacific Corporation, Ehrlichman's investment trust/holding company, with 98 percent of its common stock owned by The United Corporation. Next was Murphy Favre & Co., an old-line Spokane investment banking house, United Corp. having purchased 100 percent of its capital stock in 1928. United Diversified Securities Corporation was Murphy, Favre's investment trust company, and United Corp. owned 66 percent of the company's voting stock. Forty percent of Ferris & Hardgrove, a Seattle brokerage, had been purchased by United Corp. United Bond & Share Corporation, D.E.W.'s first investment trust, had transferred 98 percent of its common stock to United Corporation.

At the structure's base lay the originating company: Drumheller, Ehrlichman & White. And over everything, there arose Ehrlichman's huge holding company, United Corporation, a majority of whose own voting stock, finally, was controlled by Ehrlichman and his two partners.

Though their attempt was to position themselves ever deeper in the region's commercial base - with Ehrlichman, as late as September, 1929, taking a major position in the start-up of the new People's First Avenue Bank - for the greatest part, the holding company still rested on income from its trusts. This was cash flow that in 1929 seemed inexhaustible. As long as the market continued as it had, the structure seemed tapped to an inexhaustible supply. And in the first fall days of 1929, with the market continuing on course

- everything simply pointed in a single, unequivocal direction: straight up.

It was this environment, in the autumn of '29, that led Ehrlichman to an agreement with Louis Seagram, head of the $686 million United Founders Corporation. For an initial payment of $2.7 million in cash, Ehrlichman sold to Seagram's New York based, investment trust holding company, a 33 1/3 percent interest in his United Group. Ehrlichman's desire to expand his cash-short insurance division had forced his hand, leading him to give up a measure of his company's management. But by cutting against the grain, by dealing away his closely guarded control, Ehrlichman had dealt himself capital with which to grow. With cash in hand, he spent the early fall pouring the first of it down the hole of his insurance companies, priming the pump. Then, coming into October of 1929 - convinced of his long-term payback - Ehrlichman poured it all.

• • •

His Malacca walking stick on the limousine's seat beside him, Ehrlichman was driven to work as usual on the morning of October 24, though he was running a bit late. An hour earlier, from his bedroom window as he'd dressed, Ehrlichman had seen clouds building above the Cascade Mountains to the east. Now, looking out the big square windows of the Cadillac, all he could see was blue sky. Always a good sign, he thought.

The nation's economic indicators, however, had been showing other signs of late - the country's steel production was falling off, freight car loadings turning down. Saturday's market had been bad, Monday's was worse, the industrials off 12 points. His colleagues had pointed to the blue chips, it appeared that these companies were beginning to give up ground. U.S. Steel, General Electric, Westinghouse, and Montgomery Ward had all lost several points. Yet, as Ehrlichman reminded himself, volumes on the town's exchange were running high. United was selling for 50 3/8. It had never been higher.

"Man doesn't grovel in the dirt." No, not by a long shot. "...He lifts himself." Yes, he thought to himself as his driver came around to open his door. As Ehrlichman stepped to the curbside in front of his brokerage, he found himself looking up at the Exchange Building, its concrete frame rising two blocks to the north. The building hadn't been enclosed yet. Workmen were swarming over it this morning, ropes and pulleys and wooden platforms rising up the structure's sides. He would hold the contractors to May of 1930, then conduct the finest opening ceremony the city had ever seen. They would have an orchestra, open the building in time for the whole new decade - a new speculative age - and a whole floor for the new stock exchange. But even better, his real estate division had already filled it, they had leases for every last office, from the ground up.

Ehrlichman lingered on the corner, imagining this future happiness, standing on the corner until something caught his eye. It was the owlish figure of his brother-in-law, Elwood Denny, motioning him through the brokerage's windows to come in. Denny seemed distraught. But then Elwood always seemed distraught. Ehrlichman waved his polished walking stick, then, glancing a final time at his new building, stepped inside, closing the glass doors behind him.

Jim Morford had come back from his post at the exchange that afternoon, and venturing up to the executive suites, found Roscoe Drumheller and Herb White crowded around Ben's desk. Ehrlichman was sitting forward in his chair, a telephone to his ear. He was on line to United Founders in New York, as he had been, talking to his new partners throughout the day. As the company's head trader, Morford had already witnessed the scene downstairs, men crowded around the broad tape, watching the company's new partner go under...

The tape had fallen badly behind by morning. People were saying hours, though no one really knew. And it didn't really matter, everyone could see what was happening to the board in New York. And while not listed themselves, many of the securities held by their trusts were on the board - or whatever was left of them.

Morford waited, and still no one in the room said a word. Drumheller and White glanced in his direction, then looked about Ehrlichman's office from time to time, half-seeing its brass desk clock, or the easeled sketch of the Exchange Building propped at the center of the room's Oriental rug. But the gaze of both Drumheller and White always returned to Ehrlichman, to Ben listening to New York, staring at the center of his desk.

As Ehrlichman listened to his party at the other end of the line, he absent-mindedly worked a fountain pen, nib first, into the mahogany armrest of his chair. Morford had seen Ehrlichman do this before, always when he was on the phone. The resultant hole was perhaps a half-inch deep, only now Ben's hand had increased its speed, as if sending out some private code.

Opening at 50 7/8s that morning, the company's United Group had fallen badly on the Seattle Stock Exchange. And now Morford had to return there. Wanting operating orders, the trader had come upstairs, and now, after waiting a moment longer, he changed his mind.

Back on the first floor again, the trader was met with a barrage of questions. "Hey Morford! Jim! What are they doing?"

"They're on the phone."

"On the phone...!"

"To New York," Morford said.

"What's going on?"

"Not a helluva lot, they're awful quiet," said Morford, shouldering his way back into the din of his trading room, the huge sell figures chalk-smeared on its board. He said, "You know like somebody just died."

Chapter Four

GHOSTS

1

O N THE MORNING OF SATURDAY, OCTOBER 26, 1929, JOE Gottstein's North Pacific Finance Corporation was still locked up tight for the night. The brokerage's back room hadn't come abreast of the week's huge sell-off until late the night before. It was now sun-up Saturday morning, and no one was due back for their half-day's shift until eight. But that would be in an hour, and someone had just come back to work early.

Arthur Bastheim, as secretary-treasurer of North Pacific Finance, had his private key. He used it now to let himself in, locking the door behind him before walking down the hallway to his office. Bastheim was a large man with a doughy, nearly seamless face. On this October morning, the heavy-set salesman was wearing a double-breasted blue suit, and as was his custom, more out of habit than anything, he had topped this navy suit with a red bow-tie. Fifty-year-old Arthur Bastheim always wore a bow tie, it was the sign of an extrovert, he claimed. But extrovert or introvert, this morning Bastheim was a man unquestionably captivated by his own reflection, and once in his office, checking again to see he was quite alone, he opened his cloakroom door - standing in front of his closet mirror.

He had cleaned up. Those had been his words Thursday evening, the day the market was initially forced to its knees. "I really cleaned up," Bastheim had bragged to his colleagues at North Pacific. And because he had cleaned up, the broker could say what he said next. *"I've* got nothing to worry about," he told his partners. Not a worry in this world.

And, in a way, Bastheim thought, looking at the face in his closet mirror, it was all true. At least it would be now, he thought, taking the pistol from the pocket of his coat and pressing it to his temple. And then Bastheim thought... And then he did not... For Seattle's Arthur Bastheim had pulled the trigger.

• • •

By nightfall, reports of the treasurer's death could be heard echoing up and down Second Avenue, the evening's headlines posted on every corner of the street. "Seattle Broker Found Dead," declared The Times. "Friends See Fatal Shot As Echo Of Stock Crash." Second Avenue, known as "Cash Canyon" to its intimates, reverberated with the news for two full days. This was the town's first suicide directly attributed to the crash. The melodrama of this self-destruction, however, and its connection to the financial world, set the tone for what was to follow.

Forty-eight hours after Arthur Bastheim slumped in front of his cloak-room mirror, on Tuesday, October 29th, the New York Stock Exchange collapsed in earnest, support levels giving way like rotted boards beneath the panic. During it's first half hour of free-fall, volume sales on the New York exchange were at a 33 million-a-day rate, this in a market that had viewed 6 million days as huge. Before many hours had passed, it was clear none of the Big Board's stocks, not the bluest of blue chips, was to be safe. By the end of the day, an unheard of 16,410,030 sales had been recorded on the NYSE, while the vaulting DOW had been leveled to 252.38, down from September's 386.10, effectively wiping out every gain made in all twelve months of 1929.

The damage was everywhere, though perhaps the financial mansions most immediately hurt this day were those of the investment trusts. Black Tuesday saw these wonders of the "high plateau" begin to self-destruct even faster than they'd grown. For the most part, this was attributable to "lever-age," a scheme by which the greatest portion of a trust's profits went into common stock held by its management, rather than to the publicly sold "preferred." Thus, leverage worked in a rising market, with profits rising geometrically.

It was in a falling market, however, that everything worked in reverse. The trusts' sole assets were the "diversified securities" they held in the market. When these collapsed, the collapse was magnified in the management's shares of common stock. Even if, at first, the public's preferred was covered by the company's devalued stock list, management's common would immediately dip to nothing. This was not exceptional, on the contrary, given the falling market, these effects were running through the leveraged-trusts like a tremor. And it was under these circumstances that the faltering trusts attempted to support their stock prices - by repurchasing their own securities. The trusts sent their money out, and their stock came skittering back to them. As the markets fell further and further, the nation's trusts ran through their remaining capital, forced to buy their own devalued equity. And so it was that these towers of the high plateau became repositories of nearly worthless paper, and unable to continue paying dividends, went finally and gloriously bust.

But if the trusts had lurched like timber off a cliff, crashing all the way to the bottom, it took another three long years for the effects of depression to fully arrive, the Great Bad News in all its splendor. In the meantime, the city's commercial life progressed much as it had. The year 1930 witnessed more new office space opening in downtown Seattle then had been the case at the bull market's height. Then, on May 5, 1930, Ben Ehrlichman opened his Exchange Building to the public.

The town's newspapermen, the city's municipal and business leaders, all were present for Ehrlichman's opening ceremonies. Guided tours were conducted, guests shown the building's massive trading "pit," the future home of the Seattle Stock Exchange. Three stories in height, the ballroom-sized chamber had 25 specialist's posts, each cubicle equipped with its own phone. An elevated, 800 square-foot quote-board spanned the room's First Avenue end, a spectators' balcony looking down from the room's opposite wall. More popular than even the exchange floor were the building's "self adjusting" elevators, Ehrlichman's guests queuing up to take rides. For their added entertainment, in the Exchange's elevator lobby, a ten piece orchestra accompanied a German soprano singing Wagner. The building's accoustics, those in attendance agreed, were superb.

That afternoon, after the ceremonies had been concluded and the crowd had gone, Ehrlichman rode up to the building's roof. His 23-story Exchange Building was the country's largest re-inforced concrete structure west of Chicago, and, to close the day's ceremonies, he was going to the roof with several of his associates to raise the nation's flag. The day was warm, though the wind had been unexpectedly strong on the top of the Exchange that afternoon. Before the flag was run up, the group had gathered for its portrait at the base of the building's pole. Attired in a blue suit, his white homburg propped carefully in his lap, Ehrlichman was sitting on an empty nail keg, looking into the camera's eye. He had surrounded himself with D.E.W.'s officers for this photograph: Roscoe Drumheller, George Harroun, his young brother Rudy standing to his side. Rudy's 5-year-old son John had even been included. Standing at Ben's knee, the child was confronted by a single notion as the owners of the Exchange Building had posed for their portrait. On such a windy day as this, the youngster reasoned - his uncle's arm around him or not - even a grown boy could be blown from such a building's roof. It would, he was certain, be a long way to fall.

And as it happened, the youngster wasn't entirely alone in this turn of mind. Immediately after the market panic, the Exchange Building's leased tenants had vanished, finally evaporating like the dew, so that on the day of its opening, the building's initial 95 percent occupancy rate had fallen to 60, and even this showed signs of weakening. Posing before the photographer's lens, Ehrlichman was leaning forward, facing directly into the wind. The young millionaire, however, wasn't thinking of the wind, not entirely. A studied smile on his face, Ehrlichman had become conscious of something beneath his feet. As the photographer bent beneath the camera's black hood, Ehrlichman knew what it was, shivering up through the soles of his shoes - it was the Exchange Building itself - the vacant structure shuddering with every sudden gust of wind, vibrating like the costliest, emptiest, concrete box ever built west of Chicago.

• • •

2

A MONTH AND A HALF BEFORE THE CRASH, ON SEPTEMBER 3, 1929, Ehrlichman's United Group had been posted at 50 7/8. It had never been higher. His co-partner, American Founders, was selling at 117. Two-and-a-half years later, on July 8, 1932, Founders was listed on the New York Stock Exchange as selling, when it did, at four bits. Three-thousand miles west, Ehrlichman's United Group was ghosting around on the board of the Seattle Stock Exchange at 25 cents.

It was not, however, just the company's shareholders that were hurt, though the firm's many customers in the city were injured badly enough. D.E.W. had had to sell the Medical Dental Building almost immediately after the panic. The company also lost its newly completed Shopping Tower at Third and Pine, and soon after, the Rhodes Medical Center in Tacoma. At the same time, D.E.W.'s first investment trust, the United Bond & Share Corporation, went quietly extinct. In the aftermath, Ehrlichman's brother Rudy found himself wiped out, then out of the business altogether. Not long after this, Drumheller, Ehrlichman & White's former vice president took his wife and young son, loaded what few posessions they still owned into their remaining automobile - and headed off for California. Rudy Ehrlichman and his family had just enough money to stay in the motor-courts dotting the towns along the way, though each night that summer as they motored down the coast, the ex-financier and his family would hike down the cutbanks of the creeks that run along Highway 1, taking their fishing poles to catch their supper.

It was a dream of falling - and of being unable to catch one's self - falling and waiting for the bottom to appear. By 1931 the whole country was caught in it, with the bottom still nowhere in sight. In December of 1931, the Seattle Symphony Orchestra's former first clarinet, Nicholas Oeconomocous took to sitting on the corner of Fourth Avenue and Westlake. Perched on his stool, Oeconomocous played selections from the city's concert repertoire. All through the winter holidays, the clarinetist sat on his corner, wearing his black greatcoat with its red velvet cape, a high crowned hat with a wide brim, an open Owl Cigar box at his feet. The other corners of Westlake and Fourth had been commandeered by Seattleites selling apples.

It wasn't, of course, just Seattle. Times were bad everywhere, the country's markets nearly stopping their business altogether. The DOW Jones Industrial Average had fallen to 41, the nation's shrinking economy sloughing off jobs by the thousands, then jobs by the millions. Neighborhoods of the newly unemployed began a practice of naming their makeshift communities after Herbert Hoover. Seattle's version of Hooverville was a patch of shacks located on the city's industrial waterfront. By 1932 this patch had grown dramatically, stretching for nine acres along the tideflats of the city's Railroad Avenue. Men reduced to beggers and bums, Hooverville's inhabitants also included (according to the still employed sociologists who studied them), ex-university professors, former lawyers, erstwhile engineers. A brotherhood of the newly unemployed.

Old Seattle had once had a measure of experience in dealing with down-and-outers, the inevitable detritus of boom times gone bust. This, though, was something different, this new encampment growing on a scale unmatched in the city's experience. And worse, to those still employed, the quarter looked like some terrible South American slum, as if its nine acres of shelters and sheds and scrofulous lean-tos had suddenly slid off a Rio hillside, only to wash up on the shores of Elliott Bay.

In the face of this development, it took little time for the city's politics to harden, for health officials to be contacted, for laws to be re-checked. Few were finally surprised when the city's mayor, with full and official sanction, ordered Seattle's Hooverville burned to the ground, its unemployed squatters forced out into the rain. This was done twice. Its residents' response, however, was to regroup and rebuild. This was done each time.

If only a small percentage of the city's population was ever lodged at Hooverville, it yet seemed a thing that could happen to anyone: to day laborers and grocery clerks, to clarinetists and customer's men. And there was an added fillip, at least for the town's brokers, its commission men living on what could yet be sold day by day. For the Exchange Building's upper floors afforded an excellent view of Mr. Hoover's namesake, looking out south, down along the waterfront - a commanding view of the hard time's bottom line.

• • •

"God, Jim. I can't live on that! I'm not making it!"

Jim Morford didn't know what to say. What could you say? Along with every other junior officer at First National Bank, the man had had his pay cut to $200 a month. The senior men were getting $300. Everyone was just hanging on. What in the world was he supposed to say? He knew people selling apples.

"Maybe you ought to go out and get a better job," he'd said.

"And do what? What can I do?"

"Then maybe you better hang onto your job..."

When Morford's young friend had gone, Morford was left sitting at his desk. Whether he'd been consoled or not, Morford didn't know; he did know he was seeing it more than he'd like. The week before it had been Bill Morrison. Morrison ran the city's Pioneer Sand & Gravel Company, and he'd come over to tell Morford that he had just been to the bank. "Tried to give them everything I had," Morrison told him. "If they'd just cancel the notes and write 'em off. It's all I got," he'd said. The man's bank, however, hadn't complied. "What can I do?" Morrison had asked. What could he say? "Hang on," he'd said.

Hang on... It wasn't as if he weren't hanging on himself. He'd been holding on since the crash, doing every scrap of business he could, until the business just hadn't been there to do. He knew when that had begun, too. The afternoon over at the exchange, when Ehrlichman made his play for the firm's United stock. He and Ben had made their arrangements before the opening, Morford instructed to look up into the balcony at twenty minutes into the session. Ehrlichman would be standing there, ready. Morford had then gone to his post out on the new trading floor. When the time came, there was Ehrlichman giving him his signal. The deal was for $5. Morford was to bid $5 for any and all of D.E.W.'s United stock offered. There'd be a little flurry of activity, Ben had explained, telling Morford that at this stage he was certain it would be nothing of size - they'd cover it and thereby stabilize their price. So Morford made the $5 bid, and before it was even on the board, someone had hit them with 40,000 shares. God, he could remember looking up, seeing Ben's face... Ehrlichman understanding immediately. So had he. It meant - from that point on - they were busted. It had broken them. Three days later the shares were at 50 cents. And he had seen that as well, though he wished he hadn't.

He left the trading desk and began to sell after that. Though thinking about it, sitting in his office, Morford knew what he truly did was walk. Journeying down First Avenue South. Any business that was open, he'd go in and make a call. If they were still operating, they must have some money, he told himself. Maybe enough that he'd even get an order. "Hi," he'd say, "I'm Jim Morford...with Drumheller, Ehrlichman and White..." Sometimes that was all it took to have them run you out of the place. How many people had called him a crook... It was rough, thought Morford. Just to know you were in the business was enough for some. They'd insinuate you were the cause of all their troubles. Their's and everyone else's. What could you say? Nothing - all you could do was walk. "Hi, I'm Jim Morford, I have some ideas on investment that I think could make you some money..." It was a bum joke. The old broker's joke. Your two orders for the day: "Get out! And Stay Out!"

He had become good at hanging on. He had had to. And he wasn't even making his young friend's $200 a month. If it had not been for his father-in-law, for the $2,000 life insurance policy he'd left them - he and his family wouldn't even be doing that. And now they'd drawn it down to $25. Things had to turn around. They just had to. What was he to do if they didn't? "Hi, I'm Jim Morford...apples here fresh from Wenatchee..."

It was like being stuck - being unable to move. Waiting for the phone to ring, waiting for business to turn up. Waiting for someone to start wanting what you had to sell. Though even the ones that treated you nicely, sometimes that made it even harder. He remembered the old man down on Dearborn. The man had had a metal fabrication shop, and seeing it was still open, Morford had gone in. "Look, young fellow," the owner told him, asking him to sit down. "I've been around a lot longer than you have. I'd advise you to get out of this business. I've just sold the last stocks I have and put the money in a safe deposit box. That's exactly where it's going to stay. Things are really bad, and I'm afraid they're going to get a lot worse. You take my advice. Find yourself another line of work." Then he shook Morford's hand, patted him on the shoulder and wished him luck. Morford remembered thinking as he'd walked out: He could sure use it.

• • •

The bottom finally came on July 8, 1932. The DOW fell to 41.22, hovered in the low forties for most of the month, then gradually began to rise. On the last day of July, the index closed at 54.26. A year later the DOW was at 94.18. Regardless, the nation's economy had all but collapsed. Even the country's rich had been frightened, many of those still having money rushing it into gold. Those with neither money or gold had to pick through the rubble as best they could, making do with what fragments of the economy they could piece together.

In 1932, C. D. McConahy was a Seattle broker who happened to be good at putting things together. In a way, McConahy had specialized in it. The Scotsman had an unimposing, pigeon-hole-sized office in the American Bank Building. He also had a formidable independant streak. In the twenties, McConahy had conducted a business of buying Liberty Bonds from people, purchasing them in amounts as small as $25, $50, $100. Put out in World War I, the bonds were still much in the market in the twenties. The New York Stock Exchange had even lowered its "round lot" from $5,000 to $1,000 to accomodate the issue. The bonds were selling in the mid eighties, and McConahy would place advertisements in the local papers, buying the governments from individuals whenever he could. He'd then put them together in lots of $10- to $15,000, and sell them for several points above his purchase price. By doing so, by specializing in this kind of marginal trade, McConahy had made himself well-to-do by the time of the crash.

After the crash, the broker was left with little more than his license. In McConahy's case, however, this would do. Surveying the city's junked

81

economy, the man began turning up ways of making markets in junk. McConahy placed advertisements in the papers stating that he'd buy and sell the passbooks of the area's defunct savings and loan institutions. Nearly all of the city's S&L's were closed, their former customers only able to extract $10 out of their accounts every half-year. McConahy had known the savings and loans were state chartered, what he discovered, however, was that under the state's charter, the S&L's passbooks were transferable. In other words, McConahy could make a market in them. These passbooks, in effect, were stock certificates, statements showing stock ownership in a bank. McConahy would buy these passbooks for ten cents on the dollar, turning and selling them for twice that. McConahy's buyers of a particular S&L's books, were those having home mortgages with the institution. Unable to make their $100 a month mortgage payments, people could, perhaps, pay $20. By paying $20 for one of McConahy's $100 passbooks - they could then turn it in to their S&L at par. And the S&L, by law, had to take it.

McConahy, however, didn't entirely restrict his business to the city's indigent. There was, during these years, a wealthy family that had moved out to Seattle from Enid, Oklahoma. The head of this clan was in the wholesale grocery business. In addition, the family owned oil property back in Oklahoma. Moving out to Seattle in the late twenties, the family took out a $250,000 mortgage from Puget Sound Savings and Loan to put up a showcase, half-million dollar home on Harvard Avenue. Unfortunately, the arrival of the Great Depression coincided almost exactly with the completion of the family's mansion; the price of the family's oil then dropping to 15 cents a barrel. The unlucky homeowner, having a grocery business or not, found himself unable to meet his mortgage payments to Puget Sound S&L. The once wealthy Oklahoman, however, hadn't known about C. D. McConahy.

Local cannery owner August Bushman, *did*, however. And Bushman promptly made a deal with McConahy. He would pay the Scotsman $25,000 for $250,000 of Puget Sound Savings & Loan's passbooks. McConahy immediately borrowed money to buy the books against Bushman's promise to pay, bought the books for $20,000, made his commission - and allowed Bushman to buy a half-million dollar home for $25,000. And McConahy did it in just 60 days, patching together a deal only the crack-up of the Great Depression could have allowed.

GHOSTS

. . .

To the men and women living through them, the hard times seemed not to end. In 1933, one bank in every four went out of business. In all, in that one year, deposits were lost totaling $3.6 billion. From 1929 to 1933, the number of banks in the United States dropped by 42 percent, the number of banks in Washington State by 47 percent. Deposits were off 29 percent nationally, down 41 percent in the State of Washington. In those same four years, Seattle banking deposits decreased 19 percent, 61 percent in the rest of the state. The nation's brokers had panicked in 1929, in 1933, it was the banker's turn. Seattleites filled the sidewalks of Second Avenue, lining up for their turns at the teller's window, standing in line for hours to get their savings out of the bank. During the 1933 run on Seattle First National, one of its young officers was sent to the Federal Reserve branch with a shopping cart bulging with notes and securities. He returned, pushing the same shopping cart, then filled with more than a million dollars in cash. He'd been told to use the cart by his superiors, their reasoning being a suitcase would be too obvious. He'd also been told to travel the alleys between Second and Third, anything to avoid the throngs waiting out in the street.

The young Seafirst officer wasn't entirely alone in this. There was, at the time, a Seattle brokerage president who had taken to walking through the town's back alleys, disinclined to meet former customers, or to be spat on by chancing the city's sidewalks. Ben Ehrlichman followed this route day after day, going about his business in the city. Many of Ehrlichman's former brokerage clients in the city were bitter. Having bought into the firm's investment trusts, they blamed Ehrlichman for their losses. Yet, with people going broke everywhere, most had decided long before that nothing could possibly be done. The day arrived, however, when someone decided otherwise.

The man who made this decision had been Drumheller, Ehrlichman & White's chief comptroller. He had had a misunderstanding with his employers, a disagreement that had ended in his being fired. Finding himself without a job, the ex-comptroller had determined to settle accounts with the company.

TAKING STOCK

This plan took him to see Seattle's Charley Burckhardt. Burckhardt was in the ship-building business in the city. With the depression on, Burckhardt's company was building very few ships, in fact, the company was building next to none. Under these circumstances, it had been hard for Burckhardt to forget the money he'd lost on Ehrlichman's United Corp. - all the participating preferred he had purchased in '29 - having to watch it fall to nearly nothing at all.

So, when the ex-comptroller walked into the ship builder's office, saying, "You know, Mr. Burckhardt, this Class B stock of Drumheller's? The common owned by the principles of the firm? I think it has an unfair advantage over the preferred..." Charley Burckhardt promptly asked the man to sit down.

The comptroller's plan was to take Roscoe Drumheller, Ben Ehrlichman, and Herb White to court, to force them to reorganize their company. He wanted the advantages accruing to the principle's common stock, offered equally to the "preferred," still being sold to the public. If the comptroller's concern had been largely rendered moot by the depression, his anger hadn't. For in fact, the wonders of leverage used at D.E.W. in the twenties had never been publically revealed, not even by the crash. A scheme whereby the common owned by the firm's three principles had at one time risen geometrically, astronomically, was bound to interest a public whose preferred was then barely alive. And nothing had ever been done to change it.

Charley Burckhardt listened to the man, and finding himself in agreement, went off with the comptroller to find a lawyer. They ended up at the firm of Kaiser and Bailey, and soon salvos were being fired at the brokerage's offices on Second. The result was a dialogue of sorts: suit being threatened and counter-threatened, inequities revealed and rebutted, damages asserted and vehemently denied. And then the matter began to turn on how this dialogue might look in the papers... Shortly afterwards, Drumheller, Ehrlichman & White put itself through a reorganization. When it came out the other side, the advantages issuing from the firm's two classes of stock were as much alike as mirrors. The comptroller was satisfied with this conclusion, while Charlie Burckhardt, tired of spending his days in lawyer's offices, went back to building his boats. Leaving Ben Ehrlichman his company to run, and his trips down Second Avenue's alleyways.

GHOSTS

. . .

Thunk. Skrich. Kathunk. Skrich, skrich. Thunk... "Hey, who you kiddin? That was out by a mile!"

Afternoons, during idle sessions, brokers would play handball against the big, blank southern wall inside the Seattle Stock Exchange. The games were something to do, a welcome respite to the lack of action out on the floor. By the late thirties the SSE was staying open for the call market only. The call market took thirty minutes, many of these minutes being devoted to handball.

Thunk... Ed Easter, Spike Huston, Joe Lanser, Johnny Kutz, Larry Carlson - they played until their employers made them stop, pointing out to these young men that handball wasn't dignified. Then, when their dignified bosses left, the young floor brokers would start up the games again... What else was there to do?

There was very little. The exchange itself was going out of business. The Securities and Exchange Commission had required the city's new stock exchange to keep records of all its transactions. By the late thirties, the cost of keeping these accounts was greater than any moneys coming in. Then there was the question of the SSE's 20-year lease with the Exchange Building, and its rent of $5,000 a month. At the end, the institution was paying $200 a month, Ehrlichman rebating it $4,800. And though the stock exchange wasn't the only tenant in the building, it was one of few, and Ehrlichman couldn't lose money forever. Finally, with rents going by the board, the Exchange Building defaulted on all its bonds. Though by then, Ehrlichman wasn't alone, bonds all over the State of Washington were in default.

Try as he might, C. D. McConahy no longer had a corner on the market for junk. For the most part, it was all that was left. Nor was the default of the Exchange Building in any way remarkable. Among others, the 719 Second Avenue Building was in default, the Olympic Hotel was in default, the new Dexter Horton Bank Building was in default. This was the environment within which Seattle's investment community worked in the 1930s. In order that they continue to eat, they had to work, and in order to work, they had to sell. So they began to find markets for these defaulted bonds, going out to convince customers the defaulted mortgage bonds they were offering were attractively cheap. For the alternative, if bizarre in retrospect, seemed almost as valid at the time: that in the not too distant future, the building bonds of the city of Seattle might be entirely worthless.

In 1936, Jim Morford was then working for Hughbanks Inc. The Hughbanks Company was a tenant of the Dexter Horton Building, one of the few still left. By '36, the building had lost most of its tenants, its occupancy rate between 30 and 40 percent. But empty or not, the building itself was impressive, its owners having spared few expenses during its construction in the twenties. The original financing for the building had come through the sale of 6 percent first mortgage, and 7 percent second mortgage bonds. During the middle thirties, however, the building's owners underwent a voluntary reorganization. After this they provided the holders of the building's defaulted 6 percent first mortgage bonds, a package consisting of $1,000 of new first mortgage bonds, with an interest rate then cut to 3 percent, plus an additional assortment of the building's preferred and common stock.

Yet, in spite of these attempts, the new securities fell nearly as quickly as the old, sliding until the new $1,000 bonds and their bundles of stock were selling for 15 cents on the dollar. For $150, an interested party could pick up one of the 3 percent $1,000 bonds along with its stock. Which was the exact point in the argument at which Morford would begin. The first mortgage in the 1920's, he would explain, had been in the amount of $1 million. And it was a building that eventually cost several millions to build. Now he was offering it to them for 15 cents on the dollar. Even if times got worse - though how could that be possible? - surely the building was worth more than $150,000 dollars? And they were getting $30 on their balance. How could they lose?

They couldn't. At least those that elected to buy. And it was not just the Dexter Horton Building. It was the Olympic Hotel, and the Exchange Building, and the Medical Dental Building, and Seattle City Light, and Puget Power...Anyone that invested at the time, in nearly anything at all, and hung on. Made out. Though no one rang a bell - no one could offer any guarantees. And the depression would go on for years.

• • •

3

"I REMEMBER ONCE, CHICK, WHEN I WAS WITH BROWN-JEK-lin,"Jim Morford was saying. "I was pretty hungry when some woman called up. She said, What's General Motors? So I called one of the fellows and I asked, What's General Motors? And he said, Oh it's sellin' at five bucks, Jim. So I told her it was selling at five dollars. And she said, Save me one share, I'll be right down."

Charles "Chick" Badgley looked over at Morford, both men laughing over drinks at their table near the back of the Tennis Club's main dining room. In front of them, their fellow diners had begun drifting into the room in twos and threes, sitting in tuxedos at tables throughout the long, rectangular hall. This was a once-a-year occasion in the city, the annual Bond Club Christmas Party, and all the top people in the profession were in black tie and tuxedo this night. To look at the scene, at the office managers, and brokers, and financial counselors in their evening dress, at the serving bowls heaped with fresh butter clams, even at the lights of the summer homes across Lake Washington, it was possible to think the depression had ended. It hadn't. The date was Friday, December 5, 1941, and the DOW, then standing at 115, had fallen 70 points over the last four years. Making a high in 1937, the market had subsequently gone soft, ebbing away year after year. Now it appeared to be getting softer, dropping 10 points in the last two months. And both the Congress, and Franklin Roosevelt, back for his third term in the White House, seemed at a loss in devising solutions. But this Friday evening wasn't to be wasted on politics. After a decade of hard times in Seattle, the city's brokers had come to the Christmas party to have a drink, to share stories, to have a little fun.

As the dining room filled, the Tennis Club came alive with greetings and talk and the sound of laughter. Straightaway, the club staff began circulating with platters of the clams, passing around the crowded dining room, taking orders for cocktails and bottles of beer. The laughter then became easier, and louder by the moment. Until it became a roar.

"I remember one time at Blyth," said Chick Badgley, "Joseph Vance came into my office a few months before the darn thing happened. He walked up and asked me what the price of City Company was. I told him the market was $550 a share. Well, he thought that over a for minute, Jim. And then he said, Chick, I want to sell a thousand shares. You know, I didn't let on that that meant any more to me than 10 shares. So I filled out a selling order, and pushed it over for him to sign...Which he did. Then I got up and began walking over to the trading department. I hadn't gone more than ten steps when he said, Say, Chick... Wait just a minute. What's this capital gains tax I hear about? Well, I said, it's true. There's a ten percent capital gains tax. Well, he said. Just a minute. And then he took a piece of paper and started figuring. After a moment, he said, Why say, my cost is very low on that City Corp. I bought it when I sold out my lumber company in 1923. So he says, You know? My tax on that would almost be $50 a share. That means I'd only be getting slightly over $500. Then he says, Hell Bells, Chick, cancel that order... I'd *buy* stock at that price!"

"Well," said Badgley, "there went my order. But you know the effect of that? When you look at the Vance Building today, the exterior of it is covered in terra-cotta. Nice looking, but the 1411 Fourth Avenue Building next to it, that's covered in fine Wilkenson Stone. You can see the difference, and Mr. Vance had his heart set on that Wilkenson Stone. After the break, with City Corp going down to a $19 share, he got the terra-cotta. You can see it walking by today."

"He was hurt, then?"

"Well, yes, I suppose he was."

"I didn't know Mr. Vance," said Morford. "I knew Ben Ehrlichman well, though," he said. "And Ehrlichman had his sights on more than a building. You must have known Ben?"

"Of course," said Badgley.

"I believe he wanted a Northwest Empire. Ehrlichman came close to having it, too. I remember when I went to work for those fellows in '27, saw what they were making...I thought it was about the slickest deal I ever saw. A one way street. Well, you remember, Chick. It was...it was something, wasn't it? I couldn't wait to get down to the office in the morning. And this really is funny to think of, I mean, after '32. But I can remember telling my wife, when I first went to work there. I told her it was a cinch. Just stick with me, I said...You'll wear diamonds."

As Morford and Badgley continued talking, bowls of the fresh hor d'ouvres were brought round, and drinks freshened, and finally a dinner of prime rib was set out before the club members and their guests. By the end of the meal, a smiling, compactly built man had risen from his table at the front of the crowded dining room. He stood there for a moment, before tapping his water glass with a fork.

"I'm Burle Bramwell," the smiling man announced. His tuxedoed audience immediately began hollering, "Who? Who?"

"The President of the Seattle Bond Club," Bramwell began again, his smile now even broader. "I'd like to welcome you to the fifteenth annual Bond Club Christmas Party."

The audience broke into hoots and applause, and as they did, Bramwell asked his entertainment committee to stand. When these had been applauded, and were seated again, the club president offered a final, official benediction and then opened the evening's entertainment - a stock trading game - Bramwell calling out for bids from his audience.

"Remember Bank of America stock? How they'd restrict you to fifty shares?" asked Badgley, raising his voice above the shouts suddenly coming from out in the dining room.

"The thing was going up every day," said Morford.

"At Blyth, when we went down to San Francisco, we used to use it instead of expense accounts."

"You'd buy it when you got down there?"

"Yes," said Badgley. "Buy our fifty shares in the morning when we arrived, and sell it the next day when we left. It was always good for a point, maybe two. Took care of our entertainment."

"Marine Bancorp was like that. People lining up for it."

"Remember when they listed Bancorp on the San Francisco Exchange?"

"Sure."

"I was on the desk over at Blyth. Have I told you this story before?" asked Badgley.

"About Marine Bancorp? I don't suppose you have."

"Well, I was on the desk and our trader down in San Francisco got wind that they were going to list it in a few days time. It had occured to the trader down there that it might sell a bit higher down there than here. An opportunity to have a little arbitrage. So we got ready for the ten o'clock session over at the exchange in the Chamber of Commerce Building. Our man in San Francisco had sent word up, he said go over there and buy a thousand shares. Then come back and we'll sell it. But be very quiet about it.

"I remember something like that." said Morford. "That was you?"

"Yes. I went over there and, of course, I'd disguise my purchases, I'd sell a few and buy a few and then when I was ahead a thousand shares, I'd saunter out of the place. I guess people must have thought I'd done all my business. As soon as I was outside, I'd run all the way back to Blyth. When I got in the door - we'd kept an open line to our trader in San Francisco - the trader'd say: Go back and get another thousand shares! I'd just bought a thousand at 51, and the trader had just sold a thousand in San Francisco for 52. So I'd race back there and get another thousand. We kept it up for the whole hour. We'd get a point, sometimes a point and a half. And then, after that, we went back for the afternoon session. Nobody caught on. They didn't realize the San Francisco market was higher than Seattle's. By the end of the day, we'd made $25,000."

"Yes," said Morford, now grinning. "I do remember that."

"Of course," said Badgley, "the next day it came out in the papers and people could see what we'd been doing."

"And it closed shut."

"The very next morning. But it was certainly fun while it lasted."

"I'll bet. I hope Fredericks doesn't keep you hopping like that."

"Well, we try to keep busy. Say, if you don't mind my asking... I don't think I know who you're with now, Jim," said Badgley. "Are you still with Drumheller?"

"No, I'm with Al Hughbanks."

"I thought so, I'd heard you left Drumheller. You ever see them anymore?"

"Not much. The last time I saw any of them, it was Roscoe Drumheller. He was walking down Fourth Avenue. Matter of fact, as I remember it, I saw him right in front of the Vance Building. He asked how I was doing. I told him

90

I was doing all right. Asked him how things were with him. He said, Well, you know, Jim. I was all ready to sell out in 1929. Then I talked to Ben about it, and he said, "Roscoe, why don't you just stick around for six months?" So I did. And I didn't sell out." That's what he told me.

"So he stayed in..."

"Yes. I said, You know, Mr. Drumheller? If you *had* sold, and put your money into some listed blue chips, the bottom would have fallen out of them as well. But he said, no. He'd made his mind up, he had wanted to put the whole bundle into goverment bonds."

"Well, I didn't know Drumheller that well," said Badgley. "I knew Ben, of course. But I do remember in 1929, I was making $1,000 a month there at Blyth. I remember sitting at my desk projecting that out. It'd been $50 a month when I started. I could see where I'd be making $30-40,000 a year by 1933. Then I got married, and soon after, 1932 came along. In one month at Blyth, I made $80. All I was doing was hanging on, Jim."

"Yes," laughed Jim Morford. "You know, Chick? I seem to recall doing some of that myself," he said.

On Sunday, December 7, 1941, a day and a half after the Bond Club Christmas Party, the Japanese bombed Pearl Harbor. With the first Japanese bomb falling over Hawaiian soil, even in that moment before its detonation and blast, the Great Depression was finally over. The nation was at war.

Six months later and the city's apple-sellers had vanished. Seattle was working 24-hours a day, three shifts of workers shuttling back and forth to the town's war industries. Department stores, food stores, laundries, gas stations - all were staying open to accomodate workers in the area's war plants. The city's population jumped 20 percent by June of 1942. Seattle bank clearings that month ran 38 percent ahead of 1941. Housing became nearly impossible to find. Business Week described it like this: "Seattle: A Boom Comes Back."

And stayed. Deluged with orders, Boeing began adding workers in the thousands. At the peak of its war production in 1944, the airplane plant was employing 50,000 city workers. Things had again begun to move .

The Street had begun to move as well. Market advances were modest at first, but steady, the price of securities and trading volumes increasing month after month. Though there was little need for equity financing during the war, thus fewer new securities to sell, there were an abundance of war bonds, once more a staple of every broker's inventory. By 1945, the DOW had surpassed its high of 1937, closing on the last day of December at 192.84. If this high was yet half the 381.17 set by the index in 1929, no one who had gone through the Depression expected to see 381 again. Not after they's seen 41. Besides, by 1945, by the end of the war, all the country wanted - was to see what peace would bring.

Chapter Five

OUR TOWN

1

STANDING, RIDING THE NUMBER ELEVEN INTO WORK, MAC-Millan Pringle thought that Yale hadn't prepared him for this. Hell, the Navy hadn't prepared him for it. It wasn't funny...The whole month of February now - two days to go - and not a dollar, not a nickel: zero. Nothing even near his first month, when it'd been like picking plums. Even if January's $164.15 hadn't made him rich, still, thought Pringle, it had seemed so simple. Sitting there after dinner at Fred Howden's, landing his first sale... When Howden had said yes to ten shares of P. R. Mallory, Pringle had felt a jog of adrenalin, thinking to himself: "God...the guy bought it." And though it was only a six dollar commission, still, it had been his first, and he'd *kept* thinking about it. The idea you could make money over a cup of coffee and a slice of meringue pie.

Then February had rolled in, and it'd been lemons all the way around. He ought to quit - he ought to - figure something else out. The way it was going, he could distribute his Blyth cards forever, and it wasn't going pay for their second child on the way. He thought if worse came to worse, he and Sue could always go back to New York City, live with her brother again. They'd probably give him his job back at Grace National. Though the thought of New York depressed him even further. Then he tried to imagine being thirty in three years. God...he wondered what the rest of '51 had in store.

Mac Pringle got off the number eleven bus at the corner of Fourth and Pike, and walked in the rain the block south to the 1411 Fourth Avenue Building. Riding in the elevator on his way up to the building's second floor, he glanced at his wristwatch, wiping the rain off its face. 9:19. Well - progress, not perfection - that'd be his motto. Anybody asked, that's what he'd tell 'em. He was doing better than yesterday, when he'd missed the whole sales meeting. Mott had made a point of saying he'd be late to his own funeral. Hahaha. But Si was okay. The way it was though, Pringle thought, even if it wasn't funny, it still didn't pay to take any of it *too* seriously. Though it would certainly improve his humor if he could make a buck.

Walking down the hall from the elevator, Pringle had thought to set himself for the usual gibes: "Good of you to join us, Mac." "Wonderful you could be here, Pringle." Then found himself walking faster. Once in the office, however, the big, blond broker suddenly slowed his pace. For, as Pringle soon realized, no one had even seen him come in.

Not twenty feet in front of Pringle, old Burt Gottstein had been caught out at the center of the room's green linoleum, standing with his head down, a sheaf of chart-paper in his hand, his usual headlong rush across the office having been suddenly checked. Bob Whitebrook, the man Pringle shared an office with, was standing in Gottstein's way. The old broker was trying to go around the young salesman, shifting to his right, holding his charts in tight to his chest. Failing at this, he sidestepped to the left, trying to squeeze between Whitebrook and the water-cooler. Only Whitebrook, all elbows and knees, was there before him, blocking him, saying, "Oh excuse me, Burt. Pardon me, Burt. Oh, excuuse me!" And looking over at Bill Slater, and now Pringle, winking like a bastard.

"Whitebrook!!!"

Though it wasn't Pringle's name still ringing in the air, the broker stopped as if poleaxed, standing where he was, thinking: perhaps if he didn't move...For standing in the doorway of his office, his sandy hair parted smartly in the middle, his eyes like blue sparks above an immaculate black suit, there had appeared none other than The Lord God Almighty, though in this case, the Deity had assumed the form of one Edmund Maxwell, Seattle Office Manager for Blyth & Co.

"Whitey," hollered Maxwell, "get the hell out of Burt's way and get your butt in here. The rest of you men, too. Si's gonna have his sales meeting."

Sweet Jesus! thought Pringle, tossing his raincoat over the wall of his office cubicle. Thank you Lord and thank you Whitey! He'd made it. He was even going to make the sales meeting. Nobody'd even noticed him come in...

• • •

By 1951, the name of Army Air Corps Captain William C. Slater had been carved in red Washington granite for seven long years. The identity of this Seattle-boy, a 22-year-old B-24 pilot, had been inscribed in the wall of the town's Public Safety Building in 1944, there to be counted among the city's honored war dead. Ex-Army Air Corps Captain William C. Slater would allow himself to think about this sometimes, finding himself checking off client after client in Si Mott's dead files, or trying to keep from falling asleep in Burt Gottstein's training class. It never failed to give the 29-year-old Blyth salesman a funny feeling - thinking of walking down the sidewalk, coming upon his own live name cut into the dead stone like that.

Tall and trim, with a thick head of black hair, Slater looked a bit like the "Smilin' Jack," of WWII cartoon fame. And if he lacked the airman's identifying mustache, Slater was in fact the genuine article, a bona fide WWII hero. He was a native Seattleite as well, raised by his widowed mother on Queen Anne Hill. He volunteered for the Army Air Corps while still in his teens. When the country entered the war, Slater was assigned duty as a heavy-bomber pilot in Europe. Serving over the Balkans, he received The Distinguished Flying Cross when still 21 years old. It was a year after this incident, however, with German flak having destroyed two of his engines, that he had put his B-24 into the dive that etched his name on the Public Safety Building.

The machine Slater had been piloting had been hit immediately after taking off on a mission over France. With a full load of gasoline and bombs, unable to keep his crippled bomber climbing in formation, Slater had tried to evade the enemy flak by flying under the guns' radar. Putting his B-24's nose down, he directed his co-pilot to watch their wings, listened for the sound of rivets leaving the aircraft, and rode the plane down to the surface of the

Mediterranean, flying straight down, until there was nothing but whitecaps to be seen through his windscreen - waiting for the impact of the anti-aircraft rounds.

Which, as it turned out, never came. Managing on two engines, skimming 50 feet off the surface of the water, Slater brought the injured bomber into Corsica. The pilot and his crew then enjoyed a two week respite from the air war, repairing their damaged motors, spending their days sunbathing on the island's beaches, their nights in the island's wine bars.

Before these two weeks were up, however, Bill Slater's young wife received a wire from the War Department. The government regretted to inform her that William C. Slater, along with his entire crew, had been lost to German ground fire...shot down over Corsica...presumed dead. The Army then notified the city, and the city etched Slater's name into red granite.

It was a strange sensation, finally coming back to the city after the war, standing on Fourth Avenue, seeing his name that way. Not that Slater ever talked about it. Not when he went to work at the bank, or now, as a junior salesman with the only, real, silk stocking brokerage in the city. He wasn't a boastful man. Besides, what the hell was he going to say? That he'd been lucky? Everyone who had come back from the war had been lucky. But then, as far as he knew, none of their names were carved into the side of the Public Safety Building. No, it wasn't that. It wasn't exactly luck, it was something else, something harder to say... as if he'd been singled out...as if he were meant for things.

• • •

"Yes, Mrs. Wiggens. No, Mrs. Wiggens. No no, that's right Mrs. Wiggens. No, Mrs. Wiggens. I agree absolutely, Mrs. Wiggens..."

Sitting in the cubicle they shared, Mac Pringle watched as Bob Whitebrook took his desk telephone, the one on which he was now talking, placed the receiver in the bottom of his desk drawer and closed it. Then Pringle watched as Whitebrook leaned back in his chair, putting his hands behind his head, and continued on with his conversation: "Yes, Mrs. Wiggens, No, Mrs. Wiggens, *Yes,* Mrs. Wiggens..."

OUR TOWN

Even seeing it, it was hard to believe. Pringle'd heard about Whitebrook, but being in the same office with him was something else. Tall, and skinny, perhaps ten years older than himself, Whitebrook looked years younger, a bit like pictures Pringle had seen of the young Ben Ehrlichman. He'd told Pringle he had an IQ of 178, and that the family name had originally been Reichenauweichbrodt. Nineteen letters, Whitebrook had said, as if that, along with the IQ, somehow said it all. At any rate, everybody at Blyth called him "Whitey." And as far as Pringle could tell, Whitey was fearless. Though Pringle wasn't sure if fearless was precisely the right word. Maybe, thought Pringle, maybe it was the fact that Whitebrook made $70,000 a year.

After a short while, Whitebrook relented, and taking the phone out of his desk drawer, picked up again where he'd left off.

"Yes, Mrs. Wiggens. No, Mrs. Wiggens..."

And apparently the woman hadn't a clue.

"What? You do me an injustice Mrs. Wiggens. Of course. Always a pleasure to speak with *you* Mrs. Wiggens... Goodbye, Mrs. Wiggens."

Whitebrook hung up the phone and looked over at Pringle. "That was Mrs. Wiggens," he said.

"Yeah, I guess so," said Pringle, grinning.

"Mrs. Wiggens, a woman of means, thinks many things, Mac. One thing she thinks in particular...is... that I'm a genius. You know what that means, Mac?" asked Whitebrook.

"I'm afraid to guess," said Pringle.

"It means - that at least one time in her life - Mrs. Wiggens has gotten it right."

Pringle snorted, grinning from ear to ear.

"You ready then?" asked Whitebrook, and without waiting for a reply, stood up and began putting on his topcoat. Pringle stood up and did the same.

Pringle was about to be taken over to the Terminal Sales Building, there to be shown how Robert Whitebrook dealt with *his* clients. It had been Maxwell's idea, the office manager saying, "Pay attention, kid. Maybe some of it'll rub off on ya." And what the hell, thought Pringle, thinking of the month then nearly past, maybe some of it would. As the two men left the building and walked west up Pike, Whitebrook took the occasion to tell

TAKING STOCK

Pringle how he'd come to turn his own first commission. ·

"Maxwell only saw fit to hire me on the condition I go to Blyth's San Francisco training class," explained Whitebrook, who, as Pringle was beginning to learn, was less a conversationalist than a monologist. "I remember outlining that finance book all the way down on the train. You see, I was late. Or so Maxwell informed me. He was upset, afraid the others would already have finished their course work by the time I got there. So I outlined the book all the way down, and when I arrived there, it turned out nobody'd even cracked the thing, hardly been to class at all. They'd been out in the bars instead."

"Well Mac," said Whitebrook, then turning the corner on First Avenue, pulling his hat down against the rain. "I had no compunction about spending a few off-hours amongst fellow revelers. So, one evening, I found myself sitting in Joe DiMaggio's Bar. Now there was a gentleman who had obviously over-imbibed sitting next to me. Not so drunk as to be incoherent, just enough of a bag-on to, shall we say, lower his inhibitions? It seemed he wanted me to introduce him to the young stripper then displaying her wares on the stage. Ample, as I recall. Though I remember asking myself, what was in it for me? I wasn't sure. I had, however, explained that I was a stockbroker with Blyth & Co. In point of fact, Mac, I was an unlicensed trainee. At any rate, the gentleman seemed agreeable, so I took it upon myself to conclude certain arrangements between the party of the first part and the party of the second. It turned out our amply endowed hostess was none other than Monte Thompson, Miss Idaho of 1935. Who seemed more than willing... Anyway, when I returned to the bar, the man asked what stocks I might recommend. Knowing nearly nothing at all about the subject, all that came to mind was the Weyerhaeuser Timber Company. So I said, how about that one? And he wrote me a check on the spot. Later, I got a personal note from Mr. Charles R. Blyth. In it he wrote: "You're unlicensed! It's illegal! But we are glad to accept the money..."

"Well," said Whitebrook, stopping in front of the Terminal Sales Building, "we seem to have arrived."

Indeed, even if Whitebrook - then living in near splendor on a solid acre of Lake Washington lakefront, his 46 -foot Chris-Craft nestled alongside his

100

150-foot dock - had arrived in style several years before. As the weeks turned into months, as winter became summer and summer turned once again to fall, it began to look as if even Mac Pringle's ship would come in. With his poor February then behind him, in the month of September, the young Blyth-man earned $1,251.43 for himself. He found he hadn't done it over lemon meringue pie, either. He'd done it by banging on doors.

• • •

Bill Slater didn't want to think about it - of how many places he'd walked out of that morning. As if they'd been surprised, hadn't wanted to be bothered. He'd been in the Fourth & Pike Building for almost two hours, working his way up and down the hallways, finding himself now still without an order. He hated cold-calling. Every broker Slater knew hated cold-calling. And everybody breaking into the business had to do it. Standing before one final door, Slater took in another set of black enamel names on the frosted glass: "Thompson & Thompson, Foresting Consultants. Since 1919." The broker had no idea what a foresting consultant was, but you never knew. If they'd been around since 1919, they had been in business longer than he'd been alive. And, he told himself, the timber business *was* booming...

Knocking on the door and letting himself in, Slater found a large, gray-haired woman sitting facing him from behind an oak desk. Walking up and introducing himself, he noticed that the office was smallish, and that there were two further glass doors behind the receptionist, one to either side of her. Offices, Slater noticed, that were now both closed. The broker smiled, handing the receptionist his card. Maxwell always insisted this was surefire, that a Blyth card opened any door in the city. Mr. Ed Maxwell, thought Slater, hadn't been in the Fourth & Pike Building lately.

"...Yes, ma'am," the broker said, "that's right. Blyth and Company, Investment Bankers. I was just in the building on other business, and I thought, perhaps, if your employer had a few moments...?" Slater let his voice trail off, his meaning hanging in the air.

"Well," said the woman, "my son is out, but my husband is here. Would you care to talk to him?"

101

"Yes, ma'am," said Slater, who was now less certain than he'd been before. They couldn't have any real money if the wife was working. On the other hand, if they did... It was bound to be the older man that had it. "I certainly would. That would be most helpful."

The woman got up from her desk and walked back to one of the inner-offices. She then opened the door and put her head in.

"Dad?" Slater could hear her say. "There's a gentleman here from the Blyth Company. Did you want to see him?" Slater couldn't hear what else was said; he did, however, notice two card holders on the desk in front of him. Both held business cards. One set said "Norman Thompson," the other said "Norman W. Thompson." That, thought Slater, simplified things considerably.

"Young man?" The woman had opened the door to her husband's office all the way, and was then motioning for Slater to go in.

"Yes ma'am," said Slater. "Thank you."

"Young fellow, what can I do for you?" The tone hit the broker before he'd gotten halfway in the man's office. By the time Slater was all the way in, it was apparent Thompson had little intention of asking him to sit down, though the man was sitting at a desk himself, his back to the big window behind him. Norman Thompson was in his middle fifties, with a square face, small slit eyes, and a shock of snow white hair.

"Yes sir," said Slater, trying to think of how to begin. "It's Norman Thompson isn't it?"

The man eyes slit even further."That's right. Do I know you?"

"No sir. Bill Slater's my name, Mr. Thompson. I'm with Blyth and Company. Investment Bankers. I thought perhaps, if you had a moment, we could discuss certain investment possibilities..."

"You mean you want to talk to me about buying stock in the Soundview Pulp and Paper Company..."

"Well, that's certainly a fine company, of course," said Slater, thrown off by this strange tack.

"So what would you tell me about Soundview?"

Slater began to get the feeling he always got when he knew he'd be wasting his time. Though, what could he do about it now?

"Well, if you're interested in Soundview, Mr. Thompson, I can tell you it's one of the lowest cost producers in the industry. U.M. Dickey is the company's Chairman, and Mr. Dickey runs the firm with an iron-hand. The company's currently selling at $30, earning $6 and paying $3. I believe it's an inexpensive stock at the price. If you're presently invested, and you don't own stock in Soundview, it's a company you probably ought to have a position in."

"Uh huh," said Thompson, "that's about what I thought you were going to say."

Slater looked at the man.

"You want to do me a favor young man?"

"Well sure," said Slater. "If I can."

"Good, then you go back and tell your sidekick, what's his name..." Thompson reached out and picked a business card off the top of his desk.

"...MacMillan Pringle, who, by the way just walked out of here, and who also thought highly of Soundview Pulp, that I still remember a little something called the Great Depression. Now I'm sure you're a fine young fellow, Mr. Slater. But tell me, how old are you?"

"I'm 29, sir."

"Well sir, I'm not, and I can still recall the year 1934 like it was yesterday. Which, by the way, is the year Soundview Pulp and Paper went bust; they couldn't give their pulp away. And Umberto Dickey had to come in and save their backsides. The stock market is not something I ever plan on putting my money in again. Now here," he said, handing Slater back the two cards. "You can take these both with you. And good day."

Old Mac, thought Slater, walking out of Thompson's office and down the hall. It seemed he and his friend had been bumping into each other more and more lately. He wondered, as he took in the names on the next frosted glass door in front of him - then knocked three times - what in hell Pringle had said to the guy...?

• • •

By the morning of Wednesday, October 3, 1951, Mac Pringle had already earned $102.30 in sales commission for the month. Chewing on the end of a pencil, the Blyth salesman was sitting in his second floor cubicle that morning, looking down at a pad of blank paper. Let's see, Pringle thought, first looking at his calendar, then beginning to scratch figures on the yellow tablet. As he began writing down his tallies, multiplying and adding up the sums, the Yale man began humming, finally adding the words under his breath: "We're little poor lambs who've lost our way. We're little poor sheep who've gone astray. Gentleman songsters off on a spree, damned from here to...." Jesus, he said to himself, the humming suddenly stopped. God, if he kept this up they'd be able to put a down-payment on a house soon. Multiply that by 12 and... Things were finally looking up. Five more years of this and they'd be building a house in Broadmoor. Pringle leaned back in his chair, then took up his client file, opening it in his lap. He'd picked up that lumber broker in the Terminal Sales Building, Monday. And the attorney in the Vance. Then, what was his name - Patterson? The guy with Bucyrus Eerie in the Textile Tower yesterday. Unfortunately, none were exactly Norton Clapp. That was a fact. Fact was, what he really needed was...

"Pringle!!!"

...a pair of ear plugs, thought Pringle, looking up from his chair. "Be right there, Ed," called the broker. He then got up, put the tablet with his cash projections in his desk drawer, and closing it, walked over to see Ed Maxwell.

Mac Pringle, like the rest of his young confederates at Blyth, regarded Ed Maxwell with a mixture of fear and genuine fondness. For all his bellowing, Edmund Maxwell was a friend to this youngest generation in the company - a benefactor and ally - and nearly all of them owed Maxwell the fact of their employment.

Pringle had first known the man as a friend of his mother's, someone who'd been over to the house since Pringle was a boy. And he'd seen Maxwell around the Tennis Club for as long as he could remember. Once, the Blyth manager had even purchased Pringle a tennis racket - for getting good marks in school. It was just something Maxwell was in the habit of doing.

Edmund F. Maxwell was the Seattle manager of Blyth & Co. when being the manager at Blyth was adequate cause for one's celebrity. This San Francisco company had made a place for itself among Seattle's well-to-do since the 1920s. In turn, the city's Society sent the company its sons. Starting his own career in much this manner, Maxwell had been a protege of the legendary Manse Griffiths, the former manager who'd first begun the silk stocking legend of Blyth in the city. After his ascendancy to the managership, part of Maxwell's responsibility lay in seeing to the firm's continued future. During the course of his weekly social rounds to the Seattle Yacht Club, The Seattle Tennis Club, the Seattle Golf Club, Maxwell would make a point of observing - of measuring the best of the coming generation. "Mac," he had said to MacMillan Pringle, when Pringle was still an undergraduate at Yale, "there's just no question about it. You're going into the securities business, and you're going to come to work at Blyth..."

Once on the job, however, as every new broker discovered, all of this amounted to very little. On the job, in Seattle, Ed Maxwell was no mere branch manager, Edmund F. Maxwell was Blyth itself. And every young broker on the second floor of the 1411 Fourth Avenue Building had best know what that meant. The very least of it being, when one was called, one came.

"Pringle!!!"

"I'm here..." said Pringle, swinging around the corner into Maxwell's office.

"Close the door and siddown, kid," said Maxwell, pointing to the leather couch pushed against the wall of his office. In Ed Maxwell's command of the English language, if one were a Blyth salesman, and younger than forty-five, one's name was kid.

"Listen, I'm gonna give you a nice fat break, kid. I have a client who's getting herself a divorce. The husband's made a pile of money in the securities business, and it looks like the woman's gonna get a good settlement. There's undoubtedly going to be a piece of money in this for you. To tell you the truth, Mac... Frankly, I'm tired of dealing with the woman. Now, she's gonna come in here a week from this Friday. You come in then and I'll introduce you. We'll work together with her for a couple of weeks, and then I'll gradually phase myself out. How's that sound to you?"

"Great!" said Pringle.

"I thought you might feel like that," said Maxwell. "Good. Now get out of here. Go sell somethin' for crissakes. I don't want to see you around this office 'til then."

Pringle got up from the couch.

"Thanks Ed."

"For what..? Oh, one last thing," said Maxwell, holding a letter out he'd picked up off his desk. "This came with my mail this morning, I don't know what the mix-up is, but see if you can't get your personal mail sent to your home."

Pringle thanked Maxwell again and walked back to his cubicle. Sitting at his desk, the salesman couldn't help but think he was on the verge of something. If this turned out right, adding to what he'd already put together... He brought his fist down on his desktop. A stroke of luck... And it was then that Pringle noticed the letter he still carried in his hand, the letter Maxwell had given him, seeing it was from the U.S. Navy Department. The blue envelope had his name on it, but for some reason it had been sent to his brother-in-law's address in New York. His brother-in-law, whose handwriting he recognized as having re-addressed it, had sent it on to the office. Odd. Finally Pringle looked at the postmark, and saw that it was three weeks late. Then he ripped it open.

"Greetings," the letter began. "This is to inform you, Lieutenant Junior Grade MacMillan Pringle, United States Naval Reserve, that you have been recalled for..."

Pringle let the letter drop. Then he looked at his calendar. Hell, he wasn't going to be meeting anybody a week from Friday. Not at Blyth anyway. Maybe on a ship to Korea...

· · ·

2

THE SNOWS CAME EARLY TO SEATTLE IN 1953, THEN LEFT nearly a month before Christmas. The giant star on the corner of the Bon Marche shone its lights through rain that holiday season, a cold rain that arrived from a thousand miles deep in Canada, and with the arrival of the city's

Christmas holidays, seemed never to end.

Other things had picked this season for their arrival as well. The decision of United States Circuit Court Judge, Harold R. Medina, in the case of U.S. vs. Morgan Stanley, et al., had been made public less than two months before. Medina had presided over this well-publicized lawsuit for six years, a civil action in which the Justice Department had charged every major corporation in the investment banking business with collusion, conspiracy, and agreements to monopolize the securities business. Morgan Stanley; Kuhn Loeb; Smith Barney; Lehman Bros.; Kidder Peabody; Goldman Sachs; Eastman Dillon; Drexel; First Boston; and Blyth & Co, were all counted among the alleged conspirators. As one senior Blyth executive said at the time, "If Blyth hadn't been indicted, we would have been disappointed. It would have meant we weren't on the first team."

Blyth was on the team, however. Though no one seemed unduly concerned. And, perhaps, they needn't have been. Medina's 424-page opinion, when it was released, turned out to be a vindication of these industry members, pointing out the enormous importance of the investment business to the nation, while at the same time, vigorously refuting the government's charges. Where the lawyers of the Justice Department had seen conspiracy and secret agreements, Medina saw unfettered competition. The Justice Department's case - the trial lasting 309 courtroom days, the trial record itself containing 6,000,000 words - was dismissed by Medina with prejudice.

MacMillan Pringle, recently returned from Korea, first read Medina's opinion while sitting one afternoon in front of the fireplace at the Men's University Club. He had been relaxing, enjoying a noon cocktail. Strict club rules forbade members to discuss anything as impolite as business. However, Pringle thought, sitting alone, trying to thaw two year's worth of shipboard frostbite from his feet, he could think any damn thing he liked.

Reflecting on this fact, Pringle decided the only prejudices he had that Christmas were for a few of the brokers at Blyth. Someone had been picking away at his clients, prospecting them while he'd been landing half-frozen Marines onto the shores of the Yellow Sea. But what should he have expected? He'd been away two years. At least the war was finally over - and yes, he said to the steward, he would have another, and could he have two olives this time?

Ordering his drink, Pringle's attention was redrawn to the fire in front of him, to the oil painting hanging over its mantle. It was a nude, its unrobed subject's short, dark hair bobbed in the style of the 1920s. The young flapper was lying on her stomach, raising herself to her elbows from out of a rumpled bed - glancing over her shoulder at the viewer, a look of pure invitation in her eyes. The portrait was entitled "The Hottest Day In Seattle." Pringle, his feet finally beginning to thaw, felt inclined to raise his empty glass. As for being pressed for his business at Blyth, Pringle thought perhaps he and the young woman had a great deal in common. Except, perhaps, for the tiniest of things: he hadn't been planning on giving it away.

Still, sitting there bathed in the glow of the fire, it seemed clear there was little to do about his lost business anyway. So, Pringle made up his mind to start over. Working the last four days in December, he made $138.02. It hadn't been all that much, but the way it looked to him, the real money was just coming up.

· · ·

Much of the nation had expected a long and difficult slump after the war, a recurrence of the hard-times that had followed hard on the heels of other wars. It hadn't happened. In fact, the country's post-war markets scarcely flattened out. Instead, except for a short break in '46, the country's capital markets rallied into the fifties. And with excellent reason. By the mid-fifties, American workers laid off in the depression had had jobs again for more than ten years, ten years of constant post-war shortages. Though men and women were once again able to spend, there was nothing for them to buy. With the Korean War finally over, the country on a peace-time footing at last, worker's long and pent-up demand for goods - for new clothes and cars, new apartments and houses - began fueling the nation's economy.

And the Pacific Northwest's. In 1953, the region had a manufacturing payroll of $800 million, local fisherman were canning $30 million of seafood, the state's forests produced nearly 4 billion feet of timber, the Port of Seattle did $500 million in business, and Frederick & Nelson put $10 million into its deluxe department store downtown. There was more than enough money in the local economy to acquire new clothes, cars, apartments, and houses for a growing portion of the city. And if after the car and house, one were interested in investment...

The belief in putting one's money in securities had regained its former wide appeal. The market, blamed for the depression by much of the nation in the '30s, was, in the 1950s, once again held in esteem. With new jobs in the city, growing savings, and expectations of profit propelling the town's economy - Blyth once again found itself the top-selling brokerage in the city. And who better? After all, ran the unspoken understanding at the 1411 Fourth Avenue Building - wasn't it their town?

• • •

"Patten?" Arty Yorkoff was saying over the office's direct line, calling from Blyth's National Syndicate Office in New York. "Here's what we got, we're in touch with 75,000 Yellow Transit, it's coming at 20 with a buck. How much of it do your guys want out there?"

Taylor Patten was the head of trading in the Seattle office. Lanky and bespectacled, looking a bit like a stork, Patten put down his line to Yorkoff, then buzzed Si Mott, the office sales manager.

"Si, New York's bringing out 75,000 Transit, 20 with a buck. What do we want?" Mott, only slightly less stork-like, immediately pushed up from his desk, walking out to the broker's "offices," a series of half-height bull-pens built out from the building's walls.

"Alright, New York's bringing 75,000 shares of Yellow Transit, it's 20 with a buck. Who wants some? ...Slater?"

Hands quickly came up from the cubicles.

"Yeah Si," said Slater. "I can take... let me see, give me 3,000 shares."

Slater's bid was quickly followed by others, hands rising above the cubicle walls, then, as Mott made the rounds, there came the sound of voices...

"Give me 3,000 too, Si."

"I'll take two."

"Gimme three of it, Si."
"I expect I'll take five..."
"Who said five?"
"Who is it? Whitebrook?"
"Hallucinating again."
"You mean five shares?"
"That's a five with three zeros, gentlemen."
"You and what army, Whitey. Hell Si, give *me* five-thousand."

Totaling his orders, Mott returned to Patten, adding an extra several thousand for those out of the office. With New York informed, the Seattle salesmen began laying the Yellow Transit off on clients. At Blyth, each salesman's allotment of stock was called a hallucination, in short: a "hally." These "hallies" didn't become real until the entire pledge was sold and confirmed and logged into a salesman's production for the month. And if not... If a broker couldn't move the shares he'd originally solicited, couldn't manage to place the stock he'd taken into his clients' accounts, Mott would transfer the shares to someone who could. If this happened often enough, Mott would encourage the unproductive broker to find another place of employ. This, however, was the rare occasion.

For the fact was that Blyth had many of the top securities salesmen in the city, Si Mott's brokers managing portfolios for some of the town's richest individuals. At the time, the firm had the brokerage accounts of the Nordstroms, Boeings, Schwabachers, Friedlanders, Fishers, Skinners, Wymans, Fredericks, Isaacsons, Sarkowskys, McCurdys, and Weyerhaeuser heir, Norton Clapp himself. But this glittering fact cut both ways. For it was Si Mott's job to oversee the men who oversaw the largest portfolios in town.

For all the seeming profit and perquisites of being the Seattle sales manager at Blyth & Co., when reduced to the actual mechanics of the role, Mott's job was often that of being servant to the stars. Protestations of modesty aside, men do not become top brokers by reason of having low opinions of themselves, or as a result of grossly underestimating their talents for leadership and charm. So it was at Blyth. And it was precisely Mott's role to urge these players on to greater and greater production, to the proposition that, for a top salesman, profits and perks have no limit at all. The day was perhaps inevitable then, when some would begin to covet the perks and profits that went with the job Si Mott called his own.

It wasn't hard to figure out, the succession at the Seattle office being simple enough. Ed Maxwell, as Blyth branch manager in the city, was Field Marshall. Si Mott, as sales manager, his able lieutenant. Everyone else - but for the aging heads of the municipal, operations and trading departments - was in the ranks. But someday, so the logic from down in the cubicles went, the Old General must step down. And someday, so the money was being bet, Mott would be the one to step up. And on that day, some eager young man...selected by Mott himself...would assume the sales manager's position. Somebody, of course. And *someday*. That much was known.

...But when? ...And who?

• • •

On January 16, 1956, Ed Maxwell was sitting in his office speaking into the telephone. He had been doing this most of the morning, and it was now late into his lunch hour. "Well sir, I appreciate the fact of your $300,000, but the Ford Foundation has given us clear instructions to allow no one more than 100 shares. Yes, I'm afraid that's right. Well, we expect it around $70, perhaps a bit lower. That's right. So you can see...Yes, I know you want the stock, but...That's right, Blyth *is* the lead underwriter, but...Yes, I know, you mentioned that: $300,000..."

Maxwell's caller was one of many that day, just as there had been many the day before, and the day before that, for weeks now. The greater part were first-time callers, and all rang the offices at 1411 Fourth asking for just one thing: Ford.

"Well I can probably get you as much as 50 shares," Victor Denny said, leaning over his desk, making notes on a sheet of personalized stationary. "Well, that's right, the biggest common-stock offering in U.S. history. Uh huh, it's *very* hard to get. But as I said, I can probably arrange a block of 20 shares for you. Though you know...It's Mr. Owens, isn't it? Well, you know

111

Mr. Owens, I'd expect, if I can find this stock for you, that you'd consider doing some future business with me..."

"..Some additional future business, that's right," Leo Doyle was saying in the next cubicle over. "There's a possibility a little more might be floating around the day it's released, Mr. Thorston. Maybe as much as 25 shares...That's absolutely right, they *are* offering 10 million shares. But you know what, Mr. Thorston? We could probably sell it out right here in Seattle..."

"I very much appreciate that, Mr. Roth," Burt Gottstein was saying in the cubicle next to Doyle's. "Certainly - Leonard then. Though you have to understand my position, Leonard. You're not the first caller we've had here inquiring about the Ford issue over the last few weeks. Unquestionably...any future business you may care to do with me... That's fine then... 10 shares. I'll open an account for you. No, thank *you*, Leonard..."

"...company's doubled and tripled its business since the war, Mr. Wells... What? Let's see. I've got that right here," said Carl Neu, sitting on the opposite side of the wall from Gottstein. "Before taxes," said Neu, flipping through a big blue prospectus laying on his desk. "They'll earn about $1 billion before taxes," he said. "That's right, the fourth largest in the country. Well absolutely, I'd call it a blue chip. Or it's sure as heck gonna be in a few days. ... I know, Mr. Wells, but a hundred is all I can do, at least until I see what we get here at the office. Yes, of course, future business is always appreciated..."

"If it's issued at $70," Peter Rawn was explaining, pushing aside a list of names to open a copy of <u>Newsweek Magazine</u>, holding it up and holding his phone at the same time. "'...that would mean a yield of more than 5 percent, put Ford's price-earnings ratio at around 8.7 to 1, compared to GM's 10.6 to 1 and Chrysler's 7.3 to 1.' Nope, only about 10 percent's going to the institutions...," he said, laying aside the magazine. "I know, Mr. Klemmer, but you've got to figure the demand. I know you do, and there's even a chance a little more may be around the day its released... Well, I can certainly keep my eye open," Rawn said, putting a check by the man's name. "Of course, Mr. Klemmer, that's always appreciated..."

Bill Slater, on the phone himself, was speaking to a friend. This caller, was in fact, one of Slater's oldest and largest clients, a cannery owner he'd known for years.

"Well, the Ford family just didn't intervene, P. D.. I'm sure Sidney Weinburg over at Goldman Sachs thought it'd be going over there, Weinburg having been close to the Fords for years. But, the way it turned out, Charley Blyth had been to Stanford with the head of the foundation. That's it, P. D. Right, not always what you know, but..."

Slater, at the sound of laughter nearby, happened to look up from his telephone conversation to see Si Mott, talking to Mac Pringle. Pringle had said something, a joke evidently, the older man laughing, then laughing again...

"...Yes, well I think that's right," Slater was saying. "It's very prestigious for us here at Blyth. The first time a West Coast firm has really led on a major underwriting. As you say, P. D., a coup...

As Slater talked, he continued to watch his friend out the corner of his eye, Pringle now grinning at something Mott was saying. And as he did so, a notion began to assert itself, to swim up into Slater's consciousness. The notion being that Mott and Mac had become close of late. But no, thought Slater, that wasn't it. That Mac was obviously high on Mott's list... yes, and climbing... *That* was it.

"Uh huh...Uh huh...," Slater was saying. "Hundreds of new accounts, P. D. We've had customers calling for weeks. People that have never called the brokerage before. Probably never called any brokerage before. You ought to see this place, it's a madhouse... "

Yet, as dear a friend as Pringle was, Slater also knew he'd beaten Mac silly on the only list that counted. Of the 69 Blyth brokers on the West Coast last year, more than half of them older and better established, Slater had placed 28th. Mac had come in 52nd. Only four men in the Seattle office had done better, and all of them were old...

"No need to even say it," Slater reassured his friend. "No, it doesn't matter how many new accounts... Don't concern yourself, P. D. I've got you taken care of... I've got it here in black and white. 100 shares."

Still...it happened. Slater'd seen it in the army, times when a man's career *didn't* depend on what he knew...Times, Slater thought, looking over again at Pringle, when for some, things just came together. But that was all right too.

Come this time next year, he'd be *higher* than 28th. He'd sell like he'd never sold before, make it his best year ever. Instead of spinning his wheels. No, the job would still be his to have - someday. Anyway, worrying...it was a lousy waste of time. What'd they say in the Air Corps? Worrying was like a rocking chair, it kept you moving... but you never got anywhere.

Worrying over nothing...

"...Nothing no," said Slater, turning his attention again to his client. "No, don't worry P. D. I've got you at the top of the list. Trust me, we're going to keep you there," he said. "Sure I'm sure."

• • •

3

ON AUGUST 25, 1959, AFTER A FULL DAY AT THE OFFICE, Charles R. Blyth died suddenly in the library of his home. The news of Blyth's death was on the office wire the next day, and that evening Maxwell led a contingent of his younger brokers to the bar in the Washington Athletic Club. There was nothing uncommon in this. Maxwell could usually be counted on to say, "Ah, c'mon kid, we'll just go in for one." And just as usually, forget how to count by the time every one had finished their first. This night, however, Maxwell hadn't said a word.

"God, I was fired up when we left that place," Mac Pringle was saying, speaking of the time four months before, when several of the office's top brokers had gone to Blyth's 45th anniversary gathering in Santa Barbara.

"I know," said Charley Donahoe, a young municipal bond man with the firm. "I think everybody was."

"I dunno," said Pringle. "Maybe it was when Charley got up and said that about, We're the oldsters here at Blyth, and we're gonna give you young fellows the firm. I mean, Jeezus...it was a real moment."

"And talking right to us younger guys," said Bill Slater. "It was an emotional moment for everyone, Mac."

"Yeah," said Pringle. "Remember when he got up on stage, Bill? Started saying how we're gonna give you fellows the firm? And then he said, You think you're getting a lot of equity, and a lot of money and so forth..."

"...But," Slater said, finishing Pringle's anecdote, "'there's only one thing we're really giving you. And that's integrity. And... we expect you to maintain it...'"

"Right," said Pringle, "yeah, that's right. I mean I was really revved-up, I was charged after Santa Barbara."

"And four months later he's dead," said Donahoe.

"But you know what? At least we were there. We'd been included, you know? Had the privilege to see..."

"...I'll tell ya, kid," interrupted Maxwell, who had been strangely silent up to then, an unusual thing for Maxwell, a man famous in happier times for his wit. "I'll tell you exactly. You haven't seen anything yet."

"What d'you mean by that, Ed?" asked Pringle.

"Charley Blyth is now dead, gentlemen. The man is dead, understand? I think we'll all have to wait and see. See what happens and what doesn't.

The three younger men looked across the table at each other.

"What I think is - while we're doing this waiting - is you need another drink, Ed," said Donahoe.

"Charley," said Ed Maxwell, "what can I say, kid? You're a mind reader. So get the boy over here, I'll buy us all a round."

• • •

"So there I was fellows, probably the only broker in the city of Seattle with even a superficial knowledge of the Knoll Museum of Fine Arts. And..." said Bob Whitebrook, looking over at his two companions, "a somewhat greater knowledge of Gilbert and Sullivan's Patter Songs. Put the two things together and you know what they make?"

Pringle and Slater shook their heads.

"They make me a lot of money," said Whitebrook, pleased with his own bon mot. "I shouldn't tell you this...but, what the hell."

Pringle shot Slater a glance. The three men had all been in attendance at an analyst's seminar at the Olympic Hotel, and as the thing had lasted well past dark, were now sitting around a table in the Marine Room.

"Either of you fellows ever been to the Knoll Museum of Fine Arts? Famous for its bows, arrows, buffalo heads and portraits of the late Queen Esther of Estonia?"

It was suddenly Slater's turn to look over at Pringle. Both of them knew they were in for it now.

"Just as I thought," said Whitebrook. "And you know? Neither had I. But I'd found out something about the Knoll Museum of Fine Arts. That along with the place's bows and arrows and buffalo heads, it also had a foundation. Set up by none other than James J. Hill of railroad fame. A big, fat foundation, getting bigger and fatter all the time. So...I uncovered the treasurer of said foundation, a Mr. Alfred G. Muntz. I also uncovered the fact that Mr. Alfred G. Muntz had a lovely wife, who happened to be an aficionado of Gilbert & Sullivan. Who was even then involving herself in a production of Gilbert & Sullivan's "Patience." So I committed one of the patter songs from "Patience" to memory. Now, unless you're Danny Kaye, Bill, a patter song is very difficult to deliver. Nevertheless, I got it down letter perfect, and went and knocked on Mr. Alfred G. Muntz's door. I introduced myself, Mac, and said I was most interested in the Museum of Fine Arts. Where," Whitebrook whispered in an aside, "I'd never gone. Just as I was interested in the bows and arrows, not to mention the stuffed buffalo heads - which I'd never seen. That I was an amateur historian, and hoped someday to take my degree.

"I pointed out to Mr. Alfred G. Muntz that his wife was a wonderful woman, and beautiful too - and musical! His lovely wife being a fan of Gilbert & Sullivan. Are *you* interested in Gilbert & Sullivan I asked?

"'OH I LOVE IT,' said Mr. Muntz. 'CAN'T UNDERSTAND IT - BUT I LOVE IT!'

"'Well, Mr. Muntz,' I said, 'when I was at Stanford, in one of the plays I was in' - which I wasn't - 'I happened to learn one of the patter songs. But you wouldn't be interested...'

"'OH YES I WOULD! PARTICULARLY MY WIFE WOULD!'

"'Well,' I said, 'I'm just here passing by...But it goes something like this:'"

And then Whitebrook, in a nearly professional tenor, began to sing. Though he did, Slater noticed with relief, sing very softly. Pringle thought it might be the fact they were sitting in the middle of a restaurant.

"The soldiers of our Queen, are linked in friendly tether;
Upon the battle scene, they fight the foe together;
There every mother's son, prepared to fight and fall is;
The enemy of one, the enemy of all is..."

"And," said Whitebrook, taking a breath, "that's just the introduction. As I explained to Mr. Muntz, who picked up his phone and said, 'NO CALLS, PLEASE. GO ON, MR. WHITEROCK!'

"'Name is Whitebrook,' I said."

"If you want a receipt for that popular mystery;
Known to the world as a Heavy Dragoon;
Take all of the remarkable people in history;
Rattle them off to a popular tune..."

"'MY GOD!' said Mr. Muntz.

"'That's not all,' I said."

"The pluck of Lord Nelson on board of the Victory;
The genius of Bismarck devising a plan;
The humor of Fielding, which sounds contradictory;
Coolness of Paget, about to trepan..."

"'MY GOD!' said Mr. Muntz, after I'd sung the last phrase,
'YOU'VE GOT THE KNOLL MUSEUM ACCOUNT, MR. WHIT-EROCK!'

"'That's Whitebrook...' I said."

Glancing at each other, then looking at Whitebrook, Slater and Pringle could only agree.

. . .

By spring of 1962, Blyth & Co. had moved out of the 1411 Fourth Avenue Building and into spacious quarters in the new Washington Building on Fourth. The old sea-green linoleum and tiny, cell-like office cubicles were finally a thing of the past, left behind with thirty years of office history. Other things, perhaps inescapable by that time, had not been left behind however. For the firm's rivalries moved in, right along with the desks.

The office, as if at the prospect of more space, had divided itself. Like iron filings in a magnetic field, office alliances became suddenly visible, individuals aligning themselves at points of ambition and friendship and power. Two blocs came into being, one including Ed Maxwell and Si Mott and Mac Pringle. The other was comprised of Victor Denny and Leo Doyle and Bill Slater.

The forces provoking this division had been many, the first causes having arisen years before. But, as if at a single tap, the thing had finally revealed itself. And that tap - when it came - was the rise of the institutions.

Seattle's banks and insurance companies had begun to expand their investment in the late fifties. By the early sixties, the Blyth office was getting calls for local underwritings from institutions having never purchased securities before. Washington Mutual, Seattle First National, Safeco Insurance, National Bank of Commerce - all were suddenly investing in volume. Nor was it just the banks and insurance companies. Since the passage of the Taft-Hartly Act in 1947, with its creation of jointly administered pension funds, enormous pools of money had been created, capital then requiring investment. Blyth's national office, having little idea what was about to happen, paid its brokers doing this volume investment the same commission it paid out for retail. In short, a great deal of money was being made, and quickly.

But only by those senior brokers residing at the very top of the organization. Leo Doyle had half the State of Washington, Vic Denny half the Safeco

Insurance Company account, Chuck Easter, the head of the office's bond department, had half the Seattle First National Bank account, Burt Gottstein having been given the rest. The senior men at Blyth had been assigned these accounts when they'd meant next to nothing - during the depression. Even as the money began to come in, they were in the habit of paying these institutions very little attention. It was rumored Vic Denny wasn't even aware that Safeco had its offices in the University District. And this was a habit of business these men seemed neither inclined nor prepared to break. As the business coming from the institutions then grew, the frustrations of the firm's younger brokers mushroomed.

It wasn't entirely the fact the senior men hadn't shared this business with them. There was a perception among the younger players that business was being missed. The employees at the institutions doing the actual purchasing of Blyth's securities were nearly all young men, friends and peers of the junior members of the firm. The seniors felt it beneath their dignity to cultivate these young players, and the young Blyth brokers weren't being allowed to use these friendships to their advantage. Among themselves then, the junior men at Blyth began to charge these older brokers with missing opportunities, losing business, losing steps. It seemed, so the younger generation formulated it, that a change was required. The question being, not when - but how? And who'd be standing when it was over.

By the summer of 1962, Ed Maxwell still held sway as office manager in Seattle. He was, however, on increasingly shaky ground. As he had predicted, changes had come, though in Maxwell's case, they had come in the form of cautions from the corporate offices, warnings he stop mixing after-hours celebration and business. These warnings had undermined him, and with his friend Charley Blyth then dead, Maxwell could no longer be entirely certain of his own continuing role. Si Mott, for his occasional sarcasm, and for all the burdensome responsibilities of his job, was not, by nature, a decisive man. And it was largely this passivity that tied him to Maxwell's fortunes. For Mott, it was a matter of wishing to avoid hard choices, and in such a way, to sidestep alienating friends and associates. So Si Mott hung on with Maxwell, holding out for whatever was to come. Mac Pringle, desperately wanting the sales manager's job, threw his lot in with Mott. Pringle valued his friendship with Slater, but surely, when Si Mott was elevated to the managership, he would in-turn raise Pringle along with him.

Victor Denny, grandson of pioneer David Denny, one of the top producers at Blyth, president of the National Lawn Tennis Association, and a social lion in his own right, felt Maxwell had compromised his effectiveness. With his eye on the managership for himself, Denny set about building a power base, spending time with senior Blyth executives in the company's San Francisco and New York offices whenever the chance would permit. Leo Doyle was his friend Denny's alter ego. Though he had fewer personal ambitions, Doyle supported the patrician Denny in his bid to take charge of the office. Bill Slater prized his friendship with Pringle, but he was also aware of having out-performed Mac in sales year after year. He could see as well, that Pringle had long ago won over Maxwell and Mott. So Slater moved to Denny and Doyle. If, on Maxwell's eventual departure, Vic Denny were to become manager, all to the good, thought, Slater - for all concerned really. But even if Mott were to be elected, the confident Slater felt he still had a chance.

This then was the landscape when Blyth's National Sales Manager, Ralph Sheets, came to town that June.

• • •

There was a sense of seriousness about Ralph Sheets, a rigidity given off by this corporate heavyweight's ironlike self-regard. Plainly, as Blyth's National Sales Manager, Sheets was both an executive of unwavering severity, and a man with his feet fixed firmly to the ground.

So it was that on one June night, when Ed Maxwell, in full flight after a number of drinks, and on the occasion of a company dinner honoring this guest at the Tennis Club, introduced the man as "Mr. Ralph Shits," and then had the temerity to repeat himself at greater volume... Ralph was not amused. And word returned to San Francisco just as fast as Mr. Sheets.

Finally, as the old general had increasingly feared, the writing appeared to be on the wall. Less than a month later, Ed Maxwell and Si Mott were called on an unexpected trip to San Francisco. On their immediate return, Mott convened an unscheduled sales meeting. But Maxwell, not Mott, was the one to stand up.

"At the end of the month," Maxwell told those assembled in the conference room - Denny and Doyle sitting on opposite sides of the table - Slater and Pringle having found chairs side by side, Donahoe and Rawn and the rest of Maxwell's brokers ringed around the room. "I will no longer be your office manager." Maxwell's voice wavered, the man mustering his not inconsiderable dignity. "Those duties will be passed on to Si Mott... (a shuffling of feet beneath the table.) "I will expect you all to treat Si with the same respect you have been gracious enough to show me over the years..."

Slater didn't take his eyes off Mott. Pringle, not wanting to jeopardize the position with his friend - sure of his coming nod - avoided looking at the man at all. Then, as Maxwell sat back down and Mott arose, Pringle and Slater realized the man was actually saying it, the words:

"...all comes as a great surprise, as I'm sure you all can imagine. And I've not really had a chance to give the matter as close an analysis as it warrants. Nevertheless, I think it best in these matters to come right out in the open, to just state the facts. So... I've asked Pat, our able head trader, to serve as our new sales..."

And then neither Pringle nor Slater heard anything else, as the tall, boney, birdlike Taylor Patten stood up at the table before them.

· · ·

That night at dusk, Robert Whitebrook - who hadn't been at the office meeting that afternoon, having entertained the idea of retiring soon, perhaps by the age of 48 - was standing out on the balcony of his home. Whitebrook was facing south, letting his gaze run along his Lake Washington beachfront. The setting sun had turned the southern sky pink, Mt. Rainier rosy in the gathering dusk. Whitey loved this time of night, these soft summer evenings. He looked again to the mountain rising in the south, then allowed himself to admire his 46-foot Chris-Craft power cruiser, the boat riding alongside his 150-foot dock. Whitebrook admired his house, as he admired his yard, delighting in his lakefront as well.

TAKING STOCK

The Blyth man then stood up very straight, and spreading his arms as if to embrace it all, thought precisely these thoughts. "King Farouk," thought Whitey, "King Farouk's got nuthin' on me..."

The nation's economy had been recovering from the mild recession of 1960, when a charismatic new President and his Harvard economists promised to "get the country moving again." They would do this, they explained, by applying the Keynesian principles of the "new economics."

Against a background of low inflation, and a bullish earnings outlook, stock prices soared 25 percent between October 1960 and December 1961. The Street was anticipating a surge in earnings in 1962 and beyond, but the country's investors increasingly began to wonder whether they were overpaying for this good news.

Seattle, at the time, had its own good news. The city's World Fair and Century 21 Exposition opened in April of 1962. The fair was an immediate success; the city's economy was flush that spring. John Kennedy was in the White House, and the nation was at peace. And that April, the New York Stock Exchange collapsed.

As it turned out, the country's investors had been correct - stock prices had over discounted the expected earnings rise. The trigger for the break had been a confrontation between President Kennedy and the Chairman of U.S. Steel over steel pricing. By June, the market had fallen 27 percent from its December high.

However, the nation's economy remained strong. So did Seattle's. Twenty-one months later, the DOW had regained its peak of December, 1961. This was the shortest time ever elapsed to regain a former peak following a panic. And the index then continued to climb. Though no one knew it yet, and the phrase hadn't yet been coined - the "go-go" sixties were at hand.

Chapter Six

SELF-CONFIDENCE MAN

Firms and rumors of firms

"**Z**EKE?" THE CALLER TELEPHONING HOWARD "ZEKE" ROB-
bins that June morning had a phone-voice forever reminding Robbins of a Bullfrog. No pond-size frog either; on the contrary, this was a king-
sized croaker with a five-dollar cigar in its mouth.

"Zeke," the voice repeated. "What are your plans for lunch today?"

"Let me take a look," replied Robbins, keeping the receiver to his ear as he
dug out his desk calendar, "What the hell's today? Tuesday...? Looks like I'm
free." The young broker leaned back in his chair. "Where do you want to go?"

"I thought perhaps we could meet at the Olympic Hotel," Robbins' caller
explained. "I've already spoken to Carmine in the Marine Room, he's
arranged a table for us near the back."

"Okay...Are we hiding from somebody?"

"Yes...Well, our privacy may be marginally more assured that way. The
fact is, you see, Zeke - though it wouldn't pay to mention it - I've a proposition
for you. But then," the voice added, dipping to its deepest, Everett Dirkson-
like delivery, "We can speak of that later, over lunch." And with that, Robbins
found his conversation with Stephen House Herron abruptly over.

Despite this melodrama, or perhaps in part because of it, when twelve
o'clock arrived, Robbins followed Herron's curious phone request to a "t" -

stationing himself in the hotel diningroom and waiting for the broker from Dean Witter to arrive. Thirty minutes later Robbins was still waiting, and still wondering what all the mystery was about. Something was up, Robbins knew, though Herron had been impressively vague over the telephone. One point had been made abundantly clear, however: Stephen H. Herron, a top talent at Dean Witter, and, at 39 years of age, perhaps the biggest producer in Seattle, had a proposition for him. So, hidden away as well as a 34-year-old, six-foot-two, 250-pound broker can be hidden in a hotel dining room, Robbins set about deciding between the steak sandwich on sourdough and the room's Caesar's salad - and wondering. What kind of proposition? What did Herron - on this hot summer day in 1964 - what exactly did the man have in mind?

Ten years before, a 24-year-old Zeke Robbins, son of a corporate lawyer and graduate of Harvard University, had migrated to Seattle from Massachusetts. By the time Robbins reached Seattle, the native Bostonian had already bummed around much of the American continent, this youthful trek following nine months of combat with the Marines in Korea.

If in middle age the heavyset broker would look a bit like another Bostonian, House Speaker Tip O'Neil, in 1964, when still in his early thirties, Robbins was simply a large man with a pleasant laugh and a pleasingly bluff personality. In fact, Zeke Robbins was that novelty: a street-smart Harvard Man (Hasty-Pudding/Porcellian Clubs,) a clubman with few complications and no enemies at all; a friendly, Back-Bay Yankee whose first instinct was to like everyone, to trust them.

A laudable combination, and as it was joined at the head and hip with an astuteness at picking certain local stocks, it soon provided the Seattle broker a faithful clientele. Certainly by Seattle's sweltering summer of 1964, working as a customer's man for old Ben Ehrlichman's Pacific Northwest Company, Robbins had begun to make his way.

"Your table, Mr. Herron," the maitre d' had warbled, nearly bowing and scraping in his ceremony of showing the diminutive broker to his seat. In the course of these ceremonial duties, the waiter seemed utterly oblivious to Robbins' presence at the table. "Do enjoy your lunch, Mr. Herron."

"Thank you, Carmine," said the little broker. Robbins, having removed his eyeglasses to re-read the menu, was taken by surprise by Herron's arrival. Quickly now he put his glasses back on. As always, Stephen Herron struck Robbins as an uncommonly vigorous, stylish, self-assured little man. A second glance, or third, revealed that this broker in the bow tie and fire-engine-red jacket had exceedingly large eyes, a ruddy complexion, and, at the present moment, a Cuban Corona of such proportions that had the broker abruptly turned his head (without first removing the cigar), he'd have suffered cervical whiplash. Pushing a purple, three-ring binder onto the table top, Herron lowered the outsized cigar from his mouth.

"You'll have to pardon me, Zeke," he said. "Townley sprang some syndicate people on us from San Francisco. Seems they'd been looking forward to meeting me. I couldn't really break away."

"Not at all, Steve. I was just getting ready to eat the table cloth here."

"Oh, well, hell you should have eaten, Zeke. No need for ceremony around me."

"No problem," said Robbins as the waiter arrived to take their orders. "I'll just eat twice," he said. "But we better get to it, Steve. What were you saying on the phone this morning? What's this mysterious proposition?"

"Of course, Zeke, right to the point," rumbled the little broker, his voice sliding to a near croak. This exceedingly low voice, a kind of basso-profundo, was as much Herron's signature as his cigar. "In fact I do have a proposal for you," Herron said, glancing at the diners occupying tables on either side of them. "Zeke, I'm going to make a move, I'm going to start a major new brokerage in this town." His tone was suddenly conspiritorial, confidential. "Which leads me to the reason for our luncheon. I'd like you with me, Zeke," he said. "As a principle in the firm, a full partner. It's my belief you bring the right skills, the right associations, the right background to this venture. Naturally, I've given this all a great deal of thought. My concept is this: The brokerage will be a member firm, that is, we'll purchase a seat. Unlike the Merrill Lynches of this world, however, our primary focus will be here in the Northwest. We'll accommodate only the wealthiest of the area's clients. In short, we'll be exclusive. The advantage is we then needn't branch from here to California; we can remain small and profitable to ourselves. I believe the concept is right, certainly from a marketing point of view. But I'm equally confident the time for this is right as well. Witness the performance they've had at Donaldson Lufkin, at Faulkner Dawkins. Look at the firms opened by young men on Wall Street in the last few years. You know, contrary to popular opinion, they didn't break the mold in this town when Ben Ehrlichman started his companies in the twenties. I believe, Zeke, by building this firm we can accomplish an even greater success."

As Herron continued to speak, he picked up the purple, three-ring binder in front of him, turning and placing it so that Robbins could read it from his seat.

"I've written it all out," he said, opening the binder's cover. "It's all here: the concept, my personal-professional history, the firm's financial structure, the backers, the company's philosophy. You'll even notice in the back here I've devised a time-line..." As he spoke, Herron flipped pages faster than Robbins had a hope of reading them. "But I see I'm getting ahead of things. First things first, Zeke. Tell me, give me your initial reaction. I'd like to hear what you think of the idea."

"It sounds real good to me Steve. I'd love to...I've never had any plans of staying with Ehrlichman forever, you know. But lemme ask you a question. Do you really think this town'll support another brokerage?"

"Zeke," croaked Herron, taking up his enormous cigar, hoisting it up before him like a pennant. "It's simply a matter of doing the work, and of having the confidence to carry through. If that's so, then I believe the possibility of failure does not exist."

Robbins looked over at the little broker, who gazed unblinkingly back, and it was then, with a maximum of flourish, that the two men's meals were finally seen to arrive.

· · ·

"You know, Jack," said Steve Herron, rising from his host's supper table and walking into the living room, "it's early yet." The scarlet-coated broker then picked up a lighter from his host's coffee table and turned a torpedo-sized cigar to its flame. "Perhaps it's even premature to be saying this. But, if I mentioned the name Max Wyman, would your doubts be allayed?"

"Well...I really don't know, Steve," said Jack Fitzsimmons. "Maybe if I saw Wyman's signature on a check," said Fitzsimmons, thinking momentarily of joining Herron in his living room - then deciding against it. "Maybe even if I saw him signing it. But is that what you're telling me? You're telling me Max is coming along?"

"That's precisely what I'm suggesting," said Herron, sending out a cloud of cigar smoke from Fitzsimmon's living room couch. "Wyman's with us, a major participant. Ourselves, Max, Ad Fenton, Zeke Robbins, Dick Hooper, Bill Ward, Bob King, Fritz Frink..."

If the names Herron listed registered with Fitzsimmons at all, they quickly paled in comparison with the near splendor contained in the name Wyman. The 50-year-old Fitzsimmons, a big, square-jawed, no-nonsense Irishman, a colleague of young Herron's at Dean Witter and a leading producer there since the end of WWII, knew the near tidal pull Wyman's trench-like pockets would have on the venture's outcome. Fitzsimmons knew as well (as skeptical as he was about many things), the legitimacy, the cachet, the stamp of approval the Seattle timber heir's name would afford them in the investment community.

"So Wyman's coming in?"

"Max is already on board."

"What's his involvement going to be? Wyman's a busy guy, he's sure as hell not gonna peddle stocks."

"No," said Herron, his speaking voice carrying the length of the room. "Max will be assuming a quieter position. But a major one."

"How 'major' are we talking about?"

"Between you and me? A hundred, perhaps more."

"That's a pretty big chunk, Steve. Hell, Wyman'll control the whole thing."

"No, though Max's name will appear on the seat. However, Max doesn't want to own us, he just wants to take the ride up. But then, that's exactly it, isn't it, Jack? Stepping up, making up one's mind. You know, you really ought to take a look at what's happening. Look at Faulkner Dawkins, look at Donaldson Lufkin. Every one of them coming out of major firms, venturing out on their own. It's not just us, Fitz, sitting out here in Seattle. It's happening all over the Street."

"Listen, Steve, I'll tell you the way it is," said Fitzsimmons, conscious of the sounds his wife and eight children were making in other parts of the house, the two men having been left to their after-dinner discussion. "If I came in, I'd come in as a senior partner. That's the only way I'd do it. And to come up with the numbers we've discussed, to do that - hell - I'd probably have to mortgage the house here."

"Fitz, with all due respect, I think you've got it turned around..."

"Hard facts, Steve."

"Please," said Herron, "allow me..."

"God's tru..."

"Please Jack," interrupted the broker, "allow me to explain...." Herron suddenly put down his cigar, as if requiring the use of both hands. "The real fact *is,* is that we're standing in front of a wonderful opportunity here. A marvelous opportunity. You've examined the numbers, we've gone over them now. Holding the equity positions we've projected, this firm will make us a good deal of money. Shouldn't that be the only real consideration? That we can both of us build something, build something our children will benefit from twenty years from now? You know, Fitz, the truth is I've spent the last three years putting this together. Believe me then, when I say I've come to certain inescapable conclusions. First among them is the fact I want you with me - to help run this company, to be on top of things day-to-day. As a senior partner of course, hell, what else? But, and you speak of hard facts, fact *is* I'm holding the door open, Jack. And I can't hold it open forever...You'll have to help. I hope that you will."

Big Jack Fitzsimmons, sitting at his dining room table, a purple, three-ringed binder lying open before him, looked over at young Herron on his sofa. His associate's legs were crossed, his crimson jacket open, the man's outstretched arm was resting atop the rear cushions of the couch, a dirigible-like cigar once again rising between his fingers, its silver tip aimed straight at the ceiling. For a man having just given a speech, Fitzsimmons realized, Herron then seemed strangely calm - strangely, almost incredibly composed.

"I'd have to shop around," said Fitzsimmons. "Get a decent rate on a loan, Steve."

"Excellent! Good. I knew I could count on you, Fitz. And we've got much to do now. We must negotiate lease space by the fall, make our several applications to the Exchange, buy equipment, hire employees. And we'll need a name. We'll have to be thinking about that."

"Why not the fellows' names?" said Fitzsimmons. "Say, list them alphabetically?"

"Yes," said Herron, skying another cloud of smoke. "Alphabetically," he said, saying this with nearly perfect poise, and with an absolute poker face. "That would certainly be the place to start, Jack."

• • •

"All right Steve, not that you've asked, but I'll tell you anyway. It's just not feasible. Starting a member firm in this town? You and who else? And with what capital? You young fellows'll go broke. YOU'LL GO BROKE!"

Another man might have taken this warning to heart, or swallowed it whole: having it lie, then, indigestible on the gut. But not every man burns to found a member firm in the New York Stock Exchange - something Stephen Herron was actively in the process of doing. Thus, to the self-possessed young broker, his colleagues', even his confidants' bearish warnings of "you'll go broke" carried approximately the same meaning as static on the family Magnavox. In short, it remained incoherent, unintelligible, carrying no meaning for the man at all. This ex-naval officer and member of the bar, a man whose father was one of the early, leading lights at Boeing, no more believed he'd go broke than that he'd sprout wings to fly. But then, Herron didn't need wings for what he was about to do. He simply needed money. A great deal of it. And soon.

In any kind of analysis, there were only so many main connections to be identified in the Seattle of 1964. It didn't matter how Herron calculated it, the equation always came out the same. The same question, the same answer. For the way he saw it, there was only the single equation, and but one more connection to make... Wyman.

As the well-to-do lumberman's stockbroker, one of any number around town, Herron had learned something now verging on the point. Hadn't the wealthy lumberman already done everything he'd ever wanted to do? Certainly the man had had everything: an armada of ocean-going yachts, a fleet of fast planes, even a chateau in the south of France. But to have your name on a seat of the New York Stock Exchange...the citadel as it were. Yes, Herron reminded himself, he must remember there was a certain romance involved, a level of glamour - even for Wyman. Not to mention the money they'd make. Though he hadn't quite approached the wealthy Seattle lumber-king about that. Not yet. An oversight, he reflected, straightening his tie as he was ushered into the lumber company's back office, a purple notebook at his side - and something he was about to correct.

"Well, well," said the broker, his hand held straight out before him, his arm tracking like a dowser's wand as he approached the millionaire's desk. The tall, silver-haired Wyman stood up, a smile on his face. "So good of you," said Stephen Herron, clasping Wyman's open palm, "so good of you to see me, Max...."

• • •

Which, as things turned out, was true - true all the way around. Everything else had fallen into line, why would Wyman be any different? It seemed to Herron, the summer stretching golden before him, that the whole season had fallen into place. Herron could then be excused, if to him, even the country's capital markets seemed to comply, the NYSE performing as if it had been engineered by an expert. God, it was all working out, it was clicking along like he'd planned it: inevitable, determined, as ordained as the fall of a child's dominoes. Click click, click click, click...

Sitting at his corner desk at Dean Witter, Herron had glanced up one evening that summer after working through the depths of another twelve hour day. The sun was setting behind the Olympic Mountains, and, gazing out, the broker had caught his own reflection in the office window. Evaluate it as he might, study it as he might, he could see no possible impediments to the plan he'd devised. If his strategy was entirely original, thought Herron, it was also entirely right. He'd capitalize, buy the seat on the New York exchange - then stay small - and exclusive - and profitable. He'd design the firm as the limousine of Seattle brokerages. The finest location, the strongest producers, the best of everything. Against such as that, there could be no competition. Not really. Not locally owned, Herron knew. Al Foster, over at Foster & Marshall, had been forced to sell his seat three years ago. The man's loss would be his gain, a piece of luck, thought Herron. For in a very few months, he'd be the only locally owned member firm in the city.

...And with the Big Board presently red hot. Yes, he'd done everything he could to speed things on. He was already well into negotiations with Clark Dodge, the venerable old Wall Street firm, to act as the new brokerage's correspondent. And he'd been in touch with the NYSE for months, driving home details with a half dozen lawyers, and local insurance men, and accountants, and...

Yet that was less than half of it. Without the right participants, the right producers...But he'd be smart, he'd do what old Ehrlichman had never done, he'd give his men equity. That was the way you kept your people, the best ones. You sold them stock, made them owners. Yes, and he'd put them onto a whole floor, a top floor, find space in one of the new buildings opening up. And furniture, the best antiques, and new electronics, closed circuit TVs with quotes in every office, and the pneumatic carriers he'd seen, tubes that could speed a brokers' tickets to the wire desk in a few seconds, and...

Everything was right. The money would be there. The right people. The right market. He just had to keep it quiet a few months more - take the seat on the exchange - then take the whole town by the ear. He was looking forward to that, he was indeed looking forward to that.

Realizing the sky had grown dark, and that lights were going on around the town, Herron snapped on the lamp at his desk. Once again, he caught his reflection in the glass (noticing it was now brighter, his features superimposed upon the lights of the city). Yes, he thought, returning to his work: everything would be there, ready... No unseen hitches to the plan he'd devised. He'd see to that.

• • •

If the requirements of secrecy had added dash to the affair, they also added layers of complication to nearly everything at hand. Participating in the founding of this new firm, Herron's future-partners were forced to take up roles of undercover agents, field operatives, secret-service men. They'd go off to work each day, having spent their evenings plotting the new brokerage, knowing the penalties discovery could incur, complications none of them either needed or desired to take place.

Brokers are only too aware that their clients are counted amongst their brokerages' belongings. Certainly this is true of brokers' books, detailed lists of clients and client transactions. Without these, brokers have no physical record of what their clients hold, no historical account, other than their memories, of which securities these clients prefer, or require, or even, ultimately, of who all of their various clients are. And as every commission agent knows, who each client is... is the goose that lays the golden eggs.

Because this is so, when brokers depart from a brokerage (their clients, as a rule, departing with them), there is a history of blood turning suddenly bad. It's little wonder then, that disagreements along these lines (reinforced at every turn by matters of livelihood, and profit, and prestige), frequently devolve to the level of first-strike warfare, the result regularly being, upon the occasion of discovery, a broker's desk being turned out, his office locked, his books seized. And if he hasn't first copied his books...

So, in situations such as this, cautions must be observed, safeguards taken. Which often meant that in the summer of 1964, Herron's colleagues, at his suggestion, would drift up to hotel meetings at staged, ten-minute intervals, or slip quietly around corners like pulp fiction spies.

"Jesus Christ, I think that's John Riley," said Zeke Robbins, quickly looking down, speaking under his breath. "Is that John Riley? Shit, somebody take a look! Fitz! Christ on a crutch," he said, having again glanced up. "It _is_ Riley!

It _was_ John Riley, an old-time broker who happened to know all of them - the future partners now standing in front of the new IBM Building, its nearly finished 17th floor the site of their new office, their feet suddenly frozen to the sidewalk. While Riley - someone who wouldn't take long to put two and two together (or, in this case, three and three) - was proceeding directly up the sidewalk towards them.

"Get outa here, Fitz," hissed Robbins, before realizing Fitzsimmons was already halfway across the street. Looking around, Robbins saw Billy Ward spring up the street to a shop window, with John Packo tagging right behind. Both men suddenly ducked their heads, suddenly absorbed in a case display of plastic, prosthetic limbs. Robbins quickly crossed University Street, his bulk vanishing beneath the marquee of the Fifth Avenue Theatre, there to be confronted by a poster hailing "The Spy Who Came In From The Cold." This sudden dispersal, like foxes at the first whiff of the farmer, left only Max Wyman and Herron, the two walking confidently down the street. As it was, these two were only too pleased to inquire as to the unsuspecting Mr. Riley's health and well being. But then, unlike the others, Wyman and Herron were protected, unreachable, un-damageable - the big, silver-haired Wyman by reasons of wealth and the life-long independence this had afforded him; the smiling little broker, by reason of a wealth of sheer, unmitigated nerve.

Whatever would come to pass, this was indisputable. Whether it was Herron's self-confidence, his undying belief in his own abilities, or simply the fact that he'd been born with equipment standard on a government mule. Whatever it was, there were times, when this characteristic of Herron's stood him in good stead. In the spring of 1964, for example, Herron, concluding he was the exception that proved the rule (disregarding any tales of locked offices or confiscated books), decided to fly a personal sortie down to San Francisco. Once in the town, the broker had immediately gone to Witter's head office to see Eaton Taylor, and to see Dean Witter as well. Herron knew the two principles well enough, and once being seated, lost no time in announcing that he, Stephen House Herron, undoubtedly one of the company's largest producers, was planning to start a member firm of his own. By every conceivable measure, this was virtual suicide, Herron could just as well have volunteered to commit hara-kiri then and there. But this didn't seem to have dawned on the man. And if it did, it seemed never to have fazed him at all.

Why yes, he continued on, he envisioned an exclusive shop for Seattle - first-cabin all the way - a role requiring that his new brokerage stay small, and personal, and highly profitable. Rolling his bull-frog eyes, punctuating this soliloquy with blasts on his oversize cigar, the little broker instructed the two top officers in this national corporation regarding the basics. One: that there was in fact no basis for anyone's concern, there being no areas in which

Herron's limousine brokerage and the giant Dean Witter would come into conflict. And two: there was also no way anyone could stop him. He was, in a word, unstoppable. *His* story, Witter and Taylor must understand, was to be seen as cast in the classic mold, reflecting the kind of entrepreneurship that had made the American Nation what it was. And what was more, he didn't expect to be fired over this, not at all, nor was he to be in any way inconvenienced. And what was even *more,* any attempts at so doing would amount to the basest betrayal. Actions, Herron told the two, he deemed ungentlemanly - and entirely Un-American.

Instead of firing him on the spot, Witter simply sat there, listened to Herron, and then approved it all - lock, stock and any future debentures. Not only that, Witter's number two, Eaton Taylor, became Herron's angel. No one in the company, not even Townley Bale, the Seattle broker's putative boss, could block Herron's progress after that. From that moment on, whether it be public knowledge he was in start-up or not, whether brokers shouted it from the peak of the IBM Building or not, Steve Herron became virtually unfirable. Given the history of the profession, this was unbelievable end to end. Yet no one who had ever known the little broker, even briefly, ever believed this story of Herron's chutzpah to be anything but the truth, the whole truth, and nothing but. So help them God...

• • •

"So help me, Steve! Middle of Manhattan! Walking down Fifth Avenue trying to hold my damn pants up! Right Fitz? True story..."

Jack Fitzsimmons, sitting among the future partners at his now-crowded dining room table, agreed that Zeke Robbins had it exactly right. The two of them had indeed started their last day in New York searching out a pair of suspenders for Robbins. Sent to meet their Clark Dodge counterparts, the two brokers had gone no more than a block from their midtown hotel, when they heard the twang of Robbins' braces breaking.

"So, Jeezus, of course I say 'Fitz, I gotta go get some new suspenders!' And Jack's dad's store, Rogers, Peet, is just around the corner. We're hoping we can kind of slide in and out again. The less anybody knows, right? I mean, what the hell are we supposed to be doing in New York, and on a weekday... So, we kind of tiptoe in, and we're no more than two feet in the door when we both start hearing this whispering. 'It's Mr. Fitzsimmons' boy! It's Mr. Fitzsimmons' boy!' It's all the old salesmen, all these old guys that'd known Jack since he was a kid. Hell. We might've just as well hung signs around our necks."

Herron, sitting at the head of Fitzsimmon's table, a purple notebook in front of him, joined in Robbins' familiar laughter, though he paused long enough to ask, "And what did your father say to your unexpected visit, Fitz?"

"I asked him to keep it quiet, that I didn't want anyone to know. He understood," said Fitzsimmons.

"Well, I suppose that's all right then," said Herron. "We don't want Townley to suspect any more than he already does."

"Well, I dunno," said Zeke Robbins. "About what Townley knows or doesn't. Fitz's father wasn't the only one. After we'd spent the day with Giddes and his people out at Clark Dodge, Jack and I decided to stop at the World's Fair on our way back to the airport. And hell, Jack, what? We're there ten, fifteen minutes? And we run into Barbie Crutcher and Mary Jane Anderson. Or they run into us. I mean out of a million people at that damn fair, we have to run into a couple of friends' wives from Seattle. And they're both wondering what the hell we're doing there on a weekday. I ended up telling 'em some story, but Jeezus, I'll tell you, after two near misses, I was glad to get on the damn plane."

The laughter following Robbins' finale, being nervous, was now louder, and prolonged. Until Herron finally coughed, cleared his throat, and then, looking around, brought up the matter of the new company's name.

"I've the results here from Dick Riddel, fellows, and I'm afraid it's bad news. We had all agreed last week that "Northwest Securities," was to be the firm's new name. Pending the usual corporate search in the state, of course. Now according to this," said Herron, extracting a piece of stiff, letterhead paper from his notebook, "it seems the name 'Northwest Securities Company' has been appropriated by a firm in Renton. This was news to me, I'd certainly not heard of them before. Regardless, as our first choice is now unavailable, and a list of our names would mask the fact we're a corporation, I suppose we're forced to reopen the discussion. So, that being the case, do any of you have any suggestions?"

Around the table, Herron's question produced a moment's hesitation, then:

"If somebody's already taken 'Northwest Securities,' said Bill Ward, "why not call ourselves "'Pacific Northwest Securities'?"

"Bill, I think it'd get confused with Ehrlichman's 'Pacific Northwest Company,'" said Zeke Robbins.

"Then how about just 'The Northwest Company'?" said John Packo.

"You'll sound like Canuck furtrappers," said Max Wyman.

"All right, then. Why not something such as 'The Puget Sound Investment and Securities Company'?" said Jack Fitzsimmons.

"Too many words," said nearly everyone at the table.

"I really feel some combination of 'Northwest' is required," said Herron. "Simply using the name 'Puget Sound' would exclude Oregon and Idaho, Montana and Alaska.

"Maybe 'Northwest Investment and Securities Company,' then..." said Fritz Frink.

"We'd all run out of breath, Fritzy," said Robbins.

"Then I dunno, Steve," said Bob King, turning again to Herron.

"No," said Herron. "I see," he said. "In that case, I have a suggestion. You all know I've no great desire to have my own name on the door. None whatsoever, actually. My wife though, thought perhaps the name 'Herron Northwest' might fit our needs. At first, I was reluctant. After considering this for the last several days, however, I suppose I'm inclined to agree. It's short, distinctive, and clearly identifies us with our geographical market. That, after all, has to be our primary concern here."

Around the table, a second of silence, then the sound of exhaled breaths.

"Well," said Zeke Robbins, after waiting in vain for someone else to speak. "Yeah. That would identify us all right."

"Would there be any objections to so naming us?" asked Herron. "I'm sure we'll have little trouble with anyone in *Renton* over that." A point with which, in the concurrence of general laughter, the players found themselves having to agree.

"So, Max," Herron asked, moving on, smoothing the next transition, "We haven't heard from you yet. Why don't you bring us up to date on the auction?"

"Let's see," said Wyman. "Thanksgiving's the 26th? The auction will be held three days before the holiday. That would be Monday, the 23rd. I'm leaving for New York the Friday before. We've been in contact with the Clark Dodge people in New York, and they're expecting the seat to go up somewhere in the range of $200,000 to $225,000. I'll be there, at the exchange with Giddes. And I'll call as soon as I've purchased it. I think Steve here has worked out some kind of code for you guys. To let you know. You'll all have about two days then, before the exchange sends out its bulletin. Then everybody's going to know."

"That's my understanding," said Herron. "But as soon as Max phones, I'll be on the telephone to you. Whatever the conversation, if you hear me say: "Green Light," you'll know we're going. That's the signal for you all to tell your managers you're leaving."

"I'm assuming everyone has given their check to Bob here, of course," said Wyman, referring to the principals' notes for the company's capitalization.

"You know, I seem to have everybody's accounted for but Steve's," said Bob King.

"I've just been enormously busy, Bob," said Herron. "But I'll see to the matter immediately."

"Hey," said the irreverent Zeke Robbins. "You gotta pay if you wanta play, Steve-areno!"

A sentiment to which, laughing, the principals of the newly christened Herron Northwest Inc., nearly all agreed - as they sat around Fitzsimmons' dining room table, before breaking up, and getting in their cars, and heading for home.

• • •

The silver glimmer of a cinema screen, a broker holding a phone to his ear, drumming a yellow pencil on the desktop as he listens... This scene then halves, quarters, replicating itself until the screen contains eight scenes at once, eight different brokers on view, sitting at eight different, if equally cluttered desks, their busy offices visible behind them. And all are on the line with a certain, cigar-smoking broker, whose king-sized voice can be heard off-screen. Slowly, matter-of-factly, and with gathering strength, it then imparts the same message to each:

"We are, at this moment, Monday, November 23rd, as we've all anticipated, proceeding with a green light condition on the................"

All the Byzantine planning was about to pay off. Wyman had captured the membership, successfully bidding $215,000 for Herron Northwest's seat on the New York Stock Exchange. All the meetings with lawyers and architects and real-estate agents; all the applications to the NYSE; all the sweating and planning was about to pay off. Each man would give notice that Monday afternoon. Their offices on the seventeenth floor of the new IBM Building awaited them. In exactly 20 days, on Friday, the 10th of December, the partners would hold the finest opening day party Seattle had ever seen. Less than three weeks away.

Then suddenly it was less than two.

And then, with only two *days* remaining, on Wednesday, December 8th, Zeke Robbins got a telephone call.

"Zeke?" his caller asked. It was an officer at SeaFirst Bank, an old and trusted friend, and someone the broker'd told about his upcoming deal. "Let me ask you a question, Zeke," the banker had said. "Does Steve Herron have any money?"

Robbins paused, "What d'you mean? The man's one of the biggest producers in this town."

"Yeah, we've all heard *that,* but does he have any money?"

"Well hell, I assume he does. He's on the line just like the rest of us."

"Well, let me tell you something, friend. He's down here right now trying to borrow a hundred grand. And we're not going to give it to him."

Robbins suddenly found himself holding his breath, his humor suddenly fled. "Jeezus, what d'ya mean he doesn't have any money? We've already signed long-term leases. Hell, we're gonna open day after tomorrow!"

"I just thought you'd want to know, Zeke, " said the banker.

"Sure, sure, of course," said Robbins, who thanked his caller, and hung up the phone. ...And wondered what he was going to do next.

. . .

What It Is I Seek To Accomplish

I T WAS THE ACME, THE APEX, THE PINNACLE — THE ABSO-lute, unequivocal peak! If he could have stopped time, then why not this very hour? This very moment. For this was Stephen Herron's own... Hadn't it been his idea? Hadn't he been the one to to visualize it, to formulate it, to push and plot and guide it through? From the first day, hadn't it been his creation? From the first hour? Naturally it had been him, of course it had - who else? - this opening day party then: his undeniable confirmation.

Five hundred dollars worth of sculpted ice had been set at the center of their long, linen covered conference table. The icy carving was of an enormous bird, a Trumpeter Swan. But the blue bird, big as it was, seemed nearly dwarfed by its setting: a prodigal collection of crab legs. It appeared the partners had bought nearly half the fleet's catch, and in order to display this lot, caterers from the Olympic Hotel had had to lay these clawed ranks in teetering piles, stacked up next to the ice like cordwood. The danger was that if a leg was wrenched from the bottom of this pile, a guest could be buried on the spot.

This was a kind of bounty, a kind of opening-day high style that few in Seattle's business community had seen in 1964: three bars, carving chefs in their high-topped hats, floating trays of hors d'oeuvres, music, and guided tours - and the party ran for two days. Ninty-one-year-old Joshua Green was there, this river-boater turned pioneer-banker come to give Herron his best wishes and one of his silver dollars for luck. The tall, tailored, Ben Ehrlichman was there as well, the former "boy millionaire" a millionaire once again, though now in semi-retirement, and a cautious 68 years old. Jim Morford was there, looking prosperous and fit. And Townley Bale, Dean Witter's

141

manager, was there too, coming up to see where half his vanished staff had gone. Ed Maxwell was in attendance, along with with Si Mott. Mac Pringle came with Bill Slater. Max Wyman's Gig Harbor friend, Nick Bez, was very much in attendance, this airline president looking every inch the immigrant tycoon. The wealthy Skinners brothers were there, too. And managers and bankers and brokers and reporters, many of whom had but a single thing in common: knowing the legendary Herron, the celebrated little broker, who had stationed himself at the head of these throngs. Wreathed in a cloud of cigar smoke, his ruby-tipped stogie rising at his side like a sceptre, Herron stood before the office's huge, wooden wall carving - an enormous bas-relief of the five-state region emblazed with the name "Herron Northwest" - and there introduced all to all.

"Here, I'd like you to meet my associate, Zeke Robbins...young Zeke's a Harvard man, expert in local issues...So good of you to come...like to intro-duce you to my young associate, Fritz Frink. Fritz's third generation MIT... great grandfather founded the Washington Iron Works you know...So glad you could be here...introduce my associate, Bob King. Robert's Dartmouth, originally went with Haskins & Sells, (big eight, you understand)....Wonderful you could be here...introduce my associate, Max Wyman. Max's...."

And thus, with a bang, they went into business.

• • •

"So there were doubting Thomases in the industry four years ago," The Seattle Times financial columnist Boyd Burchard would write in the fall of 1968. "Professionals looked askance at the bold, plush-quartered start of Herron Northwest, Inc.... The fancy reception [that] kicked the venture off....An obvious play for the business of well-heeled investors. Fortunately, doubters of the firm's carry-through capacities seem to have doubted wrong."

Boyd Burchard had it precisely right. Former cynics in the community had indeed been silenced by the firm's ongoing success. But economic times were good, and Herron's original idea sound: that of a small, member-firm "boutique," 15 years before the Street would use the word. And then, as if simply "good" weren't enough, the "go-go" sixties began to get even better, the DOW finally roaring off like a B-52, heading out over the Pacific. Leaving a thunderous echo, and a backwash of money falling through the brokerage's doors up on the big, white IBM Building's 17th floor. Profitable years for the company, these were years before certain facets of the firm gradually came into focus.

In the beginning, the partners of Herron Northwest simply discounted certain matters, laughing them away as quirks, peculiarities, first causes, as it were. One such matter was Herron's original capital investment, money required to purchase his predominant share of equity. With his partners' bridges already burned, the seat on the exchange purchased, with long-term leases already signed, and two days left until the firm opened - at this last, and perhaps worst of all possible moments, Herron found himself unable to come up with his entire ante. This would have brought about a cavernous hole in the future firm's capital base, an eventuality preventing the company from opening at all. A difficult situation, it left Herron but a single recourse: petitioning Wyman to intercede with the bank. Though the two men kept their own counsel concerning the affair, nevertheless, by 1968 the story had risen to the status of lore within the firm. A tale of Herron finding himself cornered, and following his gambler's instincts, betting Wyman wouldn't allow a last second difficulty to pitch the other partners out of work - and to collapse their deal. And Herron, once again, had bet right.

In its telling, the story nearly always produced the same results, a kind of awed laughter. And, of course, after being told and retold, it passed into legend. This same awe that could cause a hush whenever the broker went to the line in a friendly dice game, players waiting on the master's first pass. For however askance any Doubting Thomases may have looked, Steve Herron's brokerage *hadn't* gone broke. It was, in fact, well on its feet. Those predicting failure had been dead wrong about the man. What was more, Herron had been *right*. He had had the foresight to call it right, the self-confidence to play it right. And that, after all, is what certain legends are about.

Still, one's heyday is one thing. Its morning after, however, can be brutal. Enthroned upon such a reputation for genius, a man's margin for error may be pushed to the vanishing point. And if one has ruled by fiat, led associates

143

around by the lip...in a scenario such as this, consequences may arise like Banquo's ghost. Force an agreement through that costs your associates money, or worse, begin to make a practice of it, and former acolytes can suddenly begin circling like wolves. In such a situation, things can turn even *worse* than sour, they can turn bad.

As in the Homa Oil deal for instance.

In 1966, John R. Lewis ran an over-the-counter securities shop in Seattle. Lewis had time-in-grade in the community, having begun his investment business in the twenties. Established, successful, Jack Lewis was regarded as something of an opinion leader by the community, celebrated for his stratagems in moving product out the door. As far as the Street was concerned, such an inside reputation was solid gold, and Jack Lewis had it. At the time, however, Lewis had something else as well. The man had Herron's ear.

Thus, when Lewis rang up one morning, calling before the opening of the market, bringing word on something called The Homa Corporation - Herron began puffing up faster than a frog in heat. Spun from a company called Diversa, as Lewis explained, this Texas oil venture was a true find. Moreover, the company was greatly undervalued, ignored by Texans too sophisticated to realize what was in their own backyard. Furthermore, Lewis added, it seemed that Homa was sitting on top of a bona fide oil strike, an oil basin of other-worldly, ungodly dimensions. The feisty Lewis was soon salting his conversation with talk of "smack overs,' and "well-head strength." Rising before the deal could be put to anyone else, Herron opened his mouth to say yes, and ended up snapping down a hefty chunk of Lewis' Homa stock.

But the old trader had forgotten to tell Herron something. It seemed there was a rumor that Homa's corporate management was then quietly peddling off its capital stock. A rumor that somehow never filtered back to Herron; at any rate, it didn't reach him until long after he had peppered his partners with talk of "smack-overs," and "oil basins," and "well-head strength." And, by then, of the fact he'd already committed ten percent of the firm's capital...

His colleagues' response was as if choreographed. NO, they told him. NO, they didn't want any Homa Corp. And NO! they didn't think it such a grand investment for the firm. But one moment, Herron protested, this deal was from Jack Lewis for chrissakes! His partners simply looked at him. Cornered, stymied, his story from the old trader being pricked at every turn, the royally resourceful Herron had another idea. He would send Fritz Frink, the young head of the firm's research department, down to Texas. There Frink could meet with Homa's management. Then they'd understand, then his associates would get the *real* picture.

Which was true. For when young Frink returned to deliver his analysis, he ended his courteous, if increasingly negative appraisal to the board with a somewhat picturesque assessment. "These guys," announced Frink, looking directly at Herron at the head of table, "...in my opinion, they're a buncha goddamn bums! This Homa company's a piece-a-shit!"

The President of Herron Northwest responded by rolling his eyes, and sending up a screen of blue smoke. It was from behind this screen that he was heard to croak, "Don't you think, Fritz, you're being a little judgmental?"

As it happened, Frink did not. Nor did any of the other board members. And things seemed to lurch off from there. Like the afternoon in 1968, when the Securities & Exchange Commission came walking through the door.

By itself, this was a small enough matter, an occurrence of a new broker falling in love with a certain Canadian mining issue, then ending up buying restricted "letter stock." There was but one problem with this: The rules said it was not supposed to happen. And, according to the SEC, there was but one reason for it happening: the firm's compliance officer hadn't been diligent enough in minding the store. And the firm's compliance officer was the President himself.

So changes were made, and they were made by the board over time. The effect was to move operational responsibilities increasingly away from Herron, and to give these duties to non-producing partners. Bob King, the firm's young CPA, was the main recipient of these responsibilities. In turn, Herron was told he could continue on in his customary role - as the company's top producer. Which sounded, so the rest of the board thought, excellent on paper... But by then, Herron had begun to feel the company he'd founded slipping quickly through his fingers.

• • •

A little over a year before Burchard's "doubting Thomas" article, on

TAKING STOCK

August 22, 1967, the board of Herron Northwest met to consider a proposal by Steve Herron. At the time, the broker owned 30.3 percent of Herron Northwest's equity, some 83 1/3 shares. Sitting among his associates, he had proposed the firm buy back 23 1/3 of his shares, then valued at $2,300 per, leaving him roughly 20 percent of the firm's equity, the same as the company's next largest share holder, Max Wyman. Herron offered to the board his reasons for his proposal: to effect a slight increase in the present partners' stock positions, and to create a pool of equity which could then be offered to prospective participants. This, the company agreed to, cheerfully passing Herron's proposal into law.

They were still enthusiastic, when, six months later, Herron proposed an increase in the value of firm equity to 1 1/2 times book, (the firm's capitalization divided by the number of its shares outstanding). After all, the little broker had pointed out, hadn't they been the ones to take the initial risk, to put their personal fortunes on the line? Heads nodded in affirmation around the table. Then why should new people coming in, that is, prospective partners (and by this time the partners' numbers had doubled) be given the same opportunity as those who'd created this opportunity in the first place? No reason any of the board could think of. Furthermore, the company's president had pointed out, his voice dipping significantly lower, when the time came for them to die, their widows could step out at 1 1/2 times book, which would indeed make all these final passages a bit easier. Needing no more persuasion, the partners unanimously voted this latest change into law.

All of this seemed to track right up to November 12, 1968 - when Herron, with a faintly familiar sound, as if in the fall of a final domino, stood up at a company board meeting. It was then, within the firm's sumptuous library, and without the word "widow" ever passing his lips, that the scarlet-coated President of Herron Northwest tendered half his *own* block of stock, suggesting that none other than *himself* be taken out at 1 1/2 times book. With Herron's exit money rising by 50 percent, the partners' holdings were then diluted accordingly. And this time, with shares having appreciated to $4,242.25, heads did *not* go up and down around the library's long, carved, conference table. This time smoke curled out of respective board members' ears. Big Jack Fitzsimmons, Herron Northwest's number-two man, nearly had to be restrained.

No one had to buy Herron out, though the board finally decided to do so, leaving the partners at Herron Northwest watching as agendas began falling into place. They finally locked into place, when Herron tendered both his resignation - and the last of his 60 shares - all of ten months later. "I hope for your understanding," the man's resignation letter to the board had concluded, "and respect for what it is I seek to accomplish."

Escaping at a 50 percent multiple, timing the exact peak of the bull market - in 1969, the master prepared himself to walk after four and a half years - with a total of some nearly $350,000. On an investment of a tiny fraction of that, one leveraged with a little last minute help at the bank.

· · ·

Firms and Rumors Of Firms
(The Mobius Strip)

"**Z**EKE," SAID STEVE HERRON THAT AUTUMN IN 1969. "I'M going to make a move," he said, pushing his empty lunch plate away from him. "I'm going to start a major new financial management firm in this town."

As Herron described his future plans, his bullfrog voice nearly dipping to a whisper, Robbins found himself less listening to the broker, than taking his former boss's inventory as it were. He observed that the man looked absolutely the same - after everything - the same red coat, the same ruddy complexion, the same bright tie... though, there *was something*. Herron's cigars. Of course, his king-sized cheroots were missing, no where to be seen. The little broker looked nearly disrobed without them. Perhaps he'd forgotten them back up on the 17th floor, up in offices, that at the present moment, considered the little broker persona non grata.

"I believe the time is absolutely right," Herron was explaining. "Dick

Hooper has agreed to come in with me. I feel he has the right skills to manage assets, the right associations, the right background. We've already secured space in the new SeaFirst Bank Building, and I think really, looking at it, Zeke, we've done so at the exact right time. I don't expect this market to go on much longer. And I feel very strongly that it's time to manage assets, Zeke, not people..."

The man's conversation suddenly struck Robbins as deja-vu, memory after memory looping back on itself, reminding Robbins of other discussions, other conversations   the two men had had nearly five years before. The same, yet...different.

"It's early yet, Zeke. Perhaps premature to be saying this, but..."

What was it? Zeke wondered. One of those paper loops his kids got at school, what did they call them? Those little loops with a half twist put in, you begin on the one side...

"But I've given it all a great deal of thought, and I believe we'll be on the ground floor, so to speak..."

Start out on one side, go around in a circle, then end up in the exact-same place...

"Though of course, Dick and I have taken marvelous new floor space, the best of everything, outfitted end to end, Zeke. You'll have to come up and see it."

That was it, the trick of it, you end up in the same damn place, running hellbent in the same direction: only... absolutely upside down.

"Sure," said Robbins. "I'd love to, Steve." The big, bluff, good-natured broker then paused - before adding his long familiar laugh, laying one hand on his wallet as he reached out for the bill.

Top: Bill Slater and his B-24 crew. Slater is standing at center, hand on hip. Bottom: Bob Whitebrook, the man who knew Gilbert & Sullivan by heart.

Edmund F. Maxwell, office manager with Blyth in Seattle.

Top right: Si Mott, Maxwell's number two. Bottom: Victor Denny, the man who would be king.

We are pleased to announce

the formation of

HERRON NORTHWEST
INCORPORATED

Investment Bankers

Member New York Stock Exchange • American Stock Exchange (Associate)
New York Correspondent — Clark, Dodge & Co.

1700 IBM Building • Seattle • MU 2-9150

MAX H. WYMAN, *Chairman* JOHN E. PACKO, *Vice-President*

STEPHEN H. HERRON, *President* HOWARD W. ROBBINS, JR., *Vice-President*

JOHN F. FITZSIMMONS, *Sr. Vice-Pres.* WILLIAM S. WARD, *Vice-President*

ROBERT L. KING, JR., *Secretary-Treasurer* ADDISON E. FENTON, *Vice-President*

PHILLIP F. FRINK, JR., *Research Associate*

Opposite page: Clockwise from top left, Bob King, "Zeke" Robbins, Fritz Frink, Jack Fitzsimmons, Steve Herron, Max Wyman, Bill Ward. This page, top: Announcement of Herron Northwest's opening.

Left: Mike Foster. Bottom: From left, Hal Sampson, Ron Adolphson, Bill Rex, Fred Paulsell.

A.O. Foster, the founder of Foster & Marshall.

Opposite page, top: F&M's top trader, Sid Sanders, working at the company trading desk. Bottom: F&M's old brokerage floor, before renovations by the executive committee. The Former SeaFirst Trust Department Building, purchased by F&M in the late seventies

Left: Jim Morford, Jr., Bill
Rex and Mike Kunath

The 62nd Annual
Seattle Bond Club
Christmas Party, 1988

Left: Jeff Greenstein, Gil
Powers and Stan Schill

Left: Unidentified guest, Ed
Easter and Tom Kuebler

Left: Robbins Harper, Dickenson Harper and Stu Sierer

Left: Sandy Sanders, Brook Hawkes and Gordy Powell

Left: Laura Lee, Lloyd Hara and Pat Pabst

Seattle Bond Club
Seated L-R: Theron H. Hawkes IV; Lee Miller; William J. Rex; Robert Macrae; Gordon Powell. Standing L-R: Dean Amundson; G. Bruce Kramer; Gary K. Macpherson; Robert McCullough; Lyle Amundson; Gilbert C. Powers; Fred Willis; Michael E. Dennehy; Roger Kelly; Gordon Lawrence; Joseph Suty; Charles W. Easter Jr.; J. Clark Reardon

Seattle Bond Club
Seated L-R: Philip F. Frink, Jr.; William Slater; Rodney G. Rich; Floyd Jones; Michael G. Foster. Standing L-R: George C. Harrison;
Robbins Harper; S. Michael Kunath; Richard A. Schober; James R. Adams; Larry Elvins

Seattle Bond Club
Seated L-R: William Sanders; James G. Morford; James P. Mendenhall; Phillip F. Frink, Jr.; J. Thomas Kuebler; James R. Adams.
Standing L-R: Stanton W. Frederick, Jr.; George Kauffman; Louis Lundquist; Bruce A. Keen; Andrew J. Harris; Stanley R. Schill; Richard L. Hinton; Robert Walker

Ragen MacKenzie's Fred Britt, head of the firm's municipal department.

Ragen MacKenzie's Brooks Ragen and John MacKenzie.

The market slumped badly in 1969, then plunged in 1970. On May 25, the Dow Jones Industrial Average sank 20.81 points, closing just above 640. It was the largest drop for any single day since the Kennedy assassination in 1963. And the nation's financial miseries then seemed to deepen.

The Boeing Company - reacting to a drop in demand for its airplanes, in addition to the curtailment of its SST program - laid off 65,000 workers from January 1970 to December 1971, reducing its labor force by nearly two-thirds. Unemployment rolls in the city rose to double the national average, 12 percent and over, the highest in the nation, and the worst in any major American city since the Depression. During these first two years of the decade, one hundred thousand Seattleites were out of work. A local billboard at the time read: "Will the last person leaving Seattle, please turn off the lights."

This was the Great Bear Market of the seventies - when stock prices would slide 42 percent between January 1973 and December 1974, falling farther than they had in the 1930s. A time of towering inflation and abysmal markets, it was precisely the time during which Seattle's Foster & Marshall rose to dominance in the Pacific Northwest. And the story of that, began on a winding, gravel road, on a sunny afternoon in August.

Chapter Seven

FOSTER & MARSHALL
And
THE CRITICAL MASS

Serendipity

DRIVING BACK ALONE, MIKE FOSTER HAD RELAXED INTO the steady, rolling sound of the Oldsmobile's big V-8 engine. The rumbling of the car's tuned exhaust had been amplified by cliffsides abutting the road, spines of rock hardly three feet from Foster's side window. If peaceful, there was also a touch of claustrophobia to driving the narrow highway, even at 2 o'clock in the afternoon, and even in this August sunshine - having to hug the rocky sides of the cliffs that closely. Foster's only other alternative was fairly clear, however. To his left was the line of sea and sky. While straight ahead, out across the empty, oncoming lane, there was nothing but blue Alaskan air and silence - though Foster could well imagine the sound of the ocean beneath him, the sound of the Gulf of Alaska pounding away down there, 500 feet below.

As it was, Foster was sure he had heard enough of the sea for awhile, having spent the last 48-hours on it. The firm's Anchorage clients had been

151

satisfied though, everyone even boating a fish. A welcome accident - and pure luck, he supposed. Even so, he'd have to send something to the skipper, he'd tell his secretary to take care of it when he got back to Seattle. In a way, that had become his role, certainly since the new year, since January, 1971. Keeping the company's profits up...and keeping everyone happy. Ever since the Upham sale in '61 actually, since Meyer and Marshall had departed. Though he had to reach back for that. And why bother? Look ahead. That's what his dad always said.

His father, however, wasn't the president of Foster & Marshall anymore. He was. Thirty-four years old and president of the largest locally owned brokerage in the Pacific Northwest. He had been ready for the promotion, for the presidency. His father had made sure of it. Besides, having been groomed for it or not, he'd worked hard to get to where he was. People could think whatever they liked. Though, what did any of them know about it? Or, really, about luck for that matter - except that they'd take all they could get, a notion causing a smile to appear on Foster's face. Now, all he wanted was to take the four o'clock flight back to Seattle, to get back in time for Sunday's tournament at the Tennis Club. What else? He could think of nothing. Just the drive, the Anchorage airport to the north, and sixty more miles of this winding gravel road. Though the good thing, he thought, glancing once more at the cliff sides and the sea, the fortunate thing, was that he had it all to himself. With this in mind, Foster settled once again into the steady, rolling sound of the big Oldsmobile - unaware of the lone coupe, still two miles up the road, now heading in his direction.

The winding, gravel road Foster was driving on then improved slightly, becoming a gravel straight-away chiseled into the rock cliff side. It was here that Mike Foster first sighted the car, a maroon, two-door Impala. That much he could make out, though he wondered if its occupants were seeing him at all. They must not, he decided, the way they were driving on both sides of the road. Kids, he thought - drunk, and doing eighty easy - a plume of rock and yellow dust fanning into the air behind them.

Foster took his foot from the Oldsmobile's accelerator, moving it to the brake pedal instead. As he did so, he found himself steering right, edging closer to the bare rock face of the cliff side, slowing the big car down to a crawl. Finally, nearly pressing the side of the car into the cliff-face, he began laying on his horn. They'd have to hear him, Foster thought, or see him and slide around...or hell, sail out over the cliff edge. Anything else, Foster decided, and the idiots would plow right into him. In which case they'd all be dead.

It was then, as if to test this last hypothesis, that the two drunk airmen finally beheld the new president of Foster & Marshall, noticed the man's black eyeglasses, saw his open mouth behind his tinted windshield, his arms waving back and forth in front of his face. Saw all this through bleared, half-open eyes - racing towards him at eighty miles an hour. Now who the hell was this idiot? they wondered. And then, as if to find out, the two airmen joined their new-found friend head on...

The collision startled sea birds from cliffs a quarter of a mile away. Almost as suddenly, its aftermath created long seconds of silence, time in which the yellow dust finally returned to the roadbed to settle - and a passenger door was slowly pried open. Stumbling out, now nearly sober, the two young airman from Elmendorf Air Force Base wandered dazed, but unhurt, out along the side of the road.

However, Mike Foster, for his part, didn't believe he'd be wandering away from anything. As far as he could tell, that just was not going to be possible. At least judging from as much of the car and himself as he could still see. He could make out the blue interior of the driver's compartment, now smashed and on its side, he could lower his head to see his chest, his left hand, and the automobile's floorboards, its turquoise rugs now six inches from his face. No, the big, white Tornado looked as if it had been hammered flat, looked, crazily enough, as if he were now wearing it, its steel wound around him like a sheet. Then Foster realized it had begun to feel like that too.

Though he remained conscious, what Foster was feeling, or failing to feel, as he slipped deeper into shock, was the sensory freight of multiple fractures in both legs, a number of cracked ribs, severely fractured arms, two fractured feet, and a pair of broken wrists. Only his neck and spine had escaped any kind of injury at all.

Miraculously. Luckily. But then... Mike Foster already knew about luck.

• • •

153

The Project

OVER THE YEARS SINCE ITS COMPLETION, THE FENCE SUR-
rounding Broadmoor Golf and Country Club had taken on the status of
landmark in the city's well-to-do Madison District. With a canopy of black-
green firs rising just behind it, this red brick fence marked off a neighborhood
of handsome, one- and two-story homes, the most recent of which were built
as late as 1970.

During the spring of 1972, in one of the older and larger of these homes,
a series of three-sided meetings had begun. The latest of these was at the
moment in the process of ending. It was not long after dark, and though this
hour of the evening was relatively early, Mike Foster was already braced on
his back in bed, as he had been for the last eight months, wrapped in plaster
and unable to move. The young president of Foster & Marshall, the heavy
arms of his full-body cast raised at right angles above either side of his head,
looked like some ill-fated skier, or someone who, having raised his arms
above his head, found himself incapable of again putting them down.

"Before we leave tonight, let's try to summarize, lay this out end to end..."

Foster tried to concentrate on the man speaking from the chair at the foot
of his bed. For the most part, the words, in fact, were Foster's own. But after
listening to his young friend for a time, Foster's concentration finally strayed.
Curiously, being immobilized in pounds of plaster had freed him to do just
this, given him time to daydream, to mull over old decisions, to eventually
arrive at new ones. Looking back over the time since his crash, he knew that
the single, most difficult of these had come slowly, forming itself as he had
lain in bed month after month. Good as the family's business had been over
the years, the firm was caught in one of its periodic slumps. It had been easy
enough to blame the market, but after a time, Foster had come to see his
difficulties weren't entirely due to the DOW. He had come to understand that

154

his firm needed something, something F&M apparently lacked. But that hadn't been quite it. It wasn't so much that the company needed some *thing*, as the fact it needed some *one*. Yes, as difficult as it had been for him to finally admit, Foster had seen this to be true. His business, if it were to come back in any real way, needed some ruder ambition, some further, and still larger initiative. He'd known that he would need two men to start with, to push the company from its present niche, past the efforts of those then involved. Perhaps then they could raise it to the level of dominance Foster had imagined each day while laying in bed, looking up at the ceiling of his den.

Deciding on this course of action, Foster had immediately known which men he wanted. He also knew, however, that in order to get them, he'd have to give up a portion of the family's equity. It was this decision that had resulted in the attendance of Foster's two visitors this evening, his two future employees. Both were close to Foster's own age, each was sitting in shirt sleeves and tie, having come straight over from his respective brokerage.

"First, and, of course, this is basic," said Fred Paulsell, "we all agree we have to grow the firm, tripling, even quadrupling, the company's present business. If that's not the case, I think in the not too distant future, Foster & Marshall may find itself out of business altogether." The manager of Smith Barney's office in Seattle, Paulsell had a reputation for being both persuasive and profit-oriented. Foster had pursued him for several months, repeatedly asking the young branch manager to head an expanded retail equity division at F&M. For the last month, the 32-year-old had quietly been meeting in Foster's den.

"I don't think what Freddy's saying comes as any great surprise," said Bill Rex. "Not in the current market, Mike. But you're working with what? Eighteen offices in all? I believe we could reasonably double that in four to five years." Rex, the head of the bond department at Merrill Lynch, was an old acquaintance of Foster's. He had come to Seattle as regional manager and vice president of the investment banking firm, John Nuveen & Co. Rex had been made a partner at Nuveen prior to the company filing bankruptcy in 1968. Suddenly finding himself without a job, the former vice president had taken his skills in the municipal bond market over to Merrill-Lynch. At 39, Rex was eight years older than Paulsell, as smooth as Paulsell was assertive, and the person Foster wanted to run F&M's crucial fixed-income division.

"Then beginning very soon," Paulsell said, "I see a real synergism developing for us, the pay-off of a combination of things. We begin blanketing the Northwest with offices, picking them up as we can, opening them when we have to. All the national houses are running for cover in this market, closing branches right and left. We move in right behind them."

"E. D. Jones has one-man shops in every small city in this part of the country," said Rex. "They're usually the only brokerage in the town, too. And I hear the company's getting ready to pack it up out here. We could pick their northwest offices up for rent."

"That'd give us half of Oregon," said Paulsell.

"With no one to compete against," said Rex. "And paying out relatively little money up-front. We fill the places up with decent inventory..."

"And more people to push it," said Paulsell. "Systems like E. D. Jones, their idea of one man offices is a piece of it. We begin a major recruitment, put in two, three, four guys in every office in every town in the region. Rivalry creates action. I guarantee production'll go up."

"If the market for municipals continues as it has," Rex said, then turning the subject slightly, "I don't see a problem with initial financing. As we've all discussed before, near term, our municipal bond department is going to be paying for building the firm outside Seattle. But, as things go forward, eventually, there's every reason to believe brokers in places like Aberdeen or Bend or Pendleton or Pocatello, Idaho are gonna be doing $100,000 in commissions a year."

"Or more," said Paulsell. "Professionally speaking, I don't believe brokers become human beings until they're doing in excess of $100,000 a year."

"And no reason that can't hold true across the board..." said Rex.

"Especially, I think, after we've brought in our department heads," Paulsell said. "That has to be stressed. I think it's key....that we bring in the best department heads money can buy."

"So," said Rex, ticking off the salient points, "underwritings and the market for municipals stay healthy, we pick up a sufficient number of offices, recruit brokers to fill them, put in liaison people and a communications system."

"And back everything up with solid research and our own department heads," said Paulsell.

"Then," said Rex, his voice, if anything, now more perfectly conversational, "...as Freddy said before, I think what's created is a real synergism. Given a corporate culture that supportive, that successful, Mike, a healthy bottom line has to be the outcome."

"Barring an act of God," said Paulsell, "I don't really see any other eventuality. In addition, along with a favorable bottom line, there's one further fact. Namely, we'll be on our way to making the Foster corporation the dominant regional securities firm in this part of the country."

"So, I suppose," said Rex, then glancing up at Foster, "all we really need is the signal from you, Mike. Get you back on your feet again."

The pair's future employer, propped on his back as he peered down at his two friends, could then only joke, his arms fixed in a wide "V" set high above his head.

• • •

In 1972, Foster & Marshall was the Pacific Northwest's largest locally owned brokerage, as it had been for a number of years. Headquartered in Seattle, the company operated branch offices in a dozen different towns across the state of Washington, as well as in the cities of Anchorage, Juneau, and Fairbanks, Alaska. Entrance to the brokerage was through the side of a local bank. This economical facade of the brokerage appeared as a begrudged luxury, or an afterthought. Inside, the firm's barn-sized sales area, with its half-height room dividers, ranks of identical metal desks, and rows of aluminum tube chairs, tended to corroborate this view. For here was the company's true dynamic: the 1970's cash machine, the Nothing-But-The-Basics model.

This no-frills brokerage had boomed over the last half-decade, the company hanging over the crest of the 1960s "go-go years." Foster's father had begun the firm in 1938, starting in a downtown room barely large enough for himself and a secretary. By 1968, Foster Sr. was running 240 people, and the privately held corporation did $50 million in municipals that year alone. In 1969, despite a badly slumping market, the firm moved from its old quarters in the city's Laird Norton Building, and leased 21,000 feet in SeaFirst Bank's former trust department, a Second Avenue, three-story granite box dating from the 1920s.

Foster & Marshall had been the city's first locally owned brokerage to own a seat on the New York Stock Exchange, a fact Al Foster was justifiably proud of. But, though a member firm, F&M was primarily a bond house, with municipals clearly driving the company's profits. Nevertheless, Foster & Marshall had attempted to diversify, adding both corporate underwriting and institutional departments to its sales, trading, research, municipals, and operation divisions. This was the corporate landscape confronting Rex and Paulsell on their first day at F&M, July 1, 1972. For there it was in all its lopsided glory: the strong municipal bond division shoring up the company's anemic equity's desk, an underwriting department uncoupled from the financial dealings on Wall Street, the company's "regional research" being pulled straight off the wire, straight off the Street in New York, the firm's branches left to ply their businesses virtually divorced from the main office's resources or expertise.

In this summer of 1972, there were seven departments within the firm. As President, Foster had removed himself from the company's bond desk, assuming a purely administrative function. Within this sovereignty - his Chairman of the Board father in semi-retirement - Mike Foster's position was akin to that of crown prince, though an acting one. Rex had been given charge of the firm's municipal department. If everything else was to work, and to work it would cost money, this was the pocket that would pay the bills. By far the strongest, most profitable of Foster & Marshall's divisions, all Rex's division need do was to continue its consistent profits. Paulsell was to administer the company's retail department, as well as oversee product development. This left five other departments headed by men predating the arrival of Rex and Paulsell. So it was, that in a few months time, five department heads vacated the premises on Marion Street, cleaning out their metal desks - while five others found their hand-picked way to F&M.

With Paulsell then busy overseeing the firm's new divisional supervisors, and Rex occupying himself with the company's municipal bond-machine, the need soon arose to add two other members to F&M's executive committee.

Ron Adolphson came over from Piper Jaffray to run the firm's branch system. In addition, Adolphson was to inaugurate a training program for new brokers at the firm. Hal Sampson was brought in as chief financial officer, assigned management of the company's operations department. Both were made partners, both offered the same $100,000 stock option as Rex and Paulsell. This was to be the final configuration of the executive committee: Foster, Rex, Paulsell, Adolphson and Sampson. Each was an experienced manager, employees dubbing the imperturbable Adolphson "The Rock," and all were entrusted with turning Seattle's "largest locally owned brokerage" into Foster's notion of a Northwest Dominion.

To effect this, a stage was initiated, a condition one executive committee member would later call "critical mass." This stage would be accomplished when F&M had assembled a sufficient amount of product, offices, brokers and business in order to spark a loud and rather spectacular boom. As envisioned, there was to be a market threshold, a juncture after which the name & Marshall would be as well known to the locality's least investor as it would be to the largest national on Wall Street.

This critical mass was to be the end point of the project's first phase. Once achieved, it would allow the company to take exponentially larger positions, to undertake major syndicate offerings, and thereafter, "to make them all," as one of F&M's executive officers put it, "a helluva lot of money." In order for this gathering-in to occur, the committee needed to build F&M's organization, and to do this immediately. To grow on such a scale, the committee felt they'd require the talents of a natural cheerleader. Fortunately for the executive committee, they already had one in place.

Fred Paulsell, standing several inches over six feet, and already prematurely gray in 1972, had graduated from Seattle's Garfield High School in 1957. Following high school, Paulsell went on to obtain an undergraduate degree and his M.B.A. from the University of Chicago. In 1962, the graduate went to work for Smith Barney & Co., beginning his career as an institutional broker in this blue-chip firm's San Francisco office. In 1968, when his mother became ill in Seattle, the broker persuaded his superiors to let him open an office in the northern city. There he managed a branch for Smith Barney for four years, building up the firm's operation in Seattle, before abruptly departing from the company in the summer of 1972. It was then that Foster, offering Paulsell $100,000 in F&M stock, beckoned from his den in Broadmoor.

Because he had been a branch manager in a large, national system, Paulsell understood how this kind of operation worked. It was obvious to him that Foster & Marshall was quite different, however. Though it had long had a seat on the New York Stock Exchange, F&M was primarily in the business of selling Northwest securities. Paulsell was of the opinion its brokers needed support in their efforts to sell these securities. He concluded that a regional research department could provide such support. Corporate cheerleading, performed as an art, is practiced in two opposite, if related, directions: employees are stroked to greater and greater effort; their customers are then induced to a fine and appreciative edge. A first rate research department, Paulsell reasoned, one specializing in Northwest firms, would help accomplish both these ends. With such analysis supporting them, F&M's brokers could be more persuasive - clients encouraged to take larger positions in the firm's Northwest securities. This gilt-edged research department was formed in 1973 around analyst John MacKenzie, a talented young fund-manager, formerly with Murphy-Favre in Spokane. MacKenzie had been both a client and long-time friend of Paulsell's, and once hired, Paulsell set about promoting his friend's expertise.

As an analyst, MacKenzie specialized in identifying underpriced stocks, allowing their purchase before they turned up in price. Saying this about an analyst is akin to saying a weather forecaster's job is to forecast weather. MacKenzie, however, had a solid record of being right, a record of performance Paulsell then proceeded to incorporate into F&M culture. Here was data a broker could use in recommending issues to his clients. And he could do so with a fair amount of confidence, seeing MacKenzie's stock list, even in a down market, gaining in value. Pleased with the new department's results, the executive committee continued to push . There was still much that needed to be done before the firm would achieve critical mass.

An emphasis on Northwest securities was not the only difference between F&M and its national competition. Foster & Marshall was a "regional" house, its head office located at the center of the brokerage's natural territory, in Seattle itself. Rather than see this as a disadvantage, a matter of being sequestered 3,000 miles away from Wall Street, the executive committee came to believe it to be their chief advantage.

They tried to realize this advantage by installing direct phone lines from their trading department, from their research and bond departments, as well as from their various department heads - to every branch office in the loop. This was an attempt to imbed the firm's central advantage in its daily function. No matter how much lip service is paid to entrepreneurship - brokers don't pursue their calling in a vacuum. When someone in a national operation has a problem, needs current analysis, has a question - that person needs an answer. This often means a product manager or a department head. In large, national operations, these division heads are to be found in New York City. In actuality, department heads are almost entirely inaccessible. For the individual broker, this inaccessibility creates a rift in his ability to do business. F&M's executive committee was determined to use this rift to their advantage. They would triple-stitch the organization together, so that familiar voices in Bend and Beaverton and Bellingham would each know what the other was doing, and all could then talk to department heads in Seattle by simply picking up a phone. They called it their white phone system, a white telephone with a public address speaker soldered beside it, and everyone everywhere in the F&M system would have one.

It seemed to make a difference. Liaison people and department heads drove or flew to the various offices in the organization as often as they were needed or could get away. But these same officers were on the system to one or another of their branches every day. With the advent of this direct telephone system, offices once distant from Seattle were now part of the loop. Suddenly there was less room for brokers to harbor the usual suspicions, for everyone heard the trading department at the same time, listened in on research or the bond department's transactions at the moment they were announced. Nor was it a passive system; reps could talk back to whomever they liked, or didn't.

If all this is a commonplace today, it wasn't in 1973, and in 1973, the system gave F&M an edge. They used this edge to cut a further niche - "largest, regional brokerage on the move" - and used this larger niche to lure rival brokers to the "the pleasures of working for a regional brokerage." Each phase was wedded to the next, reinforced the next, and then, almost before anyone realized it, F&M's expansion had begun in earnest.

TAKING STOCK

The company pushed out at a time when others were busy pulling back, in a recessionary cycle that saw more than a few nationals breaking for cover. The industry's response to this time of bear markets was company closures, cutbacks, security firms fleeing into merger, the disappearance of market-makers from the over-the-counter scene, and a reduction of the nation's brokers from 50,000 to less than 33,000. And it was during all this, through the bottom of this trough, that F&M added nearly 100 new employees. In one sense, Foster & Marshall was able to begin its enormous growth in the early seventies precisely because others were falling back, relinquishing offices and furniture and business machines, often for pennies on the dollar. There were other considerations as well. If most of these offices fell to F&M as bargains, many of them had also been one-man shops, a philosophy the Seattle firm spurned. From the beginning, the executive committee's plans had called for placing teams of three and four brokers in every town in the region. To accomplish this, obviously a great many brokers would be needed - and in a hurry. The company was able to accomplish this in two ways: by instituting a broker's training program, and by raiding other firms, luring brokers away from competing brokerages.

Polished over time, F&M's pitch to rival brokers grew to a serenade, a chorus of department heads meeting the prospective employees as soon as they walked in the door. What were the pleasures of entrepreneurship at F&M? For one, each visiting broker was informed, Foster & Marshall wasn't pulling its regional research off the teletype; instead, the company had a top-notch department under John MacKenzie, and was perhaps the only firm in the Pacific Northwest generating local analysis. To the branch broker working for a national, sitting at the end of a teletype wire, it was hard to overstate the attractiveness of this. The company also offered its brokers a telecommunications system as advanced as any in the nation. Add to this the fact that the firm's municipal bond department was nearly famous, stronger by several times over than any other in the Pacific Northwest. And in addition to a productive bond department, F&M could provide the aggressive broker an enormous inventory of syndicate offerings as well. This was because Foster & Marshall wasn't merely another spoke in a national organization. In fact, as they were sure the broker was well aware, Foster & Marshall was a major unto itself, one able to take considerable positions in important offerings,

162

national or regional. Furthermore, as an employee, the broker would be a name in the family of F&M, not just a number. To guarantee this was so, the company had department heads whose livelihoods depended on their being accessible to the working rep. And all of this, the broker must understand, created the firm's real foundation, its real secret: a competitive atmosphere so charged with accomplishment that new brokers couldn't possibly fail to double, even triple their present business.

With a concluding flourish, brokers were advised that unlike the nationals (who were leaving the area almost daily,) Foster & Marshall considered the Pacific Northwest home. The company had been part of the local investment scene since 1938 and wasn't about to disappear tomorrow. The firm certainly wasn't for sale, nor was it about to merge, with its head office reappearing in Chicago or New York or anywhere else. The company valued its Northwest identity, prized its own independence too much.

And, of course, it worked. Reps came over to F&M in waves. Offices spread across three time zones, extending from Alaska to Utah, each with a white phone in place, their shelves laden with inventory. Company revenues slowly began to break upward, and soon the firm's 18 offices numbered 23, then 29, then 32... By 1978, the company counted 37 offices in its system.

As portrayed in the pages of the local papers in the seventies, it all seemed a first-class mystery. How was it F&M was growing when times were bad? Why wasn't the firm afflicted in the same manner as every other stock brokerage? To read the local columns was to be told the regional company's growth came about because it was growing. If that didn't offer itself as a complete explanation, another was offered: in a down cycle for listed stocks, the brokerage had managed to wean itself away from the New York Stock Exchange. But there were problems with this as well. For one thing, the firm was primarily a bond house, and for another, by this time, everyone else was off listed stocks as well. Which left any derivable answers to the imagination. Perhaps it was mirrors - smoke and mirrors and offices tricked out on every mud-caked Main Street everywhere. Who really knew?

If this was the impression given to the general public, to insiders, the company's success was no secret at all. The precise name of this particular carnival mirror was "Advance Refunding." Here was the magic trick then underwriting F&M's growth in the seventies. And, in fact, it had nothing to do with the Big Board, or the AMEX, or the Pacific Exchange, or any stock exchange anywhere. Just the opposite. This was sleight-of-hand straight from the bond-side, right out of Rex's municipal department. That much was plain. It's actual purpose...that depended on your point of view.

The occasion: A small town's city council meeting. The time: 1975. The speaker: the town's municipal attorney. "Clearly, from the municipality's viewpoint, the purpose of advance refunding is to save the city money on interest expense. Like any other homeowner refinancing a mortgage, this city desires to lock-in the lowest rates possible on our debt obligations. In order to build the new gymnasium, we issued $5 million in bonds paying out 3 1/2 percent interest. Then along came this unexpected drop in interest rates. So we went back to the underwriter, and together arranged a new bond issue. The amount of this advance refunding is the same as the original bond issue, and of course it's used to pay off the old bonds, only now the interest the city will pay is 3 1/4. The difference saved automatically accrues to the town. In a nutshell, that's advance refunding. Which saves us money. Which, as you're all aware, is what we set out to do."

A fact, and one making towns happy across the land. However, that was only part of the equation, and from the underwriter's point of view, the least of it. An "advance" refunding, these secondary bonds were necessarily issued five years before the original bonds came due. Which left a half-decade until the funds were to be paid out to the old bond holders. In the meantime, what exactly was to be done with the money? The answer to that came from the IRS, and it was as breathtaking as it was blunt. The hypothetical town's hypothetical $5 million would be put into government treasuries, which then paid a very real 5 percent on the $5 million for five years. And the greatest part of that accrued interest - known as an arbitrage profit - would be delivered up to the underwriting brokerage...

In a down cycle for stocks, bond departments everywhere began to burn in a frenzy to deal advance refunds. Their returns were prodigious. A short and almost-famous case in point: During these years there was an advance refunding covering a water and sewer issue for the City of Richland, Washington. Over its five year life, the refunding fetched $40,000 in interest savings to the municipality. In turn, its Seattle underwriters took in $400,000.

This was called many things: a blessing, a bonanza, a godsend, and by then, even within the rooms of the Rainier Club: windfall profits. But for all that, it had been consecrated by the IRS, structured and sanctioned by this body from 1973 to October of 1977. And in these critical years - years of terrible markets and industry cutbacks - the executive committee of Foster & Marshall went forth into the Pacific Northwest, amassing offices like crazy.

. . .

The Genius Of The Crowd

ON THE DAY BEFORE THANKSGIVING, NOVEMBER 25, 1981, Albert Foster was sitting on the silk sofa in the living room of his Hawaiian townhouse, waiting for his doorbells to chime. Perched in the center of his big, overstuffed couch, Foster appeared even smaller than he was (though people tended to forget this about him), a round-faced, bantam of a man who looked a bit like Winston Churchill. Or, perhaps more accurately, a thick-set, white haired little man with the look of a British bulldog, the same pugnacious, undershot jaw - with something of the tough guy around the eyes and in the down-turned grin he passed off as a smile.

In 1981, Albert O. Foster was 76 years old, and if the man was rich, he was also worried. Several lifetimes ago, Al Foster had been a poor kid from the blue collar streets of Tacoma, the town where his father had spent his life as a linesman for the Bell Telephone Company. But Al Foster had had other plans. He'd made it through the university, gone to work, then gone into business for himself.

Thinking back, Foster supposed he'd been a comer as a young man, forever scrambling after the instant hit. He remembered his last employer during the Depression, old Burl Bramwell, nervous every day he'd employed him. Even he could laugh to think of it now. And a plunger, God-yes-he-was, a shooter, a player all his life. He'd finally built Foster & Marshall out of air, out of need, dreamed it into being at the end of the Depression, willed it, built

165

it on luck and balls and run it on a shoestring, a borrowed one at that. Then made the firm into an income machine without equal in the city. He'd put up a home in Windermere and joined every club worth joining in the whole damn town. Then, after Marshall got out, and Don Meyer... it had been entirely his show since 1961. Hell, it always had been. And now...now Mike and his young associates on the executive committee said they were going to make him some real money. Serious money! It was a joke. Hell, what they were going to do was sell off his company.

Albert Foster knew what it was, knew exactly what it was. It was a wrong idea. Wrong headed. And he wasn't going to let it happen, not to Foster & Marshall. Wasn't he still Chairman of the Board? And even better, he still held the stock. They couldn't get around that, he knew, watching as his backyard's windbreak of palms bent in an incoming squall. Sure, he'd have plenty to say about that. If Mike brought Rex and Paulsell along with him, fine. So much the better. They could all come over. They could hear what he had to say, too. They were all going hear what he had to say.

It was not as if he'd ever been stupid; he wasn't a stupid man. He'd never gotten in their way. Never tried to. Paulsell and Rex wanted to sell limited partnerships, fine. They wanted to sell moonrocks, fine. He knew how it was. He worried, sure. But then who wouldn't? Nearly his whole net worth was in the company. Still, he hadn't gotten in their way. He'd made up his mind and he meant it. When he'd turned it over to Mike, he turned it over and walked away. And really, to give them credit, they'd done a wonderful job. He had to admit that. Built the company beyond even his expectations. And now this. Out of the blue.

Al Foster looked at his wrist watch. On the phone the boy had said the 12:30 flight. Putting him at the house at one, one fifteen. Forty-five minutes to go.

Mike had also said $80 million. Better than three times book. The whole thing guaranteed by American Express. Well, he supposed they were good for it. And he supposed he was impressed. But it didn't change anything. It made no difference really. In the end, it'd be like his selling to Harris Upham, the same thing, all over again. He always thought Mike had known that. If they sold, they'd lose their independence. And without that, the rest didn't matter. Did the committee think Weill or Robinson were going to let them go off in a half-dozen different directions? Now that it was Jim Robinson's company, now that AMEX had bought Shearson - that's who'd call the shots. No matter how rich the deal looked, or what anyone said to the contrary. That's the way it worked.

He'd learned. Certainly '61 had been difficult enough, what with selling the old company...But God, he'd had to do it. Things had become intolerable; Marshall frustrating him at every turn, forever slowing him down. Sure, he'd made wrong calls. But hell, even so.... Partnerships were for the birds. He'd learned. Though working for Harris Upham had been worse.

He could remember the precise day, that morning in 1961 at the office on Marion. He'd come in early, strolled up to Sid Sanders on his trading desk. The man had been with him for nearly twenty years, probably the best trader in the city - faithful, dependable, hardworking, Sid. "Well," he'd told him, suddenly feeling disagreeable, and deciding just to say it, "I sold the whole company last night." Then walked off, as if it had been nothing at all. Hell, it'd almost been worth it. Just for that! The look on the man's face!

But of course it hadn't been worth it, sweating out the five-year non-compete Harris had covered him with. He had thought he could plan around it, selling off the partnership, selling Foster & Marshall's equities side to Harris Upham, then setting up a pure bond house, calling it Foster & Marshall Inc. But the way it happened, there he was in the old space on Marion, running Harris's equities, while Meyer and George Marshall were over at the new offices, free to do any damn thing they pleased.

He'd truly believed Marshall was going to retire, this eventuality being one of the reasons for structuring the new company as he had. But the man hadn't. And he himself couldn't be in two places at once. After that, it'd all quickly gone sour, and though he'd owned three-fifths of the company's capital stock, what could he really do? He'd ended up writing letters, long bitter letters to business associates, to syndicate partners, letters all over the Street. In the end he had tried to put Mike in charge, with Mike just a kid at the time. Finally he'd had to leave Upham and get back, just to put everything right. Partners. At least, after 1962, with the two resigning, he could put both behind him.

But that had been the least of it. Making money for someone else, that had been the worst. He'd even been forced to sell F&M's seat on the exchange, caching it with his son Gary back in New York. After he'd taken charge of Foster & Marshall Inc, under the terms of the Harris non-compete, they were then unable to repurchase it for five long years. The whole sorry deal had lost him revenues, and brokers - and branches. He'd lost Louie Ragan and his Portland branch, the best office in the bunch. Ragan had declined to go along with him, going over to Dominick & Dominick instead, taking his brokers with him. The rest of his offices he'd dealt away to Harris, forcing him, finally, once he'd gone back to F&M, to start all over again. No, on balance, if he'd had it to do over, he would never have sold out. Working for someone else had been like trying to fly in a damn birdcage. The sale money wasn't enough to make up for it. There were other, better ways he could have come up with that.

Glancing again at his front door, Al Foster imagined they would bring this up. Was certain of it. Bring up the fact he'd sold the company once himself. Paulsell or Rex or one of them. But wasn't that just the point? He'd been down that road, he'd learned. These young fellows just hadn't figured it out. And especially now, after they'd built this great distribution, some 56 offices, all over the Pacific Northwest. Why sell now? Now was the time to sit back and enjoy their incomes, bonuses as large as any in the business. Yes, he'd tell them. He'd tell them there should be a Foster & Marshall as long as there was a Pacific Northwest. It'd been his work, his brains, hell...his genius that'd carved it out, built it up to where these young fellows could make of it what they had. Now they wanted to sell it off. Selling off their own opportunities. It didn't make sense. It didn't. It made him mad.

Foster glared at his front door, then glanced again at his watch. One sixteen. Any minute now. He turned his eyes to the clattering palms bending and re-bending in the stiffening breeze, thought about them for a moment, then slowly re-crossed his legs, forcing himself to lean into the sofa's silk cushions. Of course, he knew what they would say. What Mike would say. That the deal made business sense, that's what he'd said on the phone. Better than three times book, and a quarter of a million a year for the rest of his life, for doing nothing, for having his son peddle his company. At $80 million, did the damn thing make sense after all? Selling the company he'd poured his life into? Albert O. Foster attempted to weigh this, and as he did so, the chimes at his front door announced his visitors had arrived.

Good, he thought, they're here. He'd give 'em the straight dope. And they'd sit there and listen to it. He had plenty to say - plenty - he knew that alright. And getting up, 76-year-old Al Foster put his foot down, and walked slowly to the door.

. . .

The Room at the Top of the World

TWO WEEKS LATER, THE DEAL - THE WHOLE FAT, GLORIOUS deal had blown sky-high in San Francisco. That it finally, if begrudgingly, had been blessed by A. O. Foster himself mattered not at all. In private rooms rented at the San Francisco Canlis, deep in the basement of the Fairmont Hotel, for one interminable evening, any previous understanding between the two parties appeared to have been turned on its head. On both sides of the table, those desiring the merger's successful completion found themselves doing mental loop-de-loops, their stomachs sinking around their knee caps. What, they were asking themselves, what in hell were they supposed to do now?

What they were required to do was watch - and listen. Which, as it turned out, was all any of them could do, biting their tongues in the time it all took to happen. Bill Rex was there, so was Fred Paulsell, Ron Adolphson, and Hal Sampson. Shearson's Peter Cohen was in attendance, as were the New York company's Mike Pantich and Wick Simmons. This was the audience for the evening's entertainment, a two-man play, its dual leads being Sandy Weill, Chief Executive Officer of the newly merged Shearson/American Express - and Mike Foster, Chief Executive Officer of Foster & Marshall Inc.

The evening had started smoothly enough, even sociably, the two CEOs amicable through rounds of drinks and dinner and bantering small talk. Neither, however, had flown his people into the city for a cocktail party, polite or otherwise. The time had been set aside for their respective statements to be made, for counter-statements to be presented. And when this took place, as they had all been waiting for it to take place, the deal came apart almost instantly.

To begin the discussions, Foster had introduced F&M as a company well worth the $80 million. This he announced as a matter of accomplished fact: casually, conversationally, as everyone was busy taking their first bite of dessert. Weill, suppressing a minor double take, then declared Foster's company worth $20 million less, saying this before anyone could take a second mouthful. $80 million? That was better than three times Foster & Marshall's book value. Quite a bit better. As the first company Shearson had looked at since their own sale, F&M was in an enviable position. Shearson would offer them $60 million, three times their book. Weill wasn't making any secret of the fact they wanted to move on the deal, hence the generosity of their offer. But it wasn't an offer that would last forever. Let no one make any mistakes, Weill informed them, his people had done their homework, his chief numbers man, his charge d'affaires, Peter Cohen, had done his homework. Even imagining he *gave* them the $80 million, gave them better than three times their book, what could he then tell his people back at Shearson? Hadn't he sold his own company for just three times book? It was an historic high. And wasn't Shearson the fastest-growing-best-run company in the business? As he spoke, the mercurial Weill, Wall Street's fastest-man-alive at merging brokerages, the man responsible for the giant Shearson's incredible, mushrooming growth, seemed an irresistible force. The stolid Foster however, this provincial from the Western Forests, proved nearly as movable as a stump.

They couldn't help what Weill had sold his own company for, Foster replied, putting down his fork, then, slowly, absent-mindedly picking up his dessert knife. Foster's people knew how much *his* company was worth. That figure was $80 million. And wasn't Foster & Marshall the fastest-growing-best-run company in the Pacific Northwest? Hadn't Foster built offices in 56 communities, offering distribution on a scale unmatched in the region. Wasn't that why Shearson was talking to them now? And furthermore, hadn't they attracted the West's top producers? These weren't even questions, Foster said. And if Shearson had truly done its homework, these facts would already be known.

When the shouting began, it had become tedious, a losing, and then incurably lost cause. At least that's the way the evening seemed to F&M's Fred Paulsell, who had been there in San Francisco and who was now, a week later - Christmas week in December - sitting high above the city of New York, in Shearson's headquarters on the 106th floor of Manhattan's World Trade Center. Sitting with Foster and Hal Sampson, in the book-lined offices of Sandy Weill.

Reuniting Foster and Weill after the scene in San Francisco had taken everyone's best efforts. Shearson's Wick Simmons had done most of the work on returning Weill to the table. Foster, though counseled by Paulsell, had finally come to the decision himself. The upshot, once Foster and Weill had been reunited, was that the head of Shearson upped his bid by more than $15 million. All agreed, this was an enormous distance to have come. Foster had eventually edged down three. And now - now Foster and Weill, along with James Robinson, Chairman of the Board of American Express, Hal Sampson, and Paulsell, were seated in Weill's office looking at each other across what yet remained: a difference of $1.3 million. They had been doing so all morning long.

They were close enough that Paulsell could nearly taste it. Jesus, he thought, you could feel it - the presence of money almost palpable in the place, the man's office nearly the size of houses in Seattle's Highlands. And all of it floating 106 stories above the city and the waters of the Hudson River below. The room even had a fireplace, Weill's famous marble-mantled hearthside, which, on this snowy December morning, was presently working its way through a half-dozen birch logs.

If it was going to get done, this was the time and place. Robinson and Weill were sitting side by side. Foster had been placed opposite them, arranged between Sampson and Paulsell. At the present moment, Weill was belaboring the fact that he'd already come a great distance, and elaborating on the all too obvious reasons he could go no further. It was a speech they'd all heard before.

"That just doesn't work, Mike. You're asking me to give you a higher multiple than I got for my own firm. That's something that's just impossible. How could I go back and look my own people in the eye? I mean, I understand what you're saying. I started a firm from scratch and built it up too, and just like you, I'm proud of the job I did. But there's more to it than that. What you should really be looking at is what happened to us after our sale. We grew. We're stronger. It'll happen to you guys. It'll be a wonderful experience for you."

"No one doubts that for a minute," Foster replied. "But you have to remember - you came after us, Sandy. We didn't approach you. We weren't for sale. And if we are going to sell, it has to be for a price we think is right, that covers us for all the work we've done. If what you're saying is you can't see your way clear to do that, that it just doesn't work, well, maybe it just doesn't work..."

The two men's dialogue kept doubling back on itself, looping along like a relay team, the same conversational baton being handed off time after time. Weill would stress how far he'd come, urging Foster to reassess. Foster would respond by saying how appreciative he was, adding if Weill would just come the last, remaining mile, they could all get the thing done.

They were tired - all of them - this weary theme having inched along for hours now. In the course of it, there had been emotion, recriminations, adjustments. Foster was being asked to sell off the company his father had created, and, though he had decided to do so, he was obdurate about sticking to his asking price. When Sampson, Paulsell, and Foster repaired to Weill's conference room to talk among themselves, or to call an anxious Rex, who was then awaiting developments in Hawaii, Foster would appear conflicted. Even if he got his price, was it finally a matter of letting down his father as well? Weill, for his part, was quick to intuit the emotional landscape, explaining he had gone through a similar wrenching in the sale of his own company. Nevertheless, he explained, this should be seen as the once-in-a-lifetime opportunity it was, for Foster's shareholders, his executive committee, his employees, and finally, for his family and himself. Besides, the hard fact remained, nearly $76 million could provide anyone a great deal of solace.

But it was no longer simply a matter of the remaining $1.3 million. It was that and much more, and in Mike Foster's mind these several threads converged, weaving themselves into a stiffening on this final dollar amount. If the deal was to be done, so be it. But he was going to get his price. Let Paulsell counsel him to come down all he liked, he'd pay no attention. Dammit, the company was worth every penny he was asking. No one else was going to give Weill the presence in the Northwest Shearson needed.

And really, what was $77 million, anyway? American Express had paid $900 million for Shearson not six months before. Now they were ready to move again. F&M was to be the new conglomerate's first acquisition. Once this was accomplished, Shearson/American Express expected others to follow. Weill and Robinson had admitted as much, repeatedly. Moreover, they'd seemed willing to pay to get this done. Besides, Foster thought, $77 million would be little more than pocket change to AMEX. A handsome figure to F&M's shareholders, however, and the Foster family would walk away with something like $35 million in AMEX stock. If that wasn't $900 million, well, Foster thought, it was enough.

Nine hundred employees, 56 offices, the fourth largest regional in the nation - and, inarguably, the best. Obviously, these were the reasons Weill wanted them. What Weill didn't know, couldn't know for sure anyway, were the reasons the executive committee had for selling. The committee had gone over and over this: citing the dollar amounts they'd need to upgrade their back office. And to stay competitive, they'd be required to upgrade their computer systems as well. Finally, all of them had been aware of Merrill's new C.M.A. card. Bringing a cash management service like that to market would cost F&M millions. And to have stayed current, Foster knew he would have had to have done it too. No, if Weill had his own reasons for buying, he had his own reasons for selling. He hadn't been looking, it'd just happened; perhaps a good thing it had. And now, Foster thought, now he just had to wait a little longer.

"Now I think it's time, Mike. Why don't you and I step out of the room for a second." Weill stood up from his chair, gesturing towards the conference room at the far end of his office. Foster rose and followed him, leaving Robinson, Sampson, and Paulsell talking amongst themselves. In a surprisingly few moments, when the two men returned, much of the gulf that had been separating them had disappeared. Weill had kicked in one million dollars.

"Well, we're making progress. We're now down to $300,000," the Shearson executive informed them. Smiles went quickly round the room. "So c'mon, Mike. Why don't we get this thing done."

"I thought we were," said Foster, then smiling himself.

"Well, dammit Mike, I've come a hell of a long way up from sixty million. Let's just round off the last three-hundred-thousand bucks. Make it an even seventy-six million."

"Hell no! God dammit, Sandy, that's the number."

"Okay, Mike. Great. What do you say I flip you for it then?"

"Flip for it? For three-hundred thousand?"

"Yeah. The last three-hundred-thousand dollars."

Foster looked at Weill, who was looking back at him. He then glanced over at Sampson and Paulsell.

"I'll call," said Foster at last, deciding in that moment he was certainly as much a gambler as his old man - and almost before he'd said this, Weill had put the coin in the air.

"Tails," Foster nearly shouted, finding himself looking over at the New Yorker's outstretched fist, then down at his open palm, staring at the glinting profile of George Washington, pigtail and all. In the silence of that second it seemed all he could hear was the room's fireplace crackling behind him.

"You lose," laughed Weill, dropping the quarter back into his pocket, then holding out his hand. And Foster, the soon-to-be-former CEO of Foster & Marshall, and a man suddenly millions of dollars richer, had to admit that he had.

"Congratulations," said Weill. "Congratulations," said Robinson. Then everyone else said it, too.

"There'll be a Foster & Marshall as long as there's a Pacific Northwest."

As late as November 23, 1981, while Mike Foster was busily packing his bags for Hawaii, setting out to convince A. O. of the wisdom of selling to Shearson, The Seattle Business Journal was featuring F&M on its front page, with Foster's photograph accompanying an in-depth feature on the reign of Seattle's "Leading Regional Brokerage..." The subtext was: "Up the local, full-service brokerage. Long live Foster & Marshall!"

From Foster's point of view, however, the timing of the city's business publication couldn't have been worse. Sandy Weill was preparing to meet him in San Francisco, he was about to confront his father in Hawaii, and The Business Journal had picked this time to tack him to its front page beneath a 30-point headline, the story getting three pages - with a side-bar on the executive committee. All the old refrains were brought out: Leading Local Brokerage; A. O.; 1938; The Expansion Years; The Company's Limited Partnerships; The Pacific Northwest, The Future...

"It's not our intention to go the route of our industry," Foster had told The Journal's reporter that Thanksgiving week, "whether through merger or sellout. It's not our intent to become part of a major brokerage house or insurance company." Absolutely not. And at that precise moment (his tickets in hand, his bags packed, and the taxi called), what else was he going to say? It was a nifty side-step, American Express being neither brokerage nor insurance company. The Journal's next paragraph, however, cut into the heart of the matter. "Everyone," Foster was finally quoted as saying, the quotation buried late in the article's third page: "everyone has his price - including us."

On January 1, 1982, despite the efforts of the executive committee to keep it hushed a bit longer, the story of Foster's price was all over the town's front pages. The deal had come in at $76 million, with staggering pay-outs to the executive committee, a quarter of a million a year to A. O. every year for the rest of his life, and a band of happy shareholders preparing to serenade American Express.

Not all, however, were so fortunate. With their jobs duplicated by Shearson in New York, F&M's back-office employees were turned out enmasse, while brokers that had entered the fold at F&M to work at a local brokerage, found themselves working for a national wire house, tethered out at the end of Shearson's national wire.

*Embittered at the prospect, leading managers and brokers at Foster &
Marshall began leaving soon after the news broke. Lured away with up-front
bonuses in the six figures, top producers took their talents to the competition,
settling in again as the decade got under way, gaining a solid grip on things
- at the very moment the Big Bull Market decided to come boiling up out of
the chute.*

*Of course, after that, didn't matter where a broker was - the whole Street
was making money. This state of affairs continued on, advancing like an
economist's dream come true. That is, until the Street awoke with a start on
the morning of October 19, 1987, lying flat on its back, trying to determine
what still moved, and what was broken.*

And then, then it was one year later...

BOOK THREE

Chapter Eight

TAKING STOCK

1

S EATTLE, 6:47 A.M., FRIDAY, DECEMBER 2, 1988. THOUGH
the city will once again rely on this holiday, banking on the season's
coming spree, Seattle's brokers are enduring days somewhat less than festive.
The Christmas holidays see the investment community holding vigil over its
lifeless phone banks, even as months have been put away in watching the
carpeting grow. Heavily depressed since the crash - the industry is presently
35 percent below its peak of 14 months ago. Still, after stumbling off the
precipice of October 19, 1987, the flattened DOW has again picked up, the
index recouping several hundred points. Technicians now describe the
market as buoyant, even bullish.

Yet, definitions aside, recollections of the crash still ride at the front of
everyone's consciousness. Attempting to remedy this, the nation's brokerages begin a heavy use of TV spots to regain clients frightened away by the
break. A statistical fact (endlessly repeated): many investors purchase equities when the market is oversold, when it's high - then lose by selling when
the market's low. The inference is obvious, the conclusion clear: the DOW
is now low, stocks reasonably priced, come in and buy.

But it doesn't seem to work, it doesn't appear to signify. It doesn't,
because something else seems to be at work - for all its illogic... a kind of
waiting.

TAKING STOCK

• • •

"It'll never happen again in our lifetimes!" explains Jim Adams, the bond broker sitting this early Friday morning behind the green screen of his new Quotron. Adams' partner, Gary Farber, as ironic as Adams appears upbeat, smiles, letting this edict on the next crash sail quietly by. Farber is sitting at his desk not fifteen feet away, in the same room as Adams, with several packing boxes stacked on the floor in front of him, the broker's lithographed ducks now leaning against the wall.

Adams and Farber have moved. The two partners jumped to the Seattle office of Oppenheimer & Co., exiting what had become, shortly after the crash, the gigantic Shearson/Lehman/Hutton/(Foster & Marshall) American Express. At the time of their departure, Oppenheimer was housed in the First Interstate Building along with Shearson, though 20 floors below. Now, in permanent quarters on the Columbia Tower Building's 39th floor, the two brokers sit in a glass oblong of an office with a high-rent view of the city and Sound, waiting for their phones to ring.

Negotiations with their new firm had lasted through the summer, arrangements kept secret from colleagues at Shearson. Farber had been first to be contacted; a headhunter had called him in April. The stock broker, as was his custom with these calls, had paid little attention. Placement agencies can be expected to call top brokers with some regularity, and Farber had evolved a standard reply to these queries: He wasn't interested in leaving Seattle, and he was happy at Shearson. However, if the caller knew of someone opening an institutional shop in Seattle, he'd be willing to listen. This was the broker's line, his set routine, and having delivered it, he put the call out of his mind. Then, two weeks later, Farber got a call from John Rudolf, the new manager at Oppenheimer. Rudolf received the same message. "Look," Farber told him, "I've gotten calls from Oppenheimer since they opened here in 1983. They're a great firm, but this is what I want to do. This is Gary Farber. Gary Farber wants to do an institutional business in equities. Period." Rudolf replied that he and Farber should talk.

John Rudolf had come out of Oppenheimer's corporate headquarters in New York City charged with a very specific mission: to make its Seattle office pay. Shortly after his arrival, Rudolf had fired nearly half the shop's employees in a dramatic effort to bring this about. As a result, in the early summer of 1988, there were two openings in an office committed to an institutional sales desk for the city.

As chances go, this one was staring Farber in the eye. But for Adams, who met with Rudolf soon after, the equation was somewhat different. The bond markets that spring had been bad and seemed determined to remain so. Talk on the Street was of bond department lay-offs, of protection necessarily offered by only the largest of houses - the giant Merrill Lynchs and Shearsons of the world. Shearson had nine office in the Puget Sound area alone. Oppenheimer & Co. had six offices in the entire nation.

But six offices or not, Oppenheimer had an aggressive reputation in equities, gained since its founding in 1950. Even this had foundered in the Northwest in recent years, however, until a shakeup in the company's highest management. But Oppenheimer had no reputation in Seattle on the bond-side at all. Ignoring any ideas of "protection," Adams felt if he were to make this opportunity work, he would have to establish the reputation himself.

Still, Adams had made his way before. Twenty years earlier, he had worked his way through Seattle University, attending night school, spending his days as a meat-cutter. Newly married, the father of two daughters, it took him nine years to graduate from the university's business school. In 1968, six months later, he was in tie and business suit working in the trust department of People's Bank. He stayed with the bank six years before going to Marshall & Myer as an underwriter and securities trader in 1975. Adams then moved to Shearson in 1980, quickly becoming manager of their regional bond department. He met Farber there in 1982, first encountering his future partner at the very moment, that he, Adams, was getting himself sacked.

The broker's troubles started with Shearson's sudden acquisition of Foster & Marshall, and with a letter he had written to Sandy Weill. In the letter, Adams had protested the way in which many of his people in Shearson's bond department had been fired. Having stood up for his staff, Adams was soon fired himself. Impressed, Farber had introduced himself, and became instrumental in getting Adams rehired at Shearson three months later. The partnership of the two men formed not long after.

TAKING STOCK

Through the spring the men had weighed their situation at Shearson, balancing it beside offers Rudolf was making them at Oppenheimer. What was firm? What was negotiable? Farber knew the check list he'd offered Oppenheimer's manager was fact, for the most part at least. He'd been born in Seattle, grown up in the city's Montlake district, graduated from the University of Washington in the mid-seventies. His father was a broker in Seattle as well, and Farber had spent his entire career in the city. He wasn't anxious to leave, to move his family down to San Francisco, even for an institutional job. That, as he saw it, was non-negotiable.

Farber had been somewhat less factual in describing his relations with Shearson, however. Both he and Adams had become increasingly frustrated with the brokerage. Certainly by Rudolf's call in April of 1988, the partners had begun looking for some place to go. The unhappiness of the two men derived from curbs Shearson had placed on their business. Shearson/Lehman/Hutton's Seattle office is a retail shop, albeit a very large one. The company conducts it's institutional business for the Northwest out of San Francisco. Adams and Farber, desiring to move up from their retail business, had, quite simply, attempted to get around this. They did so by pushing into trade with second and third-tier institutions, Seattle's smaller money management firms, who, because of their smaller size, were as yet untended by Shearson's institutional brokers.

Adams' and Farber's business with these management firms remained invisible to Shearson's institutional desk through the mid-eighties, its brokers busy with their own large accounts. But as the decade progressed and the largest private companies, pensions funds, and government entities began renegotiating fees they'd spend to invest their money, competition among institutional brokers became intense. Rather than pay "X" to have their volume trades done, the institutions, sensing the competition among the brokerages, began edging down to "Y." If an institutional broker did the same amount of business with these same institutions, the broker's income quickly dropped by the difference.

It was also during this period - the longest running bull market in American history - that Adams' and Farber's once small management firms began to grow. By so doing, they immediately caught the attention of Shearson's institutional brokers to the south. Squeezed on their largest accounts, these San Francisco brokers began to give the growing management shops their full attention, going after companies the two Seattle partners had serviced for years.

For Adams and Farber, however, the competition wasn't entirely confined to California. In April of 1988, a senior executive in Shearson's Seattle office opened up a trading account with one of the partners' largest institutional clients. He then did business with the client, and when questioned by Farber, denied having done it. Clients, carefully developed and jealously maintained, make up a broker's domain. Farber, feeling his had been violated, went to Shearson management. He was informed the infringement was simply "one of those things." Perhaps it was, as Farber soon told his partner, but it was also, "the straw that broke the camel's back."

The turning point for Adams came that June, during a fixed-income seminar in New York. In attendance were 144 institutional brokers from all the major desks in Shearson's institutional system. On the seminar's opening night, the seminar's organizer, a senior executive in Shearson, told Adams he was going to throw all 144 brokers into a room, and after three days, whoever walked out alive would get the company's institutional accounts. He then laughed. For Adams, however, the man's laughter didn't entirely shroud the message he had just conveyed. Several things then became clear for the broker. Shearson/Lehman/Hutton was going to eliminate all joint, overlapping sales. These, of course, were the very kinds of gray-area retail/institutional sales he and Farber were generating out of their retail office in Seattle, sales they were trying, with increasing difficulty, to protect from San Francisco.

To compound matters, over the 12 months since purchasing E. F. Hutton for $1 billion, Shearson's brokerage business had fallen off by nearly half. At the same time, the company found itself with twice as many brokers. Plainly, even for top producers, there was no longer a place for brokers unwilling to relocate, or for hybrids like retail/institutional brokers. Knowing this, Adams began wondering if management already knew he was talking to Oppenheimer. Perhaps this was the reason he'd been sent back to New York. Well, it worked either way: he'd gotten the word whether he left or whether he stayed. Finally, though, it didn't matter anymore. Farber had already made up his mind. Then, after New York, Adams had too.

• • •

"C'mon, if they wanted to keep me, Gary," Adams emphasizes, picking up at the ring of an incoming call, "it was just an inopportune thing to say."

"Institutional sales, Jim Adams..." If the broker is expecting a client, this is a disappointment. The caller is a parish priest asking for help in a fund raising drive. Adams talks to the priest for several spirited minutes, agreeing to help, offering suggestions. Farber then makes a number of calls. No calls come in.

Adams and Farber have taken all of their second tier institutional business from Shearson with them. But the payout to institutional brokers, because they necessarily write larger tickets, is less per-share than their brethren obtain in retail. In Adams' and Farber's case, their former payouts have been halved. They must now double the institutional business they turned at Shearson to stay even. Adams envisions "doubling, tripling, quadrupling our business in six to eighteen months." Farber believes they are "on track," for this. Both believe they have been given a unique opening, and enough time to take advantage of it. ("Face it, Gary, you don't go a week, or a day, or an hour and the lack of business begins to squeeze you," Adams confides in Farber later.) Top-line brokers, wooed away from the ailing Shearson, both partners now see Oppenheimer as "a tremendous opportunity." ("You know, that tenseness, it either produces sales, or it generates activity. Or hell...it doesn't!")

Then, at 8:06, both men's telephones ring.

• • •

TAKING STOCK

2

THIRTY-NINE FLOORS BELOW, AND DUE NORTH OF Oppenheimer's private brokerage suites in the Columbia Tower Building, three customers have gathered inside Charles Schwab & Company's public room. The discount brokerage's patrons sit side by side in the first of the tiny room's rows of padded seats, talking while staring up at the flickering marquee of the broad-tape, its lights running quotes from the New York Stock Exchange.

Discount brokerages such as Schwab's are the product of an historical occurrence in the community, one known throughout the industry as "Mayday." On May 1, 1975, the Securities and Exchange Commission abolished broker's fixed commissions, no longer requiring consumers to pay the same pre-set fees wherever they went. Suddenly, all was negotiable. As a result, the public quickly went shopping for bargains, and discount brokerages appeared on the scene. These shops offered customers basic buy-and-sell facilities, without luxuries such as investment advice, which remained the province of full-service brokers. The client could pay as little as a quarter of the commission the full-service brokerages would charge. In a perfected capitalism, with every citizen a shareholder, facilities such as Schwab's may take on the likeness of a public necessity. Indeed, there is an air of the municipal waiting room here, the public way station.

Installed in Schwab's front row this cool Friday morning is a man in his early 40s, wearing a new trench coat, Levis jeans, and a pair of alligator-skin boots. The man's right hand bears a ring with twelve diamonds, each stone half the size of a salmon's egg. The ring's gold setting has been cast in the shape of the Lone Star State, while its owner's accent is of a similar configuration, and about a thousand miles from home.

Seated next to the Texan is an older man, tall and thin and cleanly shaven, except for a shaft of beard spiking from the end of his chin. The beard is white, giving the man the dour appearance of the cartoonist's Uncle Sam. The third

185

is the oldest of the three, his bald head almost perfectly round. The old man's name is Pete. He's wearing an aged car coat, and he's smiling.

"Paul, why don'tcha do somethin'?" he asks, prodding his neighbor. "Make a trade, fer crissakes. Show us how its done."

The "Paul" thus addressed is the Uncle Sam sitting on Pete's left. Paul, though obviously an acquaintance, chooses to ignore the older man, preferring a sober commiseration with the Texan.

"In all that mess," the Texan is saying, staring again at the electronic tape, "there's gotta be a true course somewhere."

Paul nods his head at this. "I think I'm going to get out. Move into a money market account."

"I don't think it's gonna keep going, doin' nothin' like this."

"Most of the services are predicting it's going to go lower."

"Maybe then it's time to buy," the Texan replies. "It never does what they say it's gonna."

"Yes, that's so," answers Paul, stroking his beard, though he doesn't appear at all convinced.

Their associate, meanwhile, has gone to Schwab's front desk to place an order. This seems to have earned his neighbors' attention, and when Pete returns and seats himself, the Texan leans over to ask how its going.

"You're never up, you're never in," the old man tells him.

"Doing some selling, Pete?" his bearded-friend, Paul, then asks.

"Buyin'," the old man tells him. "I'm doin' some buyin', Pauly."

Paul nods, waggling his beard, then resumes looking up at the flickering tape running across Schwab's back wall. "It's just kind of tumbling along," he remarks to the Texan, as if he could untumble things for him. However, the Texan has fallen silent, lost in the depths of the tape above. Finally Paul adds, "I think I'll open a money market account." This seems to bring him some small satisfaction, though once again he glances at the old man, and once again begins to stroke the long white tuft on his whiskered chin.

• • •

3

A BASEBALL BAT LIES ON TOP OF PAINEWEBBER'S institutional sales desk. A toy bat, it lies next to a "Dwight Gooden Automatic Pitching machine." A maraschino-red, model Ferarri is parked next to this catapult, its remote control mechanism lying unused beside it. Next to the miniature racer looms the huge, black box of the office Telerate. Neither of the two men in the institutional sales office is looking at the machine's telecast now, its screen covered with columns coming straight from the Federal Reserve. Nor are they attending to the Ping-Pong table set up in the alcove nearby, or paying attention to the dartboard with the names of blue-chip securities printed around its border, or to the lucky putter hanging on the wall, or the miniature shuffleboard, or the miniature basketball hoop with its orange sponge balls, or the Abercrombie & Fitch blowgun darts with their leather carrying case displayed upon the room's back wall. Nor are they lingering over any of the framed photos spread about the office - one a dramatic, night-portrait of lightning striking the Seattle skyline - the rest color photographs of sweat-flecked thoroughbreds standing with their owner in the winner's circle.

They are not, for PaineWebber's, Robbins Harper, and his colleague, Jeff Wilson, are too busy waiting for something to turn up. At the present moment, they don't much care what.

"C'mon, do somethin'!" Wilson blurts, sitting at his side of the sales desk, attired in a monogrammed shirt and red necktie. "Raise the discount rate...Do *something!* We need the action!"

"I didn't hear anyone say it was going to be today," Harper replies. "Today'd be great, though."

"I think it would be, too," Wilson agrees.

"They've got the dollar back," Harper says.

"They intervene?"

"I don't know whether they intervened," Harper explains. "I didn't hear it. Seeing as how the low I saw was..."

A sharp voice suddenly drowns the two men out. The office "shoutdown," the head office analysis, rides the ether in from New York. "Looking at the Dow, we still see multiple testing intra-day on support levels underneath this market," the brokers are informed. "Levels starting around 2130, down in that 2110 area. It's held pretty well, bouncing up off there. But we do have a little bit of a down trend now within that trading range..."

"Hey," Harper counters as the voice dies away, "we haven't heard the worst yet. We've got one more hit coming in the market, then things will turn deathly silent."

"Yeah," says Wilson, "with the priority Paine puts on the retail end..."

"It's all over," Harper agrees, leaning forward in his chair, the soles of his tassled loafers now flat on the office's floor. "One big hit. And everybody spooks."

"Hey, guys, listen up!" It is the men's shoutdown again, a trader this time, spreading the word through the system. "I can bring out a couple million Duke power 7 7/8's of '96. Here's what I can do. I can produce 50 off the 10-year, two million Duke 7 7/8's. They're coming out of the Street."

"Great," says Harper as the trader signs off. "Coming out of the Street. Far be it from us to ever own anything."

Harper looks heavenward, and as he does there comes the shock of a telephone ringing. It's Jeff Wilson's.

"PaaaaaiiiiinnnneWEBBER!," Wilson jives, smiling as he fields the call. "You bet, J.R. Haha. Wow that's perfect! That's great. When'd they do that? Jesus. That's perfect. That's great. Oh, he is? Mmmmm. I hate that."

If no business is being done, Wilson is having a tete-a-tete with his horse trainer, Junior Coffey. Coffey is well known in the city, the man having been a record-setting fullback at the University of Washington in the sixties. Drafted by Vince Lombardi and the Green Bay Packers, Coffey culminated his stint in Wisconsin by winning a Super Bowl ring. Soon after that, the player returned to Seattle to begin a second career: as a trainer of thoroughbreds.

"Right. He's listed as a trainer," Wilson agrees. "So, he's here, J.R.... No, no. If the public thinks it's decent, and it goes off at less than five to one, we have a good chance of things getting tight. That's right, that's right."

TAKING STOCK

"Hello, Joey? It's Jean, Joey. You got a term 'till Feb. 10?" The "Jean," now talking on the phone is Jean Cunningham, Harper and Wilson's office assistant. The young woman's duties lie in streamlining the men's business, in pushing along the less glamorous of day-to-day details. "Joey, I told them that's what it was," the fashionable Cunningham tells her party, sitting at the end of the sales desk in an oversized jacket and a short black skirt. "And they wanta do it. I don't know. Yeah, I can find out for you. I know, but do I ever hear from you with collateral? Noooooo... Well, all I need is a little happiness from your side of the fence. Okay Joey? Sure, thanks Joe."

Harper is on the phone giving instructions to a friend from the Frank Russell Company, a multi-billion dollar Tacoma consulting firm that had just built itself a corporate showcase in that city.

"Just forget the P.O. box, okay? So...909 A Street?" Harper's voice suddenly fills with wonder. "A Street? What? You go A, B, C, down there? How many streets are there in Tacoma? Are there seven? Hahahaha, yeah? But do you have a floor? Well I know, but does the building go up more than one floor? Ooooohh, you've got a view..."

After months into the downturn, the bond broker has begun to couch his frustration in flashes of sarcasm. Yet, Harper is also astute: when doing business the broker is invariably gracious, unfailingly soft-spoken. The gentleman broker. Harper even looks the part: tall and slender, unerringly groomed, his hair prematurely gray. But then, Harper is the product of three generations of brokers and investment bankers. The Harper family counts itself among pioneer Seattle's earliest Society, the city's aspiring aristocracy. Not entirely unmindful of this, Harper, as a young man just earning his MBA, had flown out to New York City to train at Goodbody & Co, which at that time, in 1968, was the fourth largest brokerage in the country.

As it was, several months after Harper had begun his training, the fourth largest brokerage in the country went broke in the back-office panics of 1970. However, a deal was soon fashioned to have Goodbody's debts assumed by the NYSE. Once this was done, the brokerage was absorbed into Merrill Lynch, the largest retail securities firm in the world. With the merger, Goodbody's brokers had split up, some staying with Merrill, others moving to PaineWebber. Harper decided to move. PaineWebber sent him to Seattle as a retail broker in 1970.

From his earliest college days, Harper had had a decision to make: whether or not to start his career with the old William P. Harper & Son & Co. Harper's choice not to do so could be ascribed to a variety of reasons. Though, not long after, the Harper Company was sold, its ownership falling outside the family. Meanwhile, during the mid- to late-seventies, Robbins Harper developed a successful institutional business, dealing with the banks, insurance companies, and government entities in the region. By 1989, the broker was doing business with the greatest portion of the area's larger institutions, having by then established firm lines into them all.

"Hello! Hello! This is AT&T...testing the line? Can anybody hear me?" The voice bursts from Harper's central squawkbox, coming in over the broker's direct feed from PaineWebber's trading floors in Manhattan.

"Piercingly, Joe," answers Harper, picking up the receiver to listen, bypassing the public speaker. In the sudden silence, the voice of Jeff Wilson is once again heard conversing with his horse trainer over the phone.

"April 4th, Tuesday night. It's Kareem Abdul Jabaar's last time in Seattle. One for seven from the field, J.R.. Yeah. I saw they gave him a motorcycle in Milwaukee. Uh huh. A Harley Davidson. Hahahaha. What is he? Seven foot whatever. You see him going down the street on a Harley?"

Wilson puts his feet on his desk, displaying tassled, alligator loafers, now crossed one on the other. He sits directly across from Harper, the two brokers facing each other, separated by a tier of book shelves built down the center of the sales desk. A set of black phones is stationed here, (each broker has several), and various sets of call boxes. A slab of pink, adhesive "Post-Its" lies on the desk top in front of Wilson. Across its top is the message: "Just Say No... To Taxes."

"Yeah, they do, you know," Wilson is saying. "They began the season ranked because they had everybody coming back from the Rose Bowl. The team was supposed to be great, and they started out 0 and 4. Yeah, hahahaha. They finished 6, 4 and 1."

Despite present appearances, Wilson had done some business during the week. PaineWebber's New York "repo" desk had turned unusually aggressive, allowing him to move on several repurchase agreements. Under a repo, or repurchase agreement, brokerages will sell a block of securities to a lender such as an industrial corporation, or a pension fund which desires to invest its surplus cash for a short time. The brokerage contracts to buy the securities back at the end of the period, at a price amounting to an interest rate for the lender.

But this first week in December had been unusual. For months prior to this, PaineWebber had been less than competitive, offering threadbare rates to the lending institutions. These were tactical decisions made at the highest levels in New York, and the Seattle broker could do nothing about it. Still, Wilson estimated his local competitors were doing hundreds of millions of dollars of repo business a month, his company's corporate decisions left him a tiny fraction of that.

Harper reaches to pick up a call from Dick Schober, president and part owner of Harper/McLean, the current incarnation of the old Harper Company. "We're carrying two positions," Harper responds to a question from Schober. "One's a Tacoma 4 percent '05, the other is WPPSS. No, basically what we do, if we find something we like locally? We call San Francisco and say it's at Seattle Northwest Investment Company, or it's at Foster & Marshall, or William P., ask them to call and buy them for us, say we have an order. So then they just know who to call, and run the ticket that way."

His inventory of municipal bonds reduced to a scant few, Harper invites Schober to send him his company's offering circular listing the securities Schober's company presently owns. If Harper likes what he finds there, and believes he can sell several of Schober's bonds, he will have PaineWebber's San Francisco office commit the firm's capital. Both men stand to profit; still, this is a favor, and the way the game is played on this level, reciprocity being assumed, rarely is it ever demanded. Between the two - between "quid" and "pro quo" - there resides one's word, and one's reputation.

"The Orange Bowl, the Rose Bowl, one of 'em's gotta be on the first, J.R...." Still on the phone with his trainer, Wilson begins flipping through pages of the Sporting News, looking for dates of upcoming bowl games.

The framed photographs of thoroughbreds covering the walls of the institutional sales room are, for the most part, pictures of a single horse: Cruisin' Too Su. Trained by Junior Coffey, the big, chestnut mare was once owned by Wilson. In many of the photos, Wilson stands surrounded by family and friends, the tanned and smiling clan assembled next to Cruisin' Too Su's side in the winner's circle. Yet, not long after the last of these photographs was taken, Wilson lost his prize thoroughbred in a $20,000 claiming race. Picked up by a well-to-do Californian, the mare was sent off to run the southern tracks of that state. However, the opportunity arose for Wilson to recapture his horse in yet another claimer. For Cruisin' Too Su's former owner, though, there was a catch. To reclaim his winning filly, he would have had to expose himself to an $8,000 loss. Winning horse or not, Wilson declined. "It's a cold business," the young broker explained later, sitting across the sales desk from Harper, the two men waiting on the market, or the ponies, or the coming discount rate. Losing the thoroughbred had been, simply, "one of the breaks."

• • •

4

THERE IS NO JAPANESE ROCK GARDEN AT KUNATH KARREN Rinne & Atkin, nor is there a marble fireplace as was once proposed. But the partners, now housed on the top floor of Seattle's new Key Tower, have afforded themselves three times as much space - and, as they thought they must - they now have a shower. In fact, the financial counselors' new site boasts a small, if fully equipped locker room. This may come in handy after the rounds of golf that are played here, though for the most part, these are played on computer screen. This morning, however, all the games have been put away, three of the money managers arranged around the "partners room," ensconced in soft, plum, leather chairs.

This is an airy, corner room, the site of much of the partner's daily activity. There are, however, no desks here. Rather, the men are moored between pierlike counters jutting from the room's rear walls. Banks of windows rise immediately above the men's work counters. To the south, and near enough to count the occupants in its offices, rises the massif of the First Interstate Building. Far below it, orange against the white tip of the Smith Tower, stand the gantry cranes of the Port of Seattle. To the west, is the whole southern half of Elliott Bay.

Partner Jeffrey Atkin isn't looking at the view this morning, however. The 39-year-old Atkin, in pink shirt and aqua tie, is working over a sheaf of charts instead: logging fourth-quarter projections for the U.S. Tobacco Company. The chart service Atkin uses supplies data on companies delivering share-holders a minimum 3 1/2 percent yield each year. The publication's numbers are current through the first three quarters of 1988. Using these as a base, the analyst extrapolates the statistics over the next 90 days. If all holds up and Tobacco looks as if it will continue to offer a steady return, Aktin may recommend the company to Sandra Chamberlin, KKRA's young trader, who will then buy its shares for the firm's clientele.

There are many such companies - hundreds of them - and more charts to be worked this day. It is an exacting task, and Atkin's desk appears to have been cleared to accomplish it. But then Atkin's desk is always clean, for he is a clean-desk man. Not all of the partners are, however. In fact, the four seem to have arranged themselves from meticulousness to a kind of muddle. Partner Bruce Rinne, 38, his alcove only slightly less tidy than Atkin's, is at work this morning signing KKRA Christmas cards. To young Rinne's immediate left, 46-year-old Ned Karren sits tapping a yellow Eberhard No. 2, pondering mysteries revealed on two color monitors. Karren is the firm's chartist, and to a large extent, these consoles have replaced what had been the partner's master-chart. In their former offices, the technician had authored a five-foot high, mural-like graph. The chart has now been axed by a third, its remainder fixed, along with a miniture basketball hoop, to the room's front wall.

Karren's efforts are now largely carried on electronically with a powerful computer program that uses on-line, real-time market data. Karren is thus able to see the information split seconds after it's generated. Tick charts, line charts, volume charts, bar charts, interday charts, stochastic charts (raw, fast, slow, super slow). Point and figure charts, bar chart overlays, percentage envelopes, zoom-enhanced trend lines, zoom-enhanced channel lines, five minute oscillators, RSI (with optional smoothed line,) CCI (with smooth option,) Gann Fans and Fibonnaci Projections for the Elliott Wave Theorists.

And...the latest data on futures, options, commodities, stocks or cash from any one of the nation's exchanges. Taken together with the partner's portfolio service and the ubiquitous Telerate, Karren is able to plug himself into the fiscal workings of the world, his eyes peeled, his pencil tapping.

Directly behind Karren, a short pencil's throw away, is the work bay of Mike Kunath, though at the moment, the 48-year-old partner is nowhere in sight. Nor is much of Kunath's U-shaped work station, only the top two thirds of its computer monitor now visible above a mound of folders, stacked newspapers, computer print-outs, magazines, portfolios, booklets, reviews, newsletters, bulletins, and investment trade journals. Equally lost over the length of Kunath's work area are a number of its absentee owner's corn cob pipes.

Actually, Kunath has just returned from a week in Chicago and is at work this morning in the "big conference room," a large, formal chamber on the opposite end of the firm's floor space. Like the partner's room, this corner conference room is also filled with light, its windows looking out over the city to the North and West. At the center of this carpeted room resides a long, glass-topped conference table. This morning the table's surface is buried beneath manilla folders, stacks of publications, several ash trays and a number of yellow, cob pipes. There is a serious meeting in progress here: a party is being planned.

"It's one thing to have passive food," Kunath comments to Pam Klute, the firm's young marketing assistant, who sits with a yellow legal tablet poised before her. On it has been jotted "Flowers, Grand Piano, Gas Grill. Expresso Cart?"

"It's a step forward having people passing foods," the money manager continues, now rising and pacing, looking off into space.

"It's another step forward having somebody prepare it. And, in my judgment," Kunath explains, "it's a further step forward to properly set the food. If we're going to ask a restaurant to come in here, and they're not going to make any money on the deal, you want to give them the right kind of setting. We want the setting for Henry's to be considerably different from that of Queen City's..."

Twenty-seven year-old Klute listens as Kunath continues. The money manager, warming to his subject, seems increasingly satisfied as he pushes it along, quickly pacing up and down the room in his grey-striped shirt and burgundy suspenders, attending to his thoughts and to the sonorities of his own voice. "We want the lights dimmed in that area, and we'll bring in a few of their tables and chairs, and flowers on every table, and I think candelabras, and a couple of pictures from the restaurant, and we'll put the people in their own chef's outfits..."

This is no ordinary marketing meeting. These are the final preparations for the firm's upcoming Christmas party. The date, two weeks hence, is also to be billed as a housewarming for KKRA's new space, unveiling their new offices to the community. Kunath, once described by Zeke Robinson as Seattle's Sol Hurok, is in his element: the money manager as impresario.

There's an old vaudeville joke that begins: "How do you become a millionaire?" The answer: "First you get a million bucks." The humor of the old saw resides precisely in its ludicrousness, its pointlessness - until one gets the point. This isn't really a joke - it's the essence of the thing. How to become a millionaire? Go out and get it. On the go for the last 20 years, Kunath had attempted to do just that...

Mike Kunath began his career in 1968, by taking a year and a half off from Joshua Green's People's Bank to acquire an MBA. Thus fortified, the former teller went to work as a broker-trainee for Herron Northwest. Closeted with a directory and telephone, he began his business by selling securities to the local banks. This was institutional business in the city, and the young broker took to it. With the eventual sale of Herron to Piper Jaffray in 1972, Kunath found himself running the larger firm's institutional trade in the city. He stayed with the company until 1978, when his former boss at Herron, Bob King, hired him away to Bache. But the Bache Group soon became mired in the Hunt Brothers' ill-starred run at the silver market. With problems of its own, Bache was slow to deliver on promises made to its brokers. In 1980, then, Kunath found himself looking for a place to land.

One of the broker's institutional clients at the time was a man by the name of George Kauffman, an officer in the trust department at SeaFirst Bank. To a large extent, the phenomenon of the modern money manager is a product of the bank trust department. Since its inception in the middle of the last century, that is the trust department's function: investing its client's money. For

professional management, this was the wealthy individual's single alternative. However, in 1974, the Employee Retirement Income Security Act
(ERISA), eased pension eligibilty rules, resulting in an explosion of untaxed
retirement monies (something like $3 trillion in the U.S. today). The oppor-
tunities to manage huge pools of assets grew almost overnight. By the late
seventies, the monoliths of the old trust departments had begun to crack like
deep-canyon dams, as trust officers poured out to start management firms of
their own. Kunath's friend George Kauffman was looking to do exactly that.

Kunath was also acquainted with Boyd Sharp, a Shearson manager with
a long history in the community. Kunath, seeing Sharp was also looking to do
something new, introduced him to Kauffman. Three months later, the two
senior men came back to ask if Kunath knew of a bond person for them. "Of
course," the broker told them, "but given your personalities, what you really
need is someone to do your marketing." The upshot of this triumvirate was the
Sirach Corporation, one of the city's earliest money management firms and
presently one of its largest.

Kunath had moved from the sell-side to the buy-side, from selling
securities to managing assets. He liked the change of focus, liked being
concerned less with he made each month, and more with what he could
control. This was important to Kunath, important enough that two years later,
he thought of doing it all again.

It was at a Seattle Bond Club Christmas Party that Kunath first spoke of
the subject to Bruce Rinne. In 1982, Rinne was working for Ned Karren at
SeaFirst Investment Advisors, a money managing division at Seafirst Bank.
Rinne told Kunath he and his partner were looking for something to do outside
the bank, which was then beginning to have problems of its own. It was a story
Kunath had heard before, and soon a plan was evolved, a plan that included
dealing University Federal Savings & Loan as a silent partner. If anyone in
the city was equipped to start a new money management firm - Kunath was
convinced he was the one. He had been through the process two years before,
knew what was needed, and, perhaps as importantly, what was not. In 1980,
it had taken Kauffman, Sharp, and Kunath three months to get Sirach
operating. In 1982, it took Kunath, Karren and Rinne exactly 17 days to start
up their new counseling firm, from filing incorporation papers to opening
their doors. Starting that summer with $24 million under management

brought from their former firms, KKR had been profitable from its first month. The three partners, Kunath knew well indeed, had fashioned themselves a very good deal.

. . .

"Let's try the expresso guy outside the Bon Marche first. That cart'd be perfect here. And before I forget, you better go get the wine list." Kunath, buttoned into a thick, winter coat, waits for Pamela Klute to collect her materials. "It's one o'clock P. K. We've got to do it in a hurry."

"I thought your party wasn't until tonight?"

"Well, we always do a little thing over at the Tennis Club first."

"Tough life you've got, Michael."

"Hey!" Kunath laughs. "C'mon. It's the Bond Club Christmas Party, Pam." The money manager's voice rises in mimicry of comedian W. C. Fields. "Comes but once a year, my dear."

. . .

5

THE ENTRANCE TO THE CLUBHOUSE AT BROADMOOR GOLF and Country Club is filled with light this Friday night, as party-goers stroll up from the golf club's darkened parking lots below. The party was to have begun at 6:30; it is now 7:00 and the guests are still arriving beneath the club's canopy, letting themselves in through the building's varnished double doors.

Inside, down the building's short central hallway, a tray of hors d'oeuvres has been put up on a round deal-table in the member's lounge. There are flowers here, and sliced fruits, assorted cheeses, and tier after tier of glistening appetizers. These delicacies, as well as the evening's hosted bar, have acted as magnets, slowly drawing the crowd down the hallway from the club's brightly lit foyer. Before many moments have passed, the barroom starts to fill, coming alive with the sounds of greetings, and talk, and laughter. Straightaway, the staff begins circulating with platters of hors d'oeuvres, moving about the crowded barroom with cocktail trays, taking orders for highballs and bottles of beer. The laughter becomes easier, and louder moment by moment, until it becomes a roar.

Robbins Harper is here, polished and groomed, sporting a silvery bow tie imprinted with headlines from the Wall Street Journal. The broker is talking to Jim Morford Jr., his colleague at PaineWebber. Morford has arrived late, having just returned from shopping with his wife. He tells Harper this is a yearly occurrence. Harper grins and nods his head in deep agreement. No, Morford smiles, he isn't talking about Nordstrom's. He isn't talking about department stores at all. Once a year at Christmas, the broker and his wife buy a thousand dollars worth of groceries, then give them to the local missions. Morford laughs, explaining the deed off-handedly, then quickly changes the subject.

The crowd grows with new arrivals, swelling until the party goers number a hundred or more. Foster & Marshal, American Express's Bill Rex is here. So is Mike Foster, standing listening to his friend Fred Paulsell. Steve Herron is here too, Herron wearing his customary scarlet-red evening jacket. The diminutive financier's familiar foot-long cigar, however, is nowhere in sight. The distinguished bulk of Zeke Robbins is very much in evidence, and, as is his custom, the broker is in high good humor this night. A genuinely funny man with a story, Robbins is surrounded by listeners, the sound of their laughter rising above the bar. Ragan & MacKenzie's Brooks Ragan is in attendance; so is Theron "Brooks" Hawkes IV, white haired and trim, with a fierce, beaklike nose. Bill Slater has arrived; the former manager of Blyth speaking with the Bond Club's vice president, Jim Mendenhall. Paine-Webber's Jeff Wilson is here, too, as is his colleague Jean Cunningham, the tiny blonde holding her breath in a strapless black cocktail dress. Rod Rich arrives wearing a gold tuxedo. This has come to be expected, as each Christmas the city bond trader makes the rounds of the town's tux shops in order to eclipse himself year after year. Dick Hinton is in the crowd; so is Ed Easter, looking tall and spare and telling Gert Vierick that getting old is the bunk. Oppenheimer's Jim Adams speeds by on his committee member's rounds, the ebullient broker leaving eddies of people in his wake: "Hey, how're you doing!" "How's it going!" "Fantastic party!" Then the lights are dimmed, and dimmed again, calling the crowd in to dinner.

Thirteen circular dining tables have been set up in the country club's ballroom, its chandeliered ceilings and parquet floors redolent of weekend dining and dancing and teenage cotillions. At the far end of the room a fireplace is bordered by an American flag and a Christmas tree. At the front of the ballroom there is a small stage, filled with several rows of folding chairs. A dinner of prime rib is set out, and consumed amidst a roar of talk and laughter. By its end, a smiling, compactly built man with wiry, salt and pepper hair has mounted the dias.

"I'm Fritz Frink," the smiling man announces, prompting his formally attired audience to begin hollering: "Who? Who?"

"The President of the Seattle Bond Club," Frink begins again, his smile now even broader. "I'd like to welcome you to perhaps the sixty-fourth, maybe the sixty-third, maybe the sixty-fifth annual Bond Club Christmas Party."

Having commenced the ceremonies in the traditional fashion, Frink gratefully gives way as certain other of the banquet's preliminaries are observed. Much of what follows involves names given club members in the evening's program - a lampoon of an alumni club yearbook. During these proceedings the evening's entertainment committee is asked to rise for applause. All are wearing tuxedos, though many have embellished their appearance with joke-store eyeglass, plastic noses, black bristle mustachios... The correct note, perhaps, to set the scene for the night's entertainment.

The drone of a professional baritone - a mesmerized hush. As the dessert dishes are bussed and the lights go down, a man in a velvet dinner jacket and a black, spade-shaped beard steps into the light at the front of stage. This is "Mr. Balante," a Seattle hypnotist, and Mr. Balante, upon introducing himself, begins his performance by asking for volunteers from the audience. Several seconds pass before club members begin walking up to the stage in twos and threes, they continue to volunteer until the dais is filled. The volunteers sit in the folding chairs on the ballroom's stage, laughing and talking among themselves, nervously waiting for Mr. Balante to begin.

SEATTLE TIMES, MONDAY, OCTOBER 19, 1987:
WASHINGTON - President Reagan watched the stock market's plunge today "with concern."

The White House deputy press secretary Marlin Fitzwater, [speaking for the President] said there had been no consideration of halting trading as the market fell.

In a written statement, Fitzwater said consultations "confirm our view that the economy remains sound," with the longest peacetime expansion in history, record-high employment and increases in manufacturing output.

Out of the twenty-five that volunteered for the evening's hypnosis, one hour later only three remain, though the audience is only cheering for one... Prop guitar in hand, his heavily sprayed coiffure now hanging, sliding like snow off a warming roof, the star of the evening's entertainment is doing the rattle-snake-shake all over the stage - before all his laughing, slightly embarrassed brethren - lip-syncing his heart out to an Elvis Presley tune.

"Don't be cruuuuel," bwang, bwang, bwang, "to a heart that's truuuuuuuue...A-don't be cruuuel...To a heart that's truuuue..." Before the song is half over, the club member's starched shirt is unbuttoned, his tie untied, his face, as he stands swiveling his hips at center stage, radiating pure bliss. Bwang, bwang, bwang. "If ya want someone ta luv ya... want someone that's truuuuue... A-don't be cruuuuuuel..." As the record ends, Balante counts backwards from five, snaps his fingers, and his act is over - the lights coming up until even Elvis blinks. The audience then retires to the bar in earnest, a suddenly awake and notably subdued rock-n-roller among them.

TAKING STOCK

It had not all been theatrics, however. A brief, more serious note had been struck earlier in the evening when certain formalities were observed, as they had been observed every year at the Bond Club Christmas Party.

"It is my pleasure to say a few words." Notes in hand, the speaker had been Harper/McLean's Dick Schober. "...a few words about one of our distinguished guests, a man I've had the privilege of knowing and being associated with for the last eighteen years, Dickenson C. Harper."

This was the presentation of the club's Distinguished Service Awards. Dick Harper, Sid Sanders, and Ed Easter, who had begun their careers in the 1920s, were singled out for honors this night. Harper and Easter were present, but Sanders, because of a recent operation, had been unable to attend.

"...You know his patience always amazed me. And especially Dick's understanding of when the market was ready to make money for his clients. For this, and other reasons too numerous to mention, it is my pleasure tonight to honor Dickenson C. Harper."

The Harpers, father and son, had risen from their table amid loud and sustained applause, the younger man supporting his elderly father's arm.

TAKING STOCK

Harper senior, a stately old man with a clipped, white mustache, then offered his appreciation with a few simple, unadorned remarks.

THE WASHINGTON POST NATIONAL WEEKLY EDITION NOVEMBER 9, 1987

Things will never be the same, says New York investment banker Felix Rohatyn of the stockmarket roller coaster. "I'm not sure what we learned - because it was all so dizzying."

When the market can go down 700 points in almost three days, he says, and then come back in almost 300 points in two, "it's no longer a market place as we knew it..."

Rohatyn may be right: in this situation, the market more closely resembles a crap game, in which all bets can be won or lost in a single roll of the dice.

There were to be other ceremonies as well. By evening's end, a game of hi-lo has been set up on a table in the crowded bar. The card players sit with their stacks of chips and hands of stud laid out before them. For sixty-two years the Seattle Bond Club Party has ended in this manner. If the party's entertainment varies from year to year, this customary ending is not to be trifled with. And poker is its lesser form.

The deal table has been cleared of its hor d'oeuvres and the players begin collecting around it. Sleek as seals in their black formal wear, they glance about the lounge searching for someone - or something. Finally, a runner is sent out ("I know where they are"), and comes hurrying back with dice and a throwing cup. The players begin skinning back bills from rolls and hastily produced pocket clips. Money is placed beside ash trays and glasses and packets of cigarettes. The bank is made. "Make yer bets." Bills come out to the center of the table, "Awright shooter..." flow until at the rattle of the cup:

"Comin' out!"

"What's he got?"

"Six and two!"

TAKING STOCK

"All right, side bets gentlemen.
"Eight's the point."
"You in?"
"I'm in."
"Okay...The bank's tapped.
"One more time."
"Dice be nice."
"Now!...Get some!"

Afterword

FAT TUESDAY AT THE TOP

S EATTLE, TUESDAY, AUGUST 29, 1989. BROOKS RAGEN STEPS
from the elevator onto the floor of his brokerage at 7:14 a.m. In his middle fifties, slender, with deep, close-set eyes, Ragen MacKenzie's chairman looks straight ahead as he enters his company's lobby. The officer's modest executive suite is at the end of a long, glass-lined hall of brokers' offices, many of the doors standing open this morning. Ragen walks rapidly down the hallway, there being an air of earnestness about the man, a concentration even in the act of pausing now to greet his brokers. Wearing a gray, worsted, two-button pinstripe, Ragen has on black, neoprene-soled shoes, and is carrying a scarred, leather, two handled briefcase. Open at the top, Ragen's case bulges with a well-thumbed stack of newspapers and magazines. The Seattle Times, Business Week, Fortune, The Journal, Forbes, Barron's, Investor Dealer's Digest, The New York Times... All had been read the evening before, and now, before setting himself to anything new, Ragen sees that the material is passed out to his department heads. It is, after all, a competitive business, advantage often buried in the depths of each day's news. For the earnest practitioner, intent on providing his firm with an edge, the necessity for input can become near total.

Returning from the brokerage floor with his empty case, Ragen seats himself as his assistant enters his office, her arms full of business letters and

205

trade journals, client folders and magazines. It is almost 7:30, and sunny out, though outside Ragen's windows the foothills of the Olympic Mountains are nearly lost in the haze.

• • •

The DOW opens the trading day at 2738.41. Before the session is an hour old, the index stumbles a point, then several more. Still, the index is presently sixteen points above its top of August, 1987, the high before Black Monday's 508 point crash. The average has recouped nearly a thousand points over the last two years, passing its former peak several weeks ago. It is the last of the indexes to have done so. Though the current market in equities is being driven largely by the institutions, producing slightly lower volumes than two years ago, the Street is nevertheless beginning to effervesce, as confidence steadily percolates through the system. Memories of the crash are now pushed aside, and anticipation is rising as the country's wealthier individuals follow the institutions into equities. If these begin to come in volume, the assumption is that the huge retail market of '86 and '87 will follow... Talk is again being heard of a 3,000 point DOW, a 3,500 point DOW, 4,000...

• • •

Viewed from a crowded sidewalk, two blocks away, Seattle's Hoge Building stands like an antique table leg, an immense, old-fashioned, heavily ornamented table leg - sans the table. Seen from John MacKenzie's 43rd-floor office, however, the old stone hub seems simply another rooftop, in a stubble of rooftops, extending south along Second Avenue nearly an eighth of a mile below

Sitting in his office looking out on the firm's brokerage floor, Ragen MacKenzie's president, John MacKenzie, pays little attention to the Hoge this morning. In the nine months since MacKenzie moved into this cubicle-like office, however, the brokerage's present building, the firm's current high-rent office space on the First Interstate's 43rd floor, has been much in his

206

thoughts. The rent the firm pays for this space is the last, major obstruction to the streamlining MacKenzie began on his arrival. As part of that process, MacKenzie has opened a spread sheet this morning, working through its pages at his desk, the glint of a slim, silver, mechanical pencil in his hand.

At 53, with his Jack Kennedy hairdo and laid-back, boyish grin, Ragen MacKenzie's chief operating officer appears the embodiment of someone's Irish uncle. In fact, MacKenzie is Scottish. He is also bright, articulate, talented. The local investment community first noticed these qualities in the early 1970s, when MacKenzie took an ailing research department at Foster & Marshall and placed it on its feet, creating a reputation for himself as, perhaps, the city's leading stock analyst. As a result of these maiden efforts, MacKenzie was offered a seat on F&M's powerful executive committee. MacKenzie, however, declined. At Foster & Marshall, he had made the decision he would limit himself to research. When Shearson bought Foster out in 1982, a part of what it was buying was MacKenzie. Nevertheless, in the post-crash November of 1988, in a mood to retrench, Shearson dismissed the consultant. Ten days later, the fired analyst, along with many of Shearson's research department in Seattle, moved over to [the then] Cable Howse & Ragen. This was more than a lateral move for MacKenzie. Understood in his relationship with his new partner was the fact that Ragen would keep a hand on policy, leaving MacKenzie to direct day-to-day operations, overseeing the firm's institutional, retail, and bonds sales. He would no longer limit himself to research, observing while others made management decisions as he had at F&M. If decisions were to be made - and consequences to follow - MacKenzie would now make them himself.

. . .

Streamlined or not, Ragen MacKenzie pays the highest rent of any tenant-firm in the First Interstate Building. It seems, so the partners explain, incredible that this should continue into the future. In preliminary, third-party negotiations, the owners of the office building had refused to budge on the firm's lease agreement. Things become even more difficult, as Ragen and MacKenzie know both the building's owners socially. Still, knowing their landlords or not, the partners of Seattle's largest, locally owned brokerage feel they must do something about their rent.

MacKenzie's solution is to buy it down. Among the partners, he has tentatively proposed offering their landlords a sum of money, cash these men can invest as they see fit, and in light of which Ragen MacKenzie will expect a rent reduction. MacKenzie proposes this as simple quid pro quo, its feasibility, so he imagines, depending on an assumed interest rate. However, in concurrence with his partner Ragen, MacKenzie has also come up with a tentative "back door." Ragen MacKenzie can move.

Every other factor at the city's largest, locally owned brokerage has been addressed. In order to build its base, Ragen MacKenzie has opened branches in cities around the Northwest. So too, it has expanded its retail sales force in Seattle. To strengthen the firm internally, interest and trading expenses have been cut, telephone costs reduced, and a dependence on overnight air-mailers abolished. Fat, wherever it was found, was meticulously carved away. Which left the growing brokerage in an increasingly enviable cash position, and, with the summer's markets rising, increasingly unwilling to be tied to an onerous lease. So, on this afternoon of Tuesday, August 29th, Ragen and MacKenzie put on their suit coats, leave their offices and walk to the brokerage's elevators. The two officers tell the receptionist they'll be gone the rest of the afternoon. They are going to see a man about a building.

The AT&T Gateway Tower rises less than fifty yards from the site of Seattle's old Rainier Hotel. Construction for the Gateway Tower was begun in 1989, the Rainier Hotel was put up in 1889. The new tower, though yet to be enclosed, is 60 stories taller. The Rainier Hotel no longer exists. Brooks Ragen and John MacKenzie have come to see the Gateway's builder, Herman Sarkowsky, to see the man's new building, to provide themselves a glimpse into their possible future.

"It's a timeless building," Ragen and MacKenzie are informed as they stand in Gateway Associate's conference room on the 32nd floor of the 5th Avenue Plaza Building. "A building unlike any building anywhere in the world," says Jeff Miller, Sarkowsky's leasing director. "You can't go to Paris or New York or Houston or anyplace else and find a building that's got this same signature. It's creating a whole new identity for the skyline of Seattle."

FAT TUESDAY AT THE TOP

Ragen and MacKenzie listen, standing in front of a large, glass-enclosed model of the building. Sarkowsky, a tall, graying presence in a blue-gray suit, stands off to one side, his lips pursed, his eyes never leaving his young director's face.

"The main entrance to the building is at 5th and Columbia, off the corner here," says Miller, leaning down to point to the model's base. "You don't have to walk to the middle of the block to get into the building, you're drawn in from the crosswalks when you or your customers come from any other building. In through the portico then, here, where it says AT&T Gateway Tower, and into the Atrium Lobby where you're surrounded by huge potted Ficus trees growing 40 feet tall into the air..."

Theme-restaurants; pink, Carerra-polished granite siding; Otis Whisper-Ride Elevators; fiber optic cores; Honeywell airflow control systems - when the presentation is over, Ragen and MacKenzie are given white hard-hats, then asked to follow Miller and Sarkowsky out of the 5th Avenue Plaza and across the street. Nine months from completion, the AT&T Gateway stands on the corner, the building still unenclosed, its 62 open floors disappearing overhead. Ragen and MacKenzie are led past construction fences, up a series of wooden ramps and into the building's construction elevator. Bells ring, and shortly all four rise up further than the Atrium Lobby's future fig trees: 40, 60, 600 feet into the air.

· · ·

Brooks Ragen's own rise had been nearly as swift. As a high school honors graduate in 1951, he had been the winner of a full, four-year scholarship to Yale University. In 1955, he received a degree in history, graduating from the ivy league school magna cum laude. In 1956, Ragen attended law school at Stanford University, taking and passing the Oregon bar, though he had no intention of practicing law. Ragen's ambition was to enter the securities business, which he did immediately after leaving law school, moving to New York City to join the firm of Dominick & Dominick. While moving through the ranks at Dominick, Ragen attended night classes at New York University, earning a masters degree in business administration.

TAKING STOCK

In 1961, he was informed by his superiors at Dominick he could open a branch for the firm anywhere he chose. A native of Portland, Oregon, Ragen chose to open an office in Seattle. In eleven years, Ragen built this office up to 27 brokers. In 1972, he then left Dominick to open a Seattle office for Blyth Eastman Dillon, rising with Blyth from branch management to investment banking. Then in 1982, along with Tom Cable and Elwood Howse, Ragen put together a brokerage of his own: Cable Howse & Ragen. The new brokerage was a member firm in the New York Stock Exchange, and Ragen was named the firm's president. In November of 1987, Ragen bought Cable and Howse out, continuing operations for a year, before forming Ragen MacKenzie. With Ragen MacKenzie, Ragen elevated himself to chairman and chief executive officer. His firm was the largest locally owned brokerage in the city of Seattle. Brooks Ragen was 56 years old.

• • •

The elevator slows as it nears the top, the operator opens its doors, holding them open as Sarkowsky leads Ragen and MacKenzie off onto the tower's 60th floor. The floor and ceiling of the new building are bare concrete, 5/8-inch strands of wire cable strung as a railing around the floor's perimeter. At this height, though this August afternoon is warm and clear, the wind seems to blow continuously, gusting as Sarkowsky first leads, then follows Ragen and MacKenzie on a circuit of his building.

"Brooks, this may be your last chance to get on the 60th floor," Sarkowsky jokes.

Ragen smiles. "Herman," he says, making a point of venturing out in the vicinity of the railing, "it looks like a very *premium* view."

Sarkowsky smiles, though he says nothing in reply.

Nonetheless, Ragen's meaning has not been missed - the tower's eventual rent is likely to be as steep as its view. But then, it *is* premium. Off to either side of the Gateway, this vista from the 60th floor is less of known buildings and familiar avenues than it is the extraordinary, maplike fact of the city's grid, its geometry laid out below. To the south and east and north, the city's streets fan out to the horizon line, the town's low-rise buildings appearing only slightly less two-dimensional. Crowding up into the west, however, the huge office towers of the 1970s and '80s rise up from the bay. Across 5th Avenue, the black trunk of the Columbia Center seems close enough to touch. The effect of this perspective, of being high amongst the city's towers, is one of being aloft in a forest looking off through the trees, the mountains and harbor appearing as shafts of light between the columns of the Columbia Center, the Federal Building, the 4th Avenue Plaza Building, the First Interstate Building, the Key Tower...

"Look at this," says MacKenzie, stopping in front of a pair of workman's shoes placed side by side, not inches from the edge of the precipice. It appears as if their absent owner has jumped out of them, a thought immediately shared by all four men, as everyone begins to smile.

"He must have read the price tag," says Ragen.

"The what...?" asks Sarkowsky, unable to hear.

"The price, he must have seen the rent," says Ragen, and then everyone, even Sarkowsky, laughs.

The wind makes it difficult to hear, compelling Ragen, MacKenzie, and Sarkowsky, when they talk, to stand quite close together, or, as they continue their circuit around the building, to raise their voices. Benjamin Bernerd Ehrlichman had known this, forced to raise his own voice as the wind gusted over the roof of the Exchange Building, 23 stories up - and nearly 60 years ago.

All the old names: Harper and Herron and the brothers at Blyth, surely Ehrlichman and Foster. All had known these elevations, where careers and business become means to an end, that end being the definition of the self. As a result, each man's efforts had always to be new, every new attempt, each new turn. "If I didn't think I was doing something considerably different," Brooks Ragen had commented in a crowded restaurant that afternoon, "I wouldn't stay in business."

Maybe not. Yet, over the hundred-year course of the community's history, each of these players had forged a business, built a career, finally sharing in the one ambition common to all: that of dominating the industry in the Pacific Northwest. Moments must have arrived when this first seemed possible - then the days when it even seemed likely - all laying their shoulders and their fortunes and their hands to the wheel. And when it moved - when it rolled...! The Future must have felt as if they owned it.

TAKING STOCK

. . .

The circuit is now finished. If nothing is decided, all realize this has been preliminary. Sarkowsky wanted to show his new tower, these top officers of the city's largest local brokerage wanted to see it, to think about it, to let the fact of their visit run like a main circuit cable all the way back to their landlords. A friendly probe, every etiquette has been observed - now all four move into the Gateway's elevator. A button is pushed, a bell rings, the men step back from the windows of the car as the elevator begins its descent. Cables lurch as the platform gains speed, slipping down the huge, northern face of the tower. The buildings of the city slowly rise to meet it, as sirens and the sounds of the town's traffic surge up from below, growing louder...then louder still as the tiny elevator rattles down the side of the Gateway.

Down into the city and gone.

Lake City
Duprel Farm
Lichton Springs

June 1987 - October 1989

INDEX

The Northwest Center for Research Journalism is particularly indebted to the group of individuals, and the organizations behind them, who made this project possible:

Michael G. Foster
Robbins Harper
J. Thomas Kuebler
James G. Morford, Jr.
William J. Rex
The Seattle Bond Club
Kirby L. Cramer
Richard L. Hinton
Frederick O. Paulsell
John D. Penny
Ragen & MacKenzie, Inc.
Howard W. Robbins
James R. Adams
Allen Nelson
MacMillan Pringle
James S. Rogers
J. Gary Larsen
First Washington Corp.